POLICY ISSUES AFFECTING LESBIAN, GAY, BISEXUAL, AND TRANSGENDER FAMILIES

POLICY ISSUES AFFECTING LESBIAN, GAY, BISEXUAL, AND TRANSGENDER FAMILIES

****

Sean Cahill and Sarah Tobias

THE UNIVERSITY OF MICHIGAN PRESS *Ann Arbor*

Published in the United States of America by
The University of Michigan Press
Manufactured in the United States of America
♾ Printed on acid-free paper

2010 2009 2008 2007 4 3 2 1

A CIP catalog record for this book is available from the British Library.

Library of Congress Cataloging-in-Publication Data

Cahill, Sean (Sean Robert)
Policy issues affecting lesbian, gay, bisexual, and transgender families / Sean Cahill and Sarah Tobias.
p. cm.
Includes bibliographical references and index.
ISBN-13: 978-0-472-03061-3 (pbk. : alk. paper)
ISBN-10: 0-472-03061-2 (pbk. : alk. paper)
1. Gays—Family relationships—United States. 2. Lesbians—Family relationships—United States. 3. Gay couples—United States. 4. Lesbian couples—United States. 5. Children of gay parents—United States. 6. Gays—Legal status, laws, etc.—United States. 7. Lesbians—Legal status, laws, etc.—United States. I. Tobias, Sarah, 1963– II. Title.

HQ76.3.U5 C33 2006
306.85086'640973—dc22 2006021882

Parts of this work are based on information first published in a report titled "Family Policy: Issues Affecting Gay, Lesbian, Bisexual and Transgender Families," by Sean Cahill, Mitra Ellen, and Sarah Tobias, published by the National Gay and Lesbian Task Force Policy Institute (New York, 2002). The material has been significantly expanded, updated, and revised to address the unprecedented developments in gay family policies of the last four years, including debates over the family rights of same-sex couples.

ACKNOWLEDGMENTS

This publication would not have been possible without the help of many people. This book grew out of the National Gay and Lesbian Task Force's 2002 publication *Family Policy: Issues Affecting Gay, Lesbian, Bisexual and Transgender Families.* For their research assistance and other contributions at various stages of that project, we would like to thank Paula Ettelbrick, Kenneth T. Jones, Shireen Barday, Sangeeta Budhiraja, Carrie Evans, Lisa Mottet, Gautam Bhan, Brian Cahill, Pavita Krishnaswamy, Ruth McFarlane, Jill Rader, John Vang, and Lorri Jean. In addition, we especially thank Mitra Ellen, our coauthor on that study.

We thank Kara Suffredini, Jason Cianciotto, Alain Dang, Nick Ray, Shawn Clark, Urvashi Vaid, and Matt Foreman for their support and assistance with this book. Thanks also to Samuel Buggeln and Marian Cole for their design assistance. Thanks also to Jim Reische at the University of Michigan Press for committing to this project and for seeing it through, and to others at the Press for their careful work on our manuscript. We especially extend thanks to all of the families who are profiled in this book, and to all those who take a stand for fairness for same-sex couples and other LGBT families.

Sean would like to thank his family, friends, colleagues, and funders.

Sarah would like to thank her sisters, Clare and Jo, for always believing in her; Annie, Marty, Liz, John, Alicia, Jeremy, Ruwani, Keya, Melanie, Delyth, and Gill—for sustaining her through life's joys and challenges; and Beth and Talila—for the laughter, warmth, and sweetness they bring to everything. It is to them, with love, that she dedicates this text.

CONTENTS

Chapter 1

INTRODUCTION

Eugene Clark and Larry Courtney lived like many married couples, creating their lives around each other and being recognized by their families and friends as a committed couple. When Larry was offered a job in New York City in 1988, the couple relocated from Washington, D.C., and Eugene found a new position in New York. When New York City created a domestic partnership registry, the couple went to City Hall to get the closest thing to a marriage certificate available to them. When Eugene's mother became ill, they brought her from D.C. to their one-bedroom Manhattan apartment so that they could care for her during the last years of her life.

On September 11, 2001, Eugene was one of the thousands at the World Trade Center who did not come home to their loved ones that evening. Larry received a voice mail from Eugene after the first building was hit: "Don't worry, the plane hit the other building. I'm okay. We're evacuating." That was the last time Larry heard from him. Like other people who lost family members that day, Larry reported Eugene missing and filled out his death certificate and the workers' compensation forms. However, Larry was informed that since he and Eugene were not legally married, he was not considered family. The compensation would go to Eugene's father, with whom Eugene had not spoken in over twenty years.

In the midst of his intense grief, Larry had to counter this claim that he and Eugene were not family, even though they had built a life together for fourteen years. Larry joined with Lambda Legal Defense and Education Fund to educate the public, the media, and legislators about this unjust situation. On August 20, 2002, the New York State Assembly passed a bill giving the domestic partners of September 11 victims full spousal rights to workers' compensation.[1]

Unfortunately, this type of situation is far from uncommon for same-sex couples and their families. Larry Courtney's predicament was addressed in part because his life partner Eugene was killed in an attack of international significance. Although the resulting 2002 bill marks an important victory, most lesbian, gay, bisexual, and transgender (LGBT) families remain routinely discriminated against by public policy. These injustices are usually not linked to a high-profile national tragedy, and these families' stories usually do not make it to the evening news. Nevertheless, many LGBT people experience personal tragedies—such as the death of a life partner—that are compounded by a callous disregard of their family bonds. As a result, they suffer emotionally, economically, and personally.

Family policy affects LGBT individuals and influences their security and well-being throughout their lives—from childhood through young adulthood, middle age through older years, and even after death. Much public policy is based on the goal of promoting "the family," recognizing the economic and emotional interdependence of family members and giving special priority to this bond. Yet policy has historically been based on a narrow definition of family that does not encompass the bonds of LGBT people. Most policy gives preference to heterosexual married couples and their children over all other family formations. Thus, unmarried couples (both same-sex and opposite-sex), single parents, extended-family caregivers, and the children of these families are all disadvantaged. Homophobia and heterosexism compound this problem for LGBT families. Consequently, LGBT people are left with little security for their relationships, especially in times of hardship or transition.

This book will provide a comprehensive account of the discrimination that LGBT families confront. It will explore how policy changes could make LGBT families more secure. It will pay particular attention to the current political debate over how to recognize same-sex couple families.

The issue of whether or not same-sex couples should be allowed to access the institution of civil marriage emerged as a major national political controversy in the mid-1990s. During this time, same-sex relationships were decried by congressional conservatives as a threat to an abstract construct of "the family"—the heterosexual, married, and economically sustainable family—which was posited as "the backbone of this country" by Representative Bob Barr (R-GA) in 1995 and as "one of the essential foundations on which our civilization is based" by Representative Charles Canady (R-FL) in 1996. In congressional debate on July 12, 1996, Representative Barr, the architect of the 1996 Defense of Marriage Act, argued:

> [A]s Rome burned, Nero fiddled, and that is exactly what [supporters of same-sex marriage] would have us do . . . The very foundations of our so-

> ciety are in danger of being burned. The flames of hedonism, the flames of narcissism, the flames of self-centered morality are licking at the very foundations of our society: the family unit.[2]

Ironically, in the summer of 1996, congressional conservatives portrayed low-income single mothers and cohabiting unmarried heterosexual couples as selfish and narcissistic for not getting married, while those same conservatives concurrently denounced gay and lesbian couples as self-indulgent narcissists for seeking to get married. Gay and lesbian families seeking legal protections were portrayed as a threat to Western civilization and God. Representative Canady stated, "we as legislators and leaders for the country are in the midst of a chaos, an attack upon God's principles."[3] Representative Ron Packard (R-CA) argued, "throughout history, civilizations that have allowed the traditional bonds of family to be weakened, these civilizations have not survived."[4]

Anxieties related to gay couples seeking legal protections surfaced again in December 1999, when Vermont's high court ruled that same-sex couples required equal treatment under state policy. But backlash against the advances of gay people reached a peak in 2003–4, following a number of key court rulings in the United States and Canada striking down archaic sex "sodomy" laws and legalizing civil marriage for same-sex couples. Through the debate about gay marriage, many claims have been made about gay and lesbian people and their families. Anti-gay marriage activists and elected officials have also targeted gay and lesbian parenting, safe schools initiatives, and nondiscrimination laws protecting against anti-gay and anti-transgender discrimination.

The main chapters of this book can be divided into two discussions. In chapters 2 and 3, we provide an overview of what is known about LGBT families and the policy issues affecting them—ranging from discrimination to domestic partnership, from health insurance access to family and medical leave. In chapters 4 and 5, we focus on the recent political and intellectual history that frames the struggle over LGBT family policy—a struggle that occurs within the LGBT movement itself, as well as between supporters and opponents of legal equality for LGBT people.

In chapter 2, we summarize what is known about LGBT people and their families. We review recent U.S. Census data pertaining to the households of same-sex couples, paying particular attention to parenting data, including parenting data about people of color in same-sex relationships. We provide an overview of issues of adoption, foster care, and reproductive technology that affect LGBT families. We also address the unique situation of LGBT youth, who are at greater risk than other youth of experiencing homelessness, suicide, and violence and who are often unable to find support at school or in their families. We discuss the particular family issues facing LGBT elders, including unequal treatment under income support programs and Medicaid. We also consider the way in which major health-related issues—such as health insurance access, decision making, unpaid leave from work, nursing care, and domestic violence—relate to LGBT family policy.

In chapter 3, we address the options available to policymakers for recognizing same-sex relationships. We discuss civil marriage, civil unions, domestic partnerships, and reciprocal beneficiary relationships. We explore the international trend toward recognizing same-sex unions, and we provide an overview of recent court decisions in the United States and Canada that have major implications for public policy affecting LGBT families.

In chapter 4, we explore the intellectual history of the internal debates regarding family recognition within the LGBT movement. We show how marriage has historically been a controversial and contested terrain for gay men and lesbians. We discuss the hostility of radical feminism toward marriage, and we discuss the gay rights movement's early acknowledgment that gay liberation will only be achieved as a by-product of women's liberation. We explore queer theorists' claims that marriage constitutes a divisive and exclusionary form of moral regulation that should be shunned. We also address the way in which some LGBT legal scholars have sought to define family expansively in terms of functional relationships. About a decade into the AIDS epidemic, some conservative voices in the LGBT movement started to write about marriage as a means to reject so-called queer values, promote monogamy in gay relationships, and stabilize gay life; we discuss these arguments. Finally, we describe how the struggle for family recognition was reframed during the 1990s as a civil rights strategy to combat discrimination.

In chapter 5, we argue that the gay marriage issue[5] has become central in contemporary U.S. politics in large part because anti-gay activists from the religious right have successfully deployed gay rights controversies as divisive social issues since the early 1970s. Since the mid-1990s, the main focus of anti-gay politics in the United States has been opposition to civil marriage by same-sex couples. Social conservatives have consistently argued that expanding the institution of marriage to include gay and lesbian couples would undermine "the family," constructed as exclusively heterosexual. Chapter 5 examines the recent political history of the struggle for marriage equality by same-sex couples and the backlash evoked by such advances as the Massachusetts high court ruling of 2003 legalizing marriage for gay couples. It also examines the Massachusetts-based Coalition for Marriage, a network of national and local religious right groups that seeks to ban any type of partner recognition for gay couples in Massachusetts. The Coalition for Marriage is an example of the kinds of political coalitions being formed by the Christian right in America. In addition, chapter 5 reviews the role the marriage issue played in the 2004 presidential election.

In chapter 6, we consider the extent to which the pursuit of same-sex marriage is currently reflective of the priorities of the LGBT community. Some LGBT intellectuals continue to argue that marriage itself is a regressive or antidemocratic institution that should be abolished or supplemented with other forms of partner recognition. Many other voices of dissent within the LGBT community question the movement's focus on marriage. In addition to faulting the flaws of the institution, they argue that too many resources have been devoted to the marriage issue to the detriment of other concerns, such as anti-LGBT hate violence, anti-LGBT discrimination in employment and housing, and other basic concerns. Although many black gay people support marriage equality, some members of the African American community have expressed anger at the usurpation of civil rights discourse by LGBT whites. Gay activists argue, however, that the LGBT community must defend itself against the attacks of the anti-gay movement. This is also a critical opportunity to educate straight America about the real experiences facing same-sex couple families. Finally, several recent surveys indicate that marriage and partner recognition is a top priority of LGBT people, including LGBT people of color.

We intersperse chapters 2 and 3 with case studies illustrating the difficulties regularly confronted by same-sex couples whose family bonds are not recognized. The rights, responsibilities, protections, and peace of mind afforded couples through family recognition become particularly important in times of crisis. For example, Hillary Goodridge, one of the lead plaintiffs in the Massachusetts same-sex marriage case *Goodridge v. Dept. of Public Health*, reported encountering a "nightmare" after her partner Julie Goodridge gave birth to their daughter Annie. Her account was reported in the *Boston Globe*.

> After Annie emerged from Julie Goodridge's womb by cesarean section with lungs full of liquid, the infant was rushed from the operating room into intensive care, put on a ventilator and strapped to splints with intravenous tubes inserted in her tiny arms. As Julie's lesbian partner, Hillary, ran frantically from floor to floor between the neonatal unit and post-op where doctors were sewing up Julie, she was barred at different times from both Julie's and Annie's bedsides by hospital staff because she wasn't legally connected to either. She eventually saw both—by tearfully pleading with a nurse in one instance and telling staff she was Julie's sister in another—but the experience later fueled the couple's determination to make marriage an option for gays and lesbians like themselves.[6]

This book is intended for those interested in better understanding same-sex couple families in the United States, as well as other LGBT families. We hope that, as a result of reading this book, more people will challenge the discrimination LGBT families face in public policy. In highlighting these areas, it is our hope that we can help researchers, policymakers, and fellow Americans more clearly define areas of need and promote policies to respond to them. If changed uniformly, family policy would result in a world much more responsive to the economic, legal, and social issues LGBT people face in building and sustaining the relationships with those dearest to them—with their partners, their children, their families.

Chapter 2

LGBT FAMILIES AND THEIR POLICY NEEDS

WHAT DEFINES A FAMILY?

Most people in the United States consider a family to be "a group who love and care for each other," defining the term "in emotional, rather than legal or structural terms."[1] In the LGBT community, as in the larger community, these families take many forms. They include

- a same-sex couple living alone, with other family, or with friends;
- a same-sex couple with children from previous relationships or adopted or conceived during their relationship;
- a single parent raising a biological child or biological children, an adopted child, or a relative's child;
- individuals living with their families of origin or with their "families of choice," such as close friends who serve essential caregiving functions;
- multiple parent networks consisting of, for example, two couples or one couple and an individual who are raising children together;
- aunts, uncles, or grandparents raising their nephews, nieces, or grandchildren.

Although the public largely believes that a family is something more than a legal relationship and that caring for one another transcends legal boundaries, the vast majority of the policies that govern people's lives define family as a legal unit comprised of a married man and woman with their own biological or adopted children. This assumption underlying family policy does not reflect the contemporary demographic reality of American families. Almost one-third of families with children in the United States are headed by either single parents or two unmarried, cohabiting parents.[2] There are significant differences among racial and ethnic groups. Single parenting is much more prevalent among black and Latino parents than among white non-Hispanics. Black families with children are nearly four times as likely as white non-Hispanic families with children to be headed by single or unmarried parents. Hispanic families with children are two-and-a-half times as likely as white non-Hispanic families with children to be headed by a single or unmarried parent.[3]

Approximately 44 percent of adults in the United States are unmarried. According to the 2000 U.S. Census, married heterosexual couples with children comprise less than one-quarter of American households.[4] The 2000 U.S. Census found nearly 1.2 million men and women living with an unmarried partner of the same sex, or some 594,391 same-sex couples.[5]

Studies show that most lesbians and gay men aspire to have committed, loving relationships and want a stronger sense of family in their lives.[6] Although demographic research on lesbian, gay, and bisexual people is limited and most national surveys do not ask about sexual orientation, there is a significant body of research from which we can discern some trends. A series of studies from the 1970s to the 1990s found that between 64 and 80 percent of lesbians and between 46 and 60 percent of gay men report that they are in committed relationships with another person of the same sex.[7] Studies show that same-sex relationships are comparable to opposite-sex relationships in terms of quality and satisfaction in the relationship.[8] Contrary to common misconceptions, many same-sex couples are raising children, as are thousands of single lesbian and gay parents. Bisexuals and transgender people are found in both opposite-sex and same-sex relationships.

THE SAME-SEX COUPLE SAMPLE FROM THE 2000 U.S. CENSUS

Given the dearth of research on the families of same-sex couples, the samples of same-sex unmarried partners from the 1990 and 2000 U.S. Censuses are particularly important. The existence and widespread geographical distribution of same-sex couples are reflected in the 2000 U.S. Census data, in which nearly 600,000 same-sex couples self-reported as cohabiting "unmarried partners."[9] Although this number likely represents a significant undercount, it constitutes a 310 percent increase over the 145,130 same-sex households tallied in the 1990 Census. Whereas the 1990 Census found same-sex couples in about half the nation's counties, the 2000 Census documented same-sex couples in more than 99 percent of all counties across the United States.[10] If gay and lesbian people represent about 5 percent of the U.S. population,[11] as a broad range of surveys indicate, and if roughly half to two-thirds are in partnered relationships, as studies indicate, then there

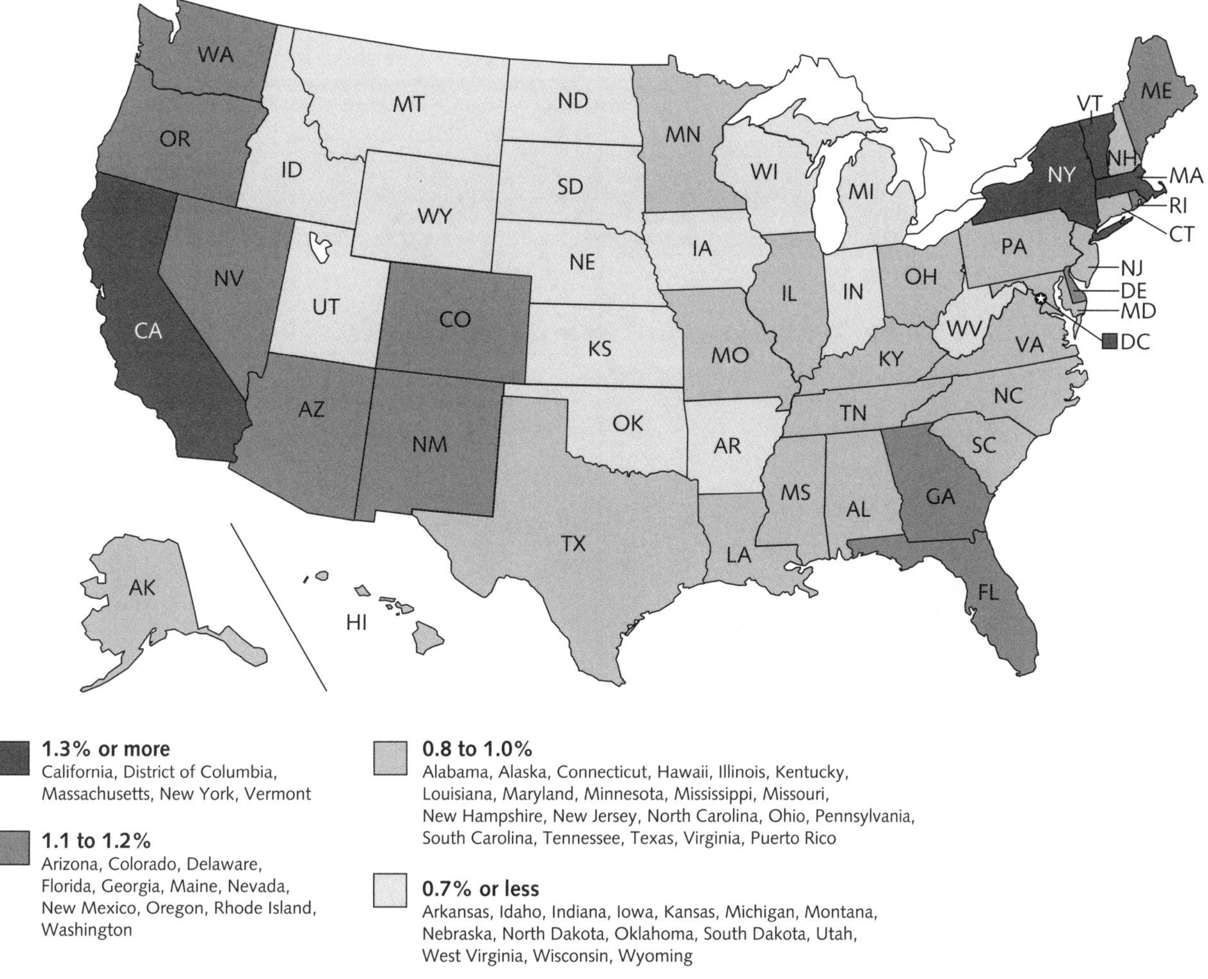

Fig. 1. Density of same-sex couples versus all coupled households.
Data from T. Simmons and M. O'Connell, *Married-Couple and Unmarried-Partner Households, 2000* [Washington, DC: U.S. Census Bureau, 2003], http://www.census.gov/prod/2003pubs/censr-5.pdf [accessed February 20, 2004]. Reproduced courtesy of the National Gay and Lesbian Task Force.

are as many as two to three million same-sex couples in the United States. However, this is a very rough estimate, and the actual number could be significantly different.

Many same-sex couples may not live together. Therefore they would not have been able to self-identify on the 2000 Census as cohabiting unmarried partners. Because of the way the U.S. Census allows same-sex cohabiting couples to self-identify, it misses many gay people, including those who are single, those whose partners have died, and people who are in a long-term same-sex relationship but who are not cohabiting with their partner. Many cohabiting gay and lesbian couples may have chosen not to indicate that they were "unmarried partners" because they did not want the government to have this information. In a country where gay people were by definition criminals under the sodomy laws on the books in fifteen states until June

2003 and in which federal, state, and local governments continue to officially discriminate in many ways, this is not surprising. Nonetheless, the U.S. Census data allow us to describe a large sample of same-sex couples, or gay and lesbian families.[12]

In 2000, same-sex couple households were reported in 99.3 percent of all U.S. counties and represented every ethnic, racial, and income group

TABLE 1. Ohio Same-Sex Households by County, 2000 Census

County	Gay	Lesbian	Total	County	Gay	Lesbian	Total
State Totals	**9,266**	**9,671**	**18,937**	Licking County	106	128	234
Adams County	18	17	35	Logan County	35	30	65
Allen County	62	66	128	Lorain County	178	204	382
Ashland County	36	40	76	Lucas County	402	479	881
Ashtabula County	75	88	163	Madison County	24	29	53
Athens County	46	52	98	Mahoning County	146	167	313
Auglaize County	10	21	31	Marion County	35	45	80
Belmont County	36	43	79	Medina County	81	82	163
Brown County	27	34	61	Meigs County	21	24	45
Butler County	208	248	456	Mercer County	15	18	33
Carroll County	22	15	37	Miami County	54	71	125
Champaign County	22	23	45	Monroe County	8	10	18
Clark County	104	102	206	Montgomery County	533	545	1,078
Clermont County	133	142	275	Morgan County	11	10	21
Clinton County	18	36	54	Morrow County	17	25	42
Columbiana County	52	72	124	Muskingum County	62	50	112
Coshocton County	18	22	40	Noble County	8	7	15
Crawford County	26	27	53	Ottawa County	20	25	45
Cuyahoga County	1,368	1,326	2,694	Paulding County	9	18	27
Darke County	27	22	49	Perry County	21	32	53
Defiance County	19	16	35	Pickaway County	23	46	69
Delaware County	106	113	219	Pike County	19	21	40
Erie County	59	44	103	Portage County	75	121	196
Fairfield County	72	99	171	Preble County	24	24	48
Fayette County	25	25	50	Putnam County	13	13	26
Franklin County	1,718	1,523	3,241	Richland County	89	85	174
Fulton County	20	32	52	Ross County	49	66	115
Gallia County	25	11	36	Sandusky County	36	44	80
Geauga County	51	51	102	Scioto County	42	66	108
Greene County	88	127	215	Seneca County	25	39	64
Guernsey County	16	18	34	Shelby County	31	38	69
Hamilton County	822	798	1,620	Stark County	224	271	495
Hancock County	65	61	126	Summit County	491	464	955
Hardin County	14	23	37	Trumbull County	130	143	273
Harrison County	13	10	23	Tuscarawas County	43	61	104
Henry County	19	17	36	Union County	17	23	40
Highland County	26	25	51	Van Wert County	16	15	31
Hocking County	13	28	41	Vinton County	13	5	18
Holmes County	30	24	54	Warren County	95	94	189
Huron County	20	31	51	Washington County	40	42	82
Jackson County	23	27	50	Wayne County	57	55	112
Jefferson County	49	55	104	Williams County	15	21	36
Knox County	42	49	91	Wood Conty	72	95	167
Lake County	128	139	267	Wyandot County	9	22	31
Lawrence County	61	56	117				

Source: Data from the 2000 U.S. Census, U.S. Census Bureau, Washington, DC, analyzed in J. Bradford, K. Barett, and J. A. Honnold, *The 2000 Census and Same-Sex Households: A User's Guide* (New York: Policy Institute of the National Gay and Lesbian Task Froce, 2002), 107.

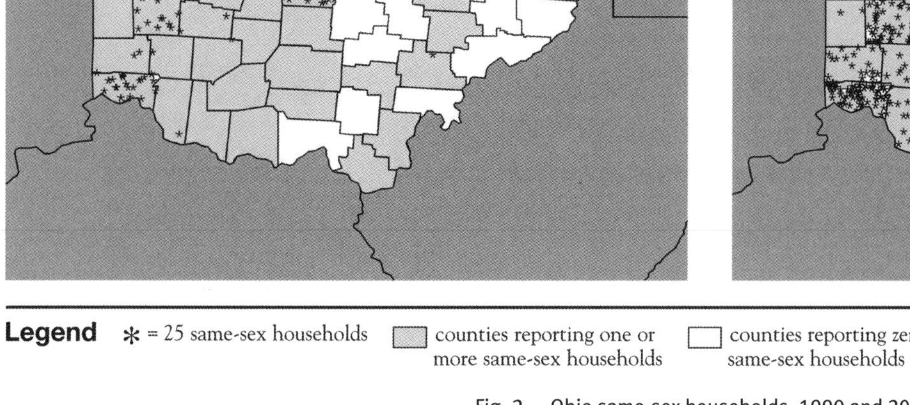

Fig. 2. Ohio same-sex households, 1990 and 2000.
Map by Kirsten Barrett.

and every adult age-group.[13] For example, about 14 percent of all same-sex couples, or eighty-five thousand same-sex couples reported on the 2000 Census, include at least one black or African American adult. Four in five of these "black same-sex couples" include two black men or two black women. The other 20 percent include one black man or woman and one man or woman of another race.[14] This and other analyses indicate that the U.S. Census's same-sex household sample reflects the racial diversity of the overall U.S. population.

PARENTING AMONG SAME-SEX COUPLES AND SINGLE GAY PARENTS

Many same-sex couples are raising children. Estimates of the number of lesbian or gay parents in the United States range from two to eight million.[15] These figures include many single parents who are lesbian, gay, or bisexual. Data from the 2000 Census indicate that 34 percent of lesbian couples and 22 percent of gay male couples[16] have at least one child under eighteen years of age living in their home.[17] While these figures may not seem that high, when compared with parenting rates among married heterosexual couples (46 percent of whom are raising children), lesbian couples on the 2000 Census parent at about three-quarters the rate of married straight couples, and gay male couples parent at about half the rate as married straight couples. Many more are parents of children who do not live with them or are "empty nesters" because their children are away at college or living on their own as adults.

RESEARCH ON CHILDREN OF LESBIAN, GAY, AND BISEXUAL PARENTS

Anti-gay groups portray parenting by gay men, lesbians, and same-sex couples as a threat to children. For example, Focus on the Family ran a full-page advertisement in the *Boston Globe* in January 2004, just as the Massachusetts legislature was reacting to the state high court's ruling legalizing marriage for same-sex couples. The ad claimed: "Same-sex marriage advocates and the Massachusetts Supreme Judicial Court are asking our state and nation to enter a massive, untested social experiment with coming generations of children. We must ask one simple question: Is the same-sex 'family' good for children?"[18] Conservative elected officials echo these claims with statements that "every child needs/deserves a mother and a father." For example, Massachusetts governor Mitt Romney said at the Republican National Convention in August 2004, "because every child deserves a mother and a father, we step forward by recognizing that marriage is between a man and a woman."[19]

The vast majority of children's advocacy organizations recognize that most lesbian and gay parents are good parents and that children can and do thrive in gay and lesbian families. Several leading professional organizations concerned with child welfare have made statements to this effect.

The American Academy of Pediatrics. "A growing body of scientific literature demonstrates that children who grow up with 1 or 2 gay and/or lesbian parents fare as well in emotional, cognitive, social and sexual functioning as do children whose parents are heterosexual."[20]

The American Psychological Association. "Not a single study has found children of gay or lesbian parents to be disadvantaged in any significant respect relative to children of heterosexual parents."[21]

The National Association of Social Workers, in conjunction with the Ameri-

can Psychological Association. "[C]hildren who retain regular and unrestricted contact with a gay or lesbian parent are as healthy psychologically or socially as children raised by heterosexual parents and . . . the parenting skills of gay fathers and lesbian mothers are comparable to their heterosexual counterparts."[22]

The American Psychoanalytic Association. "Accumulated evidence suggests the best interest of the child requires attachment to committed, nurturing and competent parents. Evaluation of an individual or couple for these parental qualities should be determined without prejudice regarding sexual orientation. Gay and lesbian individuals and couples are capable of meeting the best interest of the child and should be afforded the same rights and should accept the same responsibilities as heterosexual parents."[23]

The American Academy of Family Physicians called for their group to "establish policy and be supportive of legislation which promotes a safe and nurturing environment, including psychological and legal security, for all children, including those of adoptive parents, regardless of the parents' sexual orientation."[24]

These positions are based on decades of social science research that has discredited the overly simplistic premise that it is always in the best interest of a child to be raised by two heterosexual, married parents. For example, Silverstein and Auerbach contend:

> [O]ur research with divorced, never-married and remarried fathers has taught us that a wide variety of family structures can support positive child outcomes. We have concluded that children need at least one responsible, caretaking adult who has a positive emotional connection to them and with whom they have a consistent relationship . . . We share the concern that many men in U.S. society do not have a feeling of emotional connection or a sense of responsibility toward their children. However, we do not believe that the data support the conclusion that fathers are essential to child well-being and that heterosexual marriage is the social context in which responsible fathering is most likely to occur.[25]

In a comparison of five different family structures—families with adoptive children, two-parent families with biological children, single-mother headed families with biological children, families with a stepfather present, and families with a stepmother present—researchers concluded that there

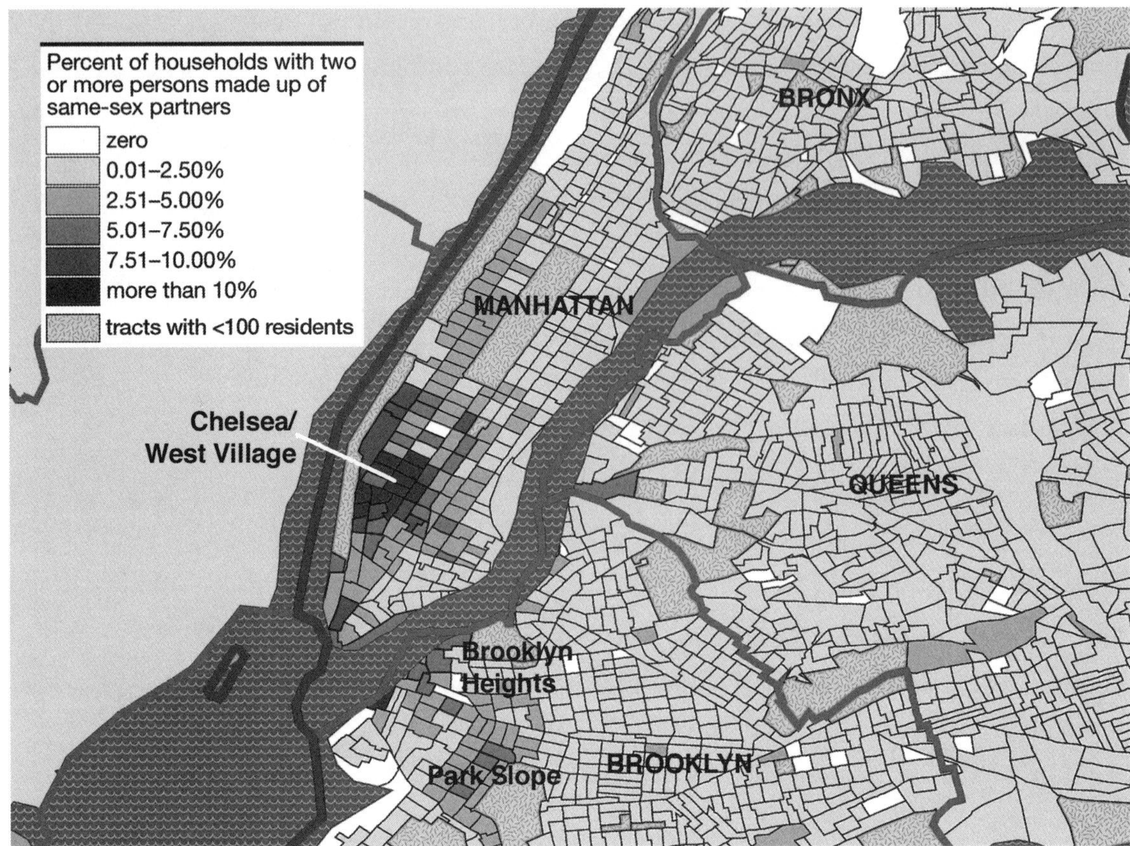

Fig. 3. Same-sex couples in New York City (based on 2000 U.S. Census data).
Reprinted from J. Bradford, K. Barrett, and J. A. Honnold, *The 2000 Census and Same-Sex Households: A User's Guide* (New York: Policy Institute of the National Gay and Lesbian Task Force, 2002), 106–7.

were no major differences in children raised by single mothers compared to the children raised in other household types. Specifically, children from single-mother households did not report any differences in well-being or parental relationships as compared to other children.[26]

Sociologists debunk the claim that heterosexual parents are more successful in raising children than are lesbian or gay couples.[27] One 12-year study found that same-sex couples were better at managing disagreements than heterosexual married couples.[28] A literature review on lesbian and gay families with children concludes that the fears some have that children from families without fathers—such as lesbian families—will suffer "deficits" in personal development are without empirical support.[29] One study of psychosocial development among preschool and school-age children finds:

> [C]hildren of lesbian mothers' scores for social competence, internalizing behavior problems and externalizing behavior problems . . . did not differ from the scores for a large normative sample of American children.

> Likewise, children of lesbian mothers reported gender-role preferences within the expected normal range for children of this age.[30]

A review of current research on various family structures reveals a clear pattern: family structure is not a strong determinate of a child's well-being, and lesbian and gay parents can raise children as well as heterosexual parents can.[31] These conclusions are likely true of bisexual parents also. Although there is a lack of research focusing specifically on bisexual parents, it is highly probable that bisexuals in same-sex relationships are included in the samples of many of these studies. Since many studies do not ask people to self-identify by sexual orientation, there are no conclusive findings on bisexual parents. The addition of such a question to all parenting studies, including those focusing on opposite-sex couples, is merited and would greatly enhance our knowledge in this area.

RESEARCH ON CHILDREN OF TRANSGENDER PARENTS

There is very little research on the children of transgender parents. The few preliminary studies that exist have found that these children are not negatively affected by their parent's gender identity. A 1978 study of sixteen children from homes with transsexuals (seven raised by male-to-female transsexuals and nine by female-to-male transsexuals) found that the children did not differ appreciably from those raised in more conventional family settings.[32]

In a 1999 survey of therapists working with transgender clients, the vast majority of respondents agreed that while a parent's gender transition was not a neutral event, a parent's postponing transitioning and maintaining secrets about his or her gender identity is much more difficult for children to handle. In addition, among the survey respondents, there was "an overall consensus that factors within the parental relationship and family constellation had significantly more bearing on the outcome for the children than the transition itself."[33] Children were more likely to adjust well to the transition when they were able to maintain close relationships with both parents. Having supportive family members and minimal conflict between parents were closely linked to good outcomes for the children. The study showed that in most cases it is unnecessary and inadvisable for a transgender parent to postpone transitioning until the child becomes an adult.[34]

Much more study is warranted into the experiences, needs, and concerns of children of transgender parents. However, the existing research contradicts the notion that it is better for children to not continue a relationship with a transgender parent. This research indicates that ending parental contact, limiting custody, or requiring a parent to postpone transitioning can all be much more harmful than helpful to the children concerned.

RACIAL DIFFERENCES IN PARENTING RATES AMONG SAME-SEX COUPLES AND LGBT PEOPLE

Some studies indicate a significant prevalence of parenting among lesbian and gay African Americans and other people of color. The National Gay and Lesbian Task Force's 2000 Black Pride Survey queried nearly twenty-seven hundred African American gay, lesbian, bisexual, and transgender people in nine cities. It found that nearly 40 percent of black lesbians and bisexual women, 15 percent of black gay and bisexual men, and 15 percent of black transgender people reported having children. Twenty-five percent of the women and 4 percent of the men surveyed at Black Gay Pride celebrations reported that those children lived with them.[35] An earlier study found that one in four black lesbians and 2 percent of black gay men lived with a child for whom they had child-rearing responsibilities. One in three black lesbians reported having at least one child, as did nearly 12 percent of the gay black men surveyed.[36]

The 1990 Census data reflecting the first time the U.S. Census allowed cohabiting gay couples to self-identify indicated that ethnic minority women in same-sex relationships may be more likely than white, non-Hispanic lesbians to have children.[37] Initial analysis of the 2000 Census data indicate much higher parenting rates among black same-sex couples than among white same-sex couples.[38] These statistics indicate that anti-gay parenting policies and laws may disproportionately affect gay, lesbian, and bisexual people of color.

The states with the highest prevalence of parenting among same-sex couple households on the 2000 Census were southern and rural states. For example, in Mississippi 31 percent of gay male couples who self-identified on the 2000 Census were raising children, as were 44 percent of lesbian couples. This compares with 22 percent of gay male couples and 34 percent of lesbian couples nationally. South Dakota and Alaska also reported high rates of parenting by same-sex couples. Some 24 percent of gay male couples and 36 percent of lesbian couples in southern states reported raising chil-

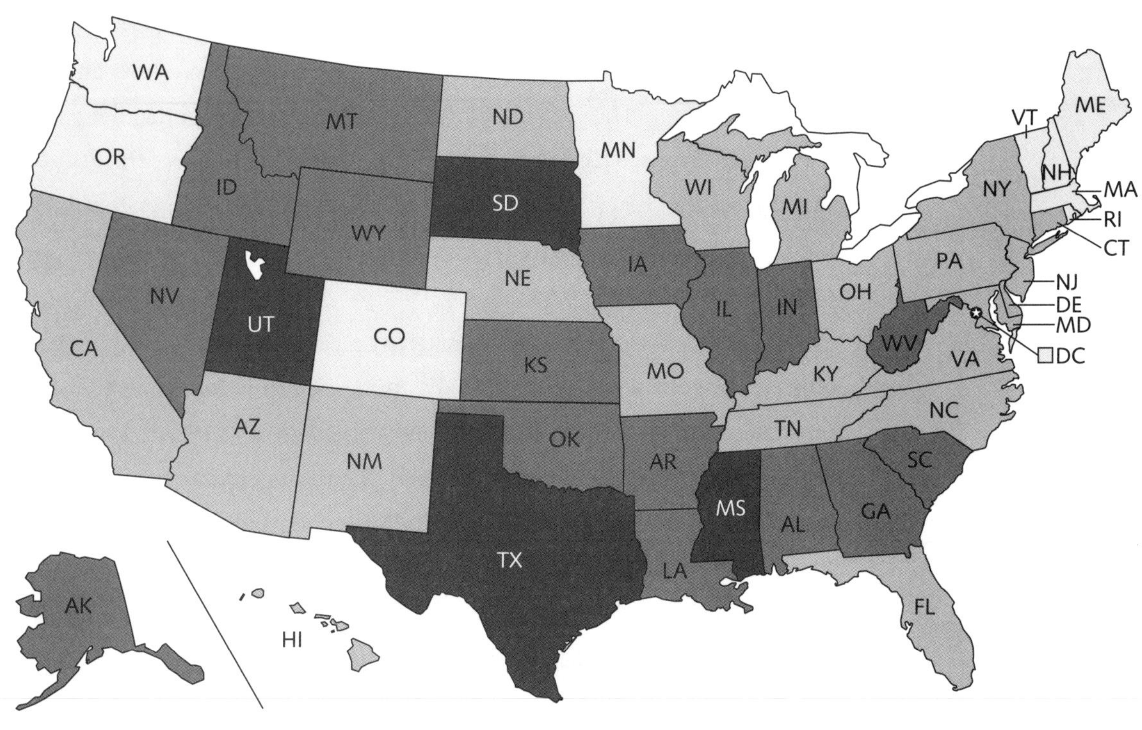

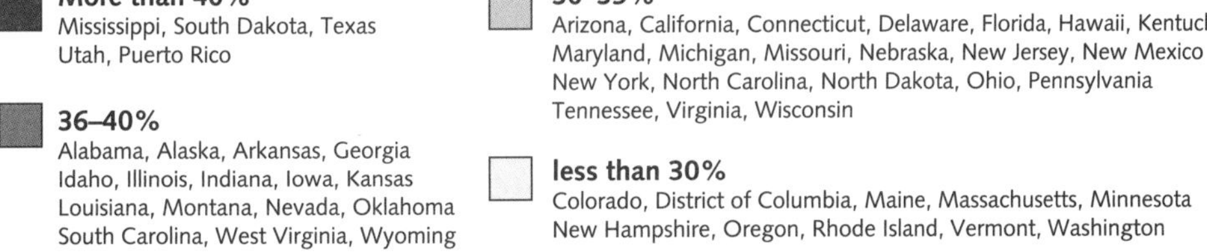

Fig. 4. Prevalence of parenting: percentage of lesbian couples raising children. Data from U.S. Census Bureau.

dren who lived in their homes. Both rates—that for gay male couples and that for lesbian couples—are two percentage points above the national average.[39] Unfortunately, most states with anti-gay parenting policies are in the U.S. South.

INCOME AND PARENTING

Despite the widespread stereotype that gay men and lesbians are wealthier than the general population, a claim frequently deployed by anti-gay groups, research shows otherwise.[40] An analysis of 1990 Census data and U.S. General Social Survey data from the late 1980s and early 1990s indicates that gay men earn about one-fifth to one-quarter less than their heterosexual counterparts. Lesbians appear to earn about the same as heterosexual women, but lesbian couples earn less than straight couples, because women, on average, earn less than men.[41] Preliminary data from the 2000 Census indicate similar earnings between same-sex couple households and opposite-sex couple households.[42] Yet lesbian couples in particular earn less, on average, than married opposite-sex couples. For example, the 2000 Census reported that black female same-sex couples (black lesbian couples) earn nine thousand dollars less in average household income than black married opposite-sex couples.[43]

Even when same-sex couples earn the same as heterosexual married couples, they often pay more in taxes and are eligible for fewer elements of the social safety net, such as Social Security survivor benefits. For example, domestic partner health insurance, when offered, is taxed as income. In comparison, spousal health insurance, which married heterosexual couples can access, is tax-exempt.[44]

Low- and moderate-income gay families confront obstacles because many public policies and private employers do not recognize their families. Poor lesbians and gay men grapple with a welfare system that increasingly favors married heterosexual couples over single parents and all unmarried couples, including same-sex couples.[45] Homeless same-sex couples may be unable to apply for public housing as a family. Gay youth are often mistreated in state-run foster care systems.

The lack of equal access to marriage and adoption forces many gay couples to spend thousands of dollars on legal documents to protect their families—documents that are not always upheld in court or respected by hospitals, banks, and other institutions. Those who cannot afford such legal fees can find their families without even minimal protections in times of crisis. Gay individuals and families in need of social services may experience hostility, discrimination, and even proselytizing at the hands of social service providers under the faith-based initiative.[46]

A FAMILY STORY

A Profile of Akilah Monifa and Ruth Bolden

When Akilah Monifa and Ruth Bolden decided they wanted to have a child, they didn't realize the full extent of hurdles they would face. Living in California, a state with relatively positive gay parenting laws, and specifically in the San Francisco Bay Area, which is known to have a selection of services for gay and lesbian families, they thought they were well situated. Initially, they decided to use donor insemination and began researching fertility clinics to find one that would meet their needs. Calling fertility clinics that primarily served lesbians, they soon discovered that most did not carry sperm from donors of color. The apologetic tone of the responses was no comfort to the two African American women, who were frustrated that the clinics were clearly not seeking to serve them.

Akilah and Ruth began calling out-of-state clinics throughout the country. Common responses to their explanation that they were two women seeking to have a child were "We serve families," "This is a Christian-based organization," and "We don't serve your kind." They also continued to experience difficulty in finding places that had a range of sperm donors of color. When they asked if a sperm bank might have sperm from a Jewish person of color (Ruth is Jewish), they were asked, "Why would you want that?!" Akilah describes fertility clinics as, "akin to country clubs," with various mechanisms for selecting their clientele. After much effort, they eventually found a place that met their needs. Unfortunately, Ruth was unable to carry her pregnancies to full term. Akilah and Ruth then decided to pursue adoption.

The couple enrolled in an adoption class and joined a support group. They decided they would like an open adoption where the family maintains contact with the birth mother and the child has the option of having a relationship with her. They also wanted a child of African descent. Again they began the process of researching agencies, and again they were turned away with statements like "We have never worked with gays or lesbians, so we are probably not the best agency for you." Some agencies said that Ruth, who is biracial and light-skinned, should pass as white because it would increase the couple's likelihood of being chosen. Eventually they found an agency that had worked both with African American couples and with gay and lesbian couples, but it soon became clear that even this was not enough. The agency had not previously worked with African American gay or lesbian couples, which Akilah says was "probably the reason they were not able to make a match." She believes this was reflected in the way the agency representatives talked to African American birth mothers and would regularly ask if they would be willing to have a gay or lesbian adoptive couple.

Fortunately, the next agency they worked with in New York took a different approach. When an African American birth mother said she would like her child to be raised by a single woman, it took only one question for the birth mother to say that she would consider a lesbian couple. She looked over and approved Akilah and Ruth's application. In January 2001, four years after deciding they would like to raise a child, Akilah and Ruth became proud parents of a baby girl, Isabella Bolden Monifa.

Reflecting on the process, Akilah notes the multiple subtle ways in which assumption of parents' heterosexuality pervades society. One recurrent problem is that forms ask parents or prospective parents to fill out "mother" and "father." "It is so easy to change forms to say 'parent' and 'parent,' and this would be inclusive of anyone who is acting as a parent, like a grandparent," Akilah says. Ruth and Akilah have experienced this problem with fertility clinics, adoption agencies, social service agencies, hospitals, and even California birth certificates. This is despite the fact that California is one of a few states that allows simultaneous joint adoption by gay and lesbian parents. Akilah also marvels at how the fact that Isabella has two mothers seems to make curious people feel free to ask completely inappropriate questions, even in front of Isabella. "Which one of you is the mother?" (to which Ruth and Akilah respond, "Both of us") is often followed by "Who is the real mother?" (again, the response is "Both of us") and then even "Who gave birth to her?" or "Did you adopt her?"

Akilah knows her daughter will face challenges because of her race and because she has two mothers. But the fact that society has changed its attitude toward those who are adopted and those who are gay—both categories that were seen as shameful secrets—makes Akilah feel more optimistic about the future. In the meantime, she and Ruth strive to do their best: they love Isabella, talk honestly to her, tell Isabella her adoption story, and teach her that it's not a big deal to say, "I have two mommies."

Source: Adapted from S. Cahill, M. Ellen, and S. Tobias, *Family Policy: Issues Affecting Gay, Lesbian, Bisexual, and Transgender Families* (New York: Policy Institute of the National Gay and Lesbian Task Force, 2002).

ADOPTION AND CUSTODY ISSUES

Some lesbian, gay, and bisexual parents discover or come to terms with their sexual orientation while they are married to someone of the opposite sex, trying to live life as a heterosexual. When these marriages end, parents are often confronted with custody challenges. In nearly every state, custody decisions must be determined according to the "best interests of the child." Even so, application of this general rule varies greatly from state to state and even from judge to judge. The District of Columbia is currently the only jurisdiction in the country that has a statute explicitly guaranteeing that sexual orientation cannot, in and of itself, be a conclusive factor in determining custody or visitation.[47] But even some very conservative courts have recently shifted away from considering the sexual orientation of a parent in custody decisions.[48] However, in Tennessee in 2002, a gay father was jailed for two days for revealing his sexual orientation to his son.[49] In the same year, Alabama chief justice Roy Moore—later famous for refusing a U.S. Supreme Court order to remove a sculpture of the Ten Commandments from Alabama's Supreme Court—denied a lesbian mother custody of her children based on the criminalization of homosexuality under the state's sodomy law. "Common law designates homosexuality as an inherent evil, and if a person openly engages in such a practice, that fact alone would render him or her an unfit parent," Moore wrote in justifying his decision to deny the mother custody. Moore also wrote approvingly of the state's right to imprison or even execute homosexuals.[50]

Prior to the June 2003 *Lawrence v. Texas* ruling overturning archaic sex laws, such "sodomy" laws as Alabama's were frequently used to deny gay men, lesbians, and bisexuals consideration as prospective adoptive parents and even custody of or visitation with their own biological children.[51] In some parts of the country, divorce courts routinely impose cohabitation restrictions preventing noncustodial parents from living with unmarried partners in order to be able to maintain visitation rights. In forty-nine states, gay men and lesbians cannot marry their partners. Due to the current ban on marriage for same-sex couples in most states, gay relationships are by definition cohabiting relationships in most jurisdictions. In this sense, noncohabitation requirements unfairly discriminate against gay and lesbian parents.[52]

When same-sex couples jointly raise children, one parent almost always lacks a biological or adoptive relationship to the children. Appellate courts in fifteen states have found that a coparent who met specified standards had a legal right to seek visitation and/or custody of a child he or she had raised.[53] But there have also been numerous cases in which the coparent was left without visitation or custody rights.[54] Several gay organizations and individuals authored a set of ethical standards for child custody disputes in same-sex relationships to avoid court litigation.[55]

Gay and lesbian adults are among the thousands who adopt children each year. Some adopt children they are raising with a partner (often the biological child of their partner), thereby creating a legal bond where a familial one already exists. Some are chosen by family members or close friends to adopt a child upon the death or incapacitation of the child's own parents. Many adopt through public or private agencies, domestically and internationally. Some work through intermediaries to identify women wishing to have their babies adopted and to reach agreements directly with those birth mothers.

ANTI-GAY LAWS AND REGULATIONS CONCERNING ADOPTION AND FOSTER PARENTING

Most U.S. states permit adoptions by single individuals, including gay men, lesbians, and bisexuals. However, a few states explicitly prohibit or regularly deny adoptions and foster parenting by gay people. Many states deny lesbian and gay couples the ability to jointly adopt a child or the option for one parent to adopt a child that already has a legal bond to the other parent. In contrast, married couples are free to pursue joint adoption, and stepparent adoption by a spouse tends to be a simple process.

At least seven states limit, in some fashion, the ability of gay men, lesbians, or same-sex couples to adopt or foster parent.[56] Four states—Florida, Mississippi, Nebraska, and Oklahoma—have express restrictions on gay adoption. Thanks in part to Anita Bryant's "Save Our Children" campaign

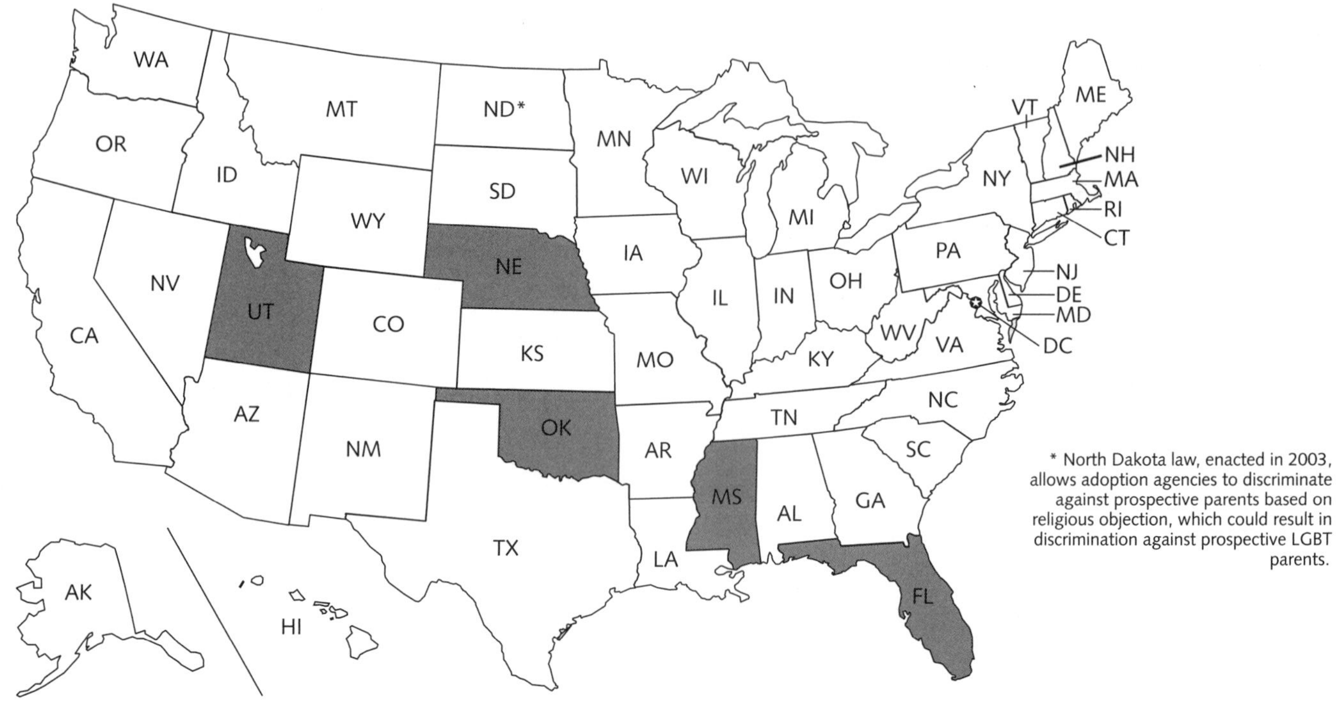

States with Laws Restricting Gay Adoption

Nebraska — Nebraska policy, by 1995 directive of the then director of Nebraska's Department of Social Services, prohibits adoption by individuals "who are known by the agency to be homosexual or who are unmarried and living with another adult." An amendment to the Nebraska state constitution restricting marriage to opposite-sex couples was struck down in 2005. The state is appealing that decision.

Florida — Florida law, enacted in 1977, expressly prohibits "homosexual" individuals from adopting.

Mississippi — Mississippi law, enacted in 2000, expressly prohibits "adoption by couples of the same gender."

Oklahoma — Oklahoma law, enacted in 2004, expressly prohibits the "state, any of its agencies, or any court" from recognizing "an adoption by more than one individual of the same sex from any other state or foreign jurisdiction." The ACLU is challenging this prohibition.

Utah — Utah law, enacted in 2000, prohibits adoption "by a person who is cohabitating in a relationship that is not a legally valid and binding marriage" under Utah state law. (Cohabiting is defined as "residing with a person and being involved in a sexual relationship with that person.") The law also prohibits the placement of foster children with unmarried couples. The Utah state constitution restricts marriage to opposite-sex couples.

Fig. 5. Adoption laws in the United States as of January 2006.
Reproduced courtesy of the National Gay and Lesbian Task Force.

that overthrew Miami-Dade County's sexual orientation nondiscrimination law in 1977, Florida has explicitly banned adoptions by "homosexuals" for more than a quarter century. Mississippi bans "same-sex couples" from adopting. In 1995, the director of Nebraska's Department of Social Services issued a directive banning "known" homosexuals and unmarried couples from adopting. Oklahoma passed an anti-gay adoption law in May 2004, banning recognition of joint or second-parent adoptions by same-sex couples who move to Oklahoma from another state. A fifth state, Utah, has an implied, de facto restriction on adoption by gay people and same-sex couples. Utah bans adoption by "cohabiting" unmarried couples. In 2003, in the wake of a high-profile adoption by a gay male couple, a sixth state, North Dakota, passed a law that allows adoption agencies that receive state con-

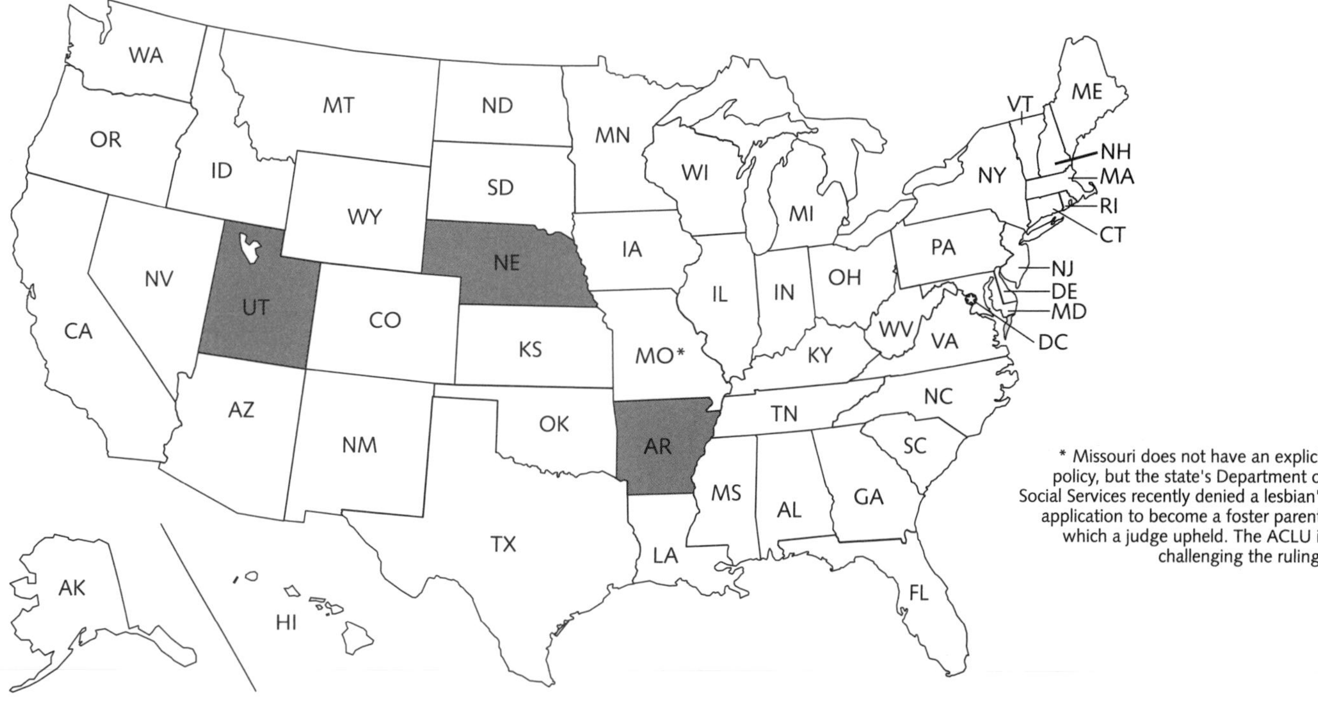

States with Laws Restricting Foster Parenting

Arkansas — Arkansas policy, adopted in 1999, expressly prohibits a person from serving as a foster parent if he or she is a homosexual or "if any adult member of that person's household is a homosexual." A 2004 court decision striking down this policy is currently being appealed.

Nebraska — Nebraska policy, by 1995 directive of the then director of Nebraska's Department of Social Services, prohibits the placement of foster children with individuals "who are known by the agency to be homosexual or who are unmarried and living with another adult." An amendment to the Nebraska state constitution restricting marriage to opposite-sex couples was struck down in 2005, and the state is appealing that decision.

Utah — Utah law, enacted in 2000, prohibits the placement of foster children with "a person who is cohabitating in a relationship that is not a legally valid and binding marriage" under Utah state law. (Cohabiting is defined as "residing with a person and being involved in a sexual relationship with that person.") The Utah state constitution restricts marriage to opposite-sex couples.

Fig. 6. Foster care regulations in the United States as of January 2006. Reproduced courtesy of the National Gay and Lesbian Task Force.

tracts and licenses to refuse to place children with prospective parents to whom they object on religious grounds. This means adoption agencies could refuse to place children with gay individuals or couples, as well as unmarried opposite-sex couples, single mothers, divorced people, and many others.

At least three states—Arkansas, Nebraska, and Utah— prohibit gay and lesbian individuals and/or same-sex couples from serving as foster parents. Since 1999, the Arkansas Child Welfare Agency Review Board has banned gays and lesbians from foster parenting. This ban was struck down in December 2004; as this book went to press, the state was appealing the ruling to a higher court. Nebraska also prohibits gay men and lesbians from foster parenting. Arkansas and Utah prohibit foster parenting—either explicitly or implicitly—by same-sex couples. Even in many states where lesbians and gay men are technically able to adopt or foster parent as individuals, judges sometimes intervene to prevent the placement of a child with a lesbian or gay parent.

JOINT AND SECOND-PARENT ADOPTION

Adoptions that codify the parental relationship of both parents are essential to ensuring the rights and security of children of same-sex couple parents. When a child is not biologically related to either parent, a joint adoption allows both parents to simultaneously adopt a child. During the 1980s, lower courts in the San Francisco Bay Area began granting same-sex couples the right to adopt children jointly and simultaneously. Since then, courts have been allowing such adoptions more frequently. Joint adoption is currently available in the District of Columbia, California, Connecticut, Massachusetts, and Vermont.[57]

A second-parent adoption allows the biological or adoptive parent to retain his or her parental rights, while consenting to the adoption of the child by his or her partner. Second-parent adoptions have been in use since 1985, when Alaska granted one of the first to a same-sex couple. Since the mid-1980s, courts in nearly two dozen states have approved second-parent adoptions.[58] In 2000, the Connecticut legislature created a mechanism for joint and second-parent adoptions.[59] Second-parent adoptions are generally possible only when a third party does not already have legal parental rights. While courts in twenty-two states have permitted second-parent adoptions by gay partners and while laws in three states explicitly permit second-parent adoption by a gay partner, children of same-sex couples in most states still live with the economic and emotional insecurity of not having their relationship with their second mother or father recognized. In four states, courts have ruled that the state's adoption law does not allow for second-parent or stepparent adoption by gay partners.[60]

Without the legal protections that come with adoption, a child can be left without access to basic benefits, including health insurance and inheritance rights. If the legally recognized parent dies, a child may be removed from the custody of his or her other parent, unless that parent has been designated the child's guardian in a will. If a child of gay parents becomes sick, the legal parent's partner may be unable to authorize medical treatment and may even be denied hospital visitation rights.

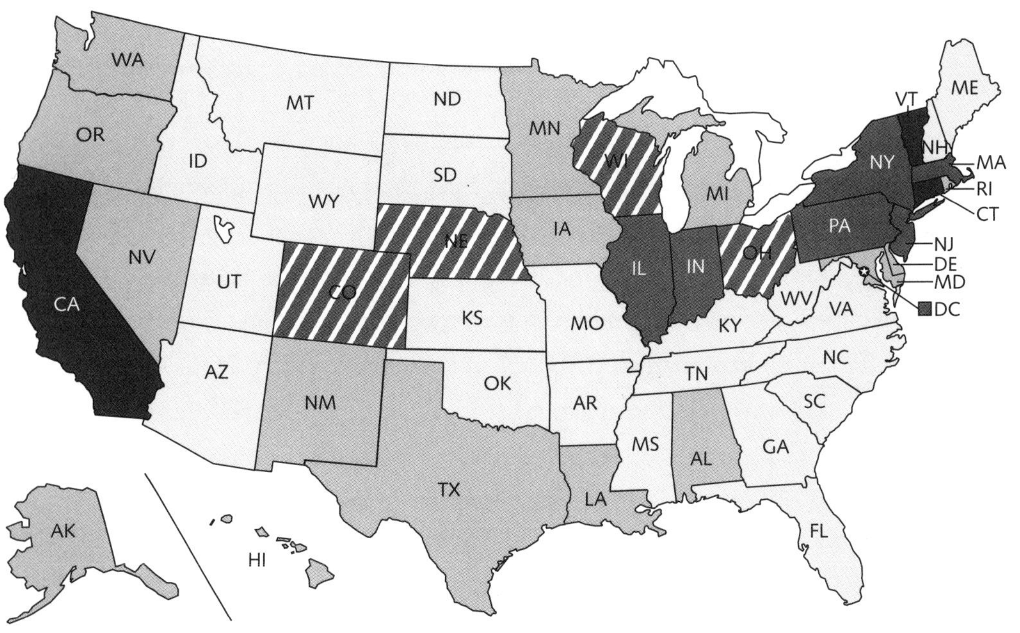

States where second-parent adoption is authorized by statute (3 states):
California, Connecticut, Vermont[1]

States where appellate courts have ruled that the state adoption law permits second-parent adoption (7 states and the District of Columbia):
California, District of Columbia, Illinois, Indiana, Massachusetts, New York, New Jersey, Pennsylvania[2]

States where trial courts have granted second-parent adoptions (15 states):
Alabama, Alaska, Delaware, Hawaii, Iowa, Louisiana, Maryland, Michigan, Minnesota, Nevada, New Mexico, Oregon, Rhode Island, Texas, Washington

States where appellate courts have ruled that the state adoption law does NOT permit second-parent adoption (4 states):
Colorado, Nebraska, Ohio, Wisconsin[3]

States where it is unclear whether the state adoption law permits second parent adoptions. (22 states):
Arizona, Arkansas, Florida, Georgia, Idaho, Kansas, Kentucky, Maine, Mississippi, Missouri, Montana, New Hampshire, North Carolina, North Dakota, Oklahoma, South Carolina, South Dakota, Tennessee, Utah, Virginia, West Virginia, Wyoming

A second-parent adoption is a legal procedure that allows a same-sex parent to adopt his or her partner's biological or adoptive child without terminating the legal rights of the first parent. States must honor second-parent adoption judgments from other states.*

* See *Russell v. Bridgens,* 647 N.W.2d 56 (Neb. 2002) (Nebraska must recognize second-parent adoption granted in Pennsylvania, even though Nebraska would not have permitted such an adoption); *Starr v. Erez,* COA99-1534 (N.C. Ct. App. Nov. 27, 2000) (North Carolina must honor second-parent adoption granted in Washington state). In May 2004, the Oklahoma legislature approved changes to the state adoption code so that the state "shall not recognize an adoption by more than one individual of the same sex from any other state or foreign jurisdiction." (Okla. Stat. Ann. tit. 10, § 7502-1.4 [2004]). A challenge to this statute is pending. See *Finstuen et al. v. Edmonson et al.,* CV-04-1152C (W.D. Okla. Dec. 7, 2004) (allowing suit to proceed).

1. Cal. Fam. Code § 9000(f) (2004) (registered domestic partners only); Conn. Gen. Stat. § 45a-724(3) (2004) (superseding *In re Adoption of Baby Z.,* 724 A.2d 1035 (1999)); Vt Stat. Ann. tit. 15A, § 1-102(b) (2004) (codifying *In re Adoption of B.L.V.B. & E.L.V.B.,* 628 A.2d 1271 [Vt. 1993]).

2. *Sharon S. v. Superior Court of San Diego County,* 73 P.3d 554 (Ca. 2003) (state's adoption law extends to same-sex couples not registered as domestic partners); *In re M.M.D. v. B.H.M.,* 662 A.2d 837 (D.C. 1995); *In re Petition of K.M. & D.M.,* 653 N.E.2d 888 (Ill. App. Ct. 1995); *In re Adoption of K.S.P.,* 804 N.E.2d 1253 (Ind. Ct. App. 2004); *In re Adoption of M.M.G.C.,* 785 N.E.2d 267 (Ind. Ct. App. 2003); *In re Adoption of Tammy,* 619 N.E.2d 315 (Mass. 1993); *In re Jacob, In re Dana,* 660 N.E.2d 397 (N.Y. 1995); *In re the Adoption of Two Children by H.N.R.,* 666 A.2d 535 (N.J. Super. 1995); *In re Adoption of R.B.F.& R.C.F.,* 803 A.2d 1195 (Pa. 2002).

3. *In re Adoption of T.K.J. and K.A.K.,* 931 P.2d 448 (Colo. Ct. App. 1996); *In re Adoption of Luke,* 640 N.W.2d 374 (Neb. 2002); *In re Adoption of Doe,* 719 N.E.2d 1071 (Ohio Ct. App. 1998); *Interest of Angel Lace M.,* 516 N.W.2d 678 (Wis. 1994).

Fig. 7. Second-parent adoption in the United States as of January 2005. Reproduced courtesy of the National Gay and Lesbian Task Force.

ACCESSING REPRODUCTIVE TECHNOLOGY

Donor Insemination

Donor insemination is a method that lesbians have used increasingly since the 1980s to conceive children. While some states have laws specifying that a sperm donor is not a legal father, most states have not addressed this issue directly. As a result, lesbians sometimes confront issues related to the paternity of the child born out of a donor insemination agreement. If they have acquired the sperm of an anonymous donor through a sperm bank, they can avoid challenges to their parental relationship and the integrity of their lesbian family. If they have used the sperm of a known donor, they run the risk of the man concerned ultimately demanding a parental role in their family. This can occur even when a preexisting arrangement mandates the contrary.

Although reproductive rights are usually understood to include the right to terminate an early-term or health-threatening pregnancy, for lesbians they also involve the right to access the technology that enables noncoital pregnancy. Many (perhaps most) sperm banks, fertility clinics, and doctors still balk at providing services to lesbians and gay men seeking to create a life.[61] No U.S. state expressly denies access to fertility clinics to lesbians, gay men, and/or unmarried couples, though in practice many individual clinics do. However, most big cities have at least one clinic that serves these prospective parents. But the cost of such services is out of reach of many lesbian individuals and couples. While fourteen states mandate medical insurance coverage of reproductive assistance, such coverage is usually limited to cases of infertility, and lesbian couples are often not seen as qualifying, because such assistance is not viewed as a medical necessity in the same way as an infertile heterosexual couple's need for assistance is deemed a necessity.[62] Consequently, donor insemination at a medical facility is often not an option available to low-income lesbians.

Some in the marriage movement and the fatherhood movement have strongly criticized donor insemination. Founded in conservative think tanks during the 1990s, the marriage and fatherhood movements now have key representatives in policymaking positions within the Bush-Cheney administration. David Blankenhorn, cofounder of the fatherhood movement along with Bush-Cheney appointees Wade Horn and Don Eberly, has advocated laws restricting access to fertility clinics to married heterosexual couples only. Blankenhorn has reserved particular vitriol for lesbian couples who choose to have a child with the help of a male friend or an anonymous sperm donor. In his 1995 book *Fatherless America: Confronting Our Most Urgent Social Problem*, in a chapter titled "The Sperm Father," Blankenhorn wrote: "The Sperm Father . . . is also a convenience father, the ideal solution for women who want to create manless families . . . [He] is also a fantasy father . . . for women, the fantasy of the little girl left alone to play with her dolls, no boys allowed."[63] Culturally, Blankenhorn added, "the rise of the Sperm Father constitutes nothing less than father killing . . . represents the final solution."[64]

Reiterating his claim that "every child deserves a father and that unwed childbearing is wrong," Blankenhorn called for cutting off the use of fertility clinics as an option for prospective lesbian mothers and other unmarried women. New laws should prohibit sperm banks and others from selling sperm to unmarried women, Blankenhorn argued, and should limit the use of artificial insemination to cases of married couples experiencing fertility problems. "In a good society, people do not traffic commercially in the production of radically fatherless children," Blankenhorn wrote.[65]

Surrogacy

While not nearly as widespread as the use of donor insemination by lesbians, gay men at times utilize surrogacy arrangements to create biological children. There are indications that parenting through surrogacy might be an increasingly frequent phenomenon. For example, in Los Angeles, an agency called Growing Generations was created to provide surrogacy services to the gay community. In the surrogacy process, the woman carrying the child may be a genetic parent to the child or a "gestational surrogate" carrying the fertilized egg of another woman.[66] The man involved often provides his own sperm, though not always. Like donor insemination agreements, surrogacy agreements can be formal or informal.[67] Surrogacy is a matter of controversy, with many states discouraging or limiting the practice.

Twenty-three states have passed laws dealing with surrogacy agreements.[68] Arizona and the District of Columbia have statutes that prohibit surrogacy. Michigan, New York, Washington, Florida, Nevada, New Hampshire, Virginia, and West Virginia technically prohibit payments to surrogates, but the laws in these states have many loopholes. Florida, Virginia, and New Hampshire presume that the two partners in the couple who contracts with the surrogate are the legal parents, while North Dakota and Utah attribute legal parentage to the surrogate and her husband.[69] For gay couples, the issue of legal parentage is a particularly important one. To preserve the integrity of their family, they need to be certain that the surrogate will not ultimately sue for custody. Usually, only the biological father is considered the legal parent.

THE STAKE OF BLACK SAME-SEX COUPLES IN THE MARRIAGE DEBATE

For at least two decades, the religious right has followed a clear strategy of pitting gay people against people of color. They have argued, incorrectly, that nondiscrimination laws concerning sexual orientation constitute "special rights" that threaten the civil rights of "legitimate minorities." A 2004 report by Concerned Women for America is titled "Homosexuals Hijack Civil Rights Bus."[70]

While racism and anti-gay bias are indeed different and while the situation of gay people in this country is quite different from that of African Americans, anti-gay groups are wrong to portray legal protections for gay people as a threat to people of color. (Of course, many gay people are also people of color.) In fact, U.S. Census data indicate that black same-sex couples may benefit more than white gay couples from the ability to marry and will be hurt most by the slew of anti-gay family amendments that have been adopted in more than a dozen U.S. states. This is because black lesbian couples are parenting at almost the same rate as black married couples and because black same-sex couples parent at twice the rate of white gay couples. They also earn less, are less likely to own a home, and are more likely to hold public sector jobs.[71]

Half of black female same-sex households (52 percent) are raising children. Households of black lesbian couples are almost as likely as households of black married opposite-sex couples to include a child of one or both of the adults (52 versus 58 percent). Nearly one third (32 percent) of the households of black male same-sex couples include one or more children. (Forty-four percent of all black same-sex households, male and female, report that they are raising at least one child under the age of eighteen.)

Black same-sex couples earn twenty thousand dollars less per year than white same-sex couples and are less likely to own the home they live in. They also earn less than black married opposite-sex couples. Black lesbian couples earn ten thousand dollars less in annual household income, on average, than black married straight couples; black gay male couples earn the same as black married opposite-sex couples.

Black same-sex couples are almost as likely as black married opposite-sex couples to report living in the same residence as five years earlier, a key indicator of relationship stability. Anti-gay groups frequently claim that same-sex relationships are unstable and typified by infidelity and promiscuity. Although maintaining the same residence for five years does not speak to infidelity (which is also widespread among heterosexual relationships), it can serve as a proxy for relationship stability.

Black same-sex partners are about 25 percent more likely than white gay partners to hold public sector jobs, which may provide domestic partner health insurance. Eight of the eleven state anti-gay marriage amendments approved in November 2004 ban or threaten domestic partner benefits provided through state and local governmental entities. In Georgia, domestic partner health coverage offered by Atlanta, Decatur, and Dekalb counties is in peril. In Ohio, unmarried but partnered employees of Ohio University, Ohio State University, Cleveland State University, and Youngstown State University could lose partner health coverage and other employer-provided benefits. The same goes for employees at the University of Michigan, Michigan State University, and the University of Utah. (In many cases, both opposite-sex and same-sex couples are affected.) Following the November 2004 election, Michigan governor Jennifer Granholm stripped state employees of domestic partner health insurance, claiming that she was forced to make this move because Michigan voters approved an amendment stating that "the union of one man and one woman in marriage shall be the only agreement recognized as a marriage or similar union for any purpose."[72]

Census data show that black men and women in same-sex households report serving in the military at high rates despite the risk of losing their income and benefits because of the ban on lesbian and gay people serving openly. In fact, partnered black women in same-sex households report veteran status at nearly four times the rate of black married women (11 percent vs. 3 percent). This finding is significant given that black women are discharged from the military under the "Don't ask, don't tell" policy at rates far exceeding their representation among service members: although they make up less than 1 percent of the military, they represent 3 percent of all discharges made under the "Don't ask, don't tell" policy.

The data on black same-sex couples from the 2000 Census underscore the hypocrisy of the Bush administration's aggressive attempts to deprive same-sex couples equal marriage rights while touting its multimillion-dollar African American Healthy Marriage Initiative as a way to strengthen the African American family. Denying the protections that come with marriage disproportionately hurts the ability of gay and lesbian African American couples to save money, provide for their children, buy a house, or prepare for retirement. Anti-gay leaders and organizations have long sought to divide the black and gay communities, speaking as if there are no black lesbian and gay people experiencing discrimination under key family policies. In fact, U.S. Census data clearly identify a large population of black same-sex couples in the United States, nearly half of whom are parents living with their children. These families have the same hopes and aspirations as other

American families. They deserve the same protections and opportunities to benefit from state and federal policies designed to promote family formation, stability, home ownership, and other values that contribute to community strength and the common good. Those who care about racial and economic justice should reject discriminatory antifamily amendments to our state and federal constitutions.

THE IMPACT THAT INITIATIVES PROMOTING HETEROSEXUAL MARRIAGE AND FATHERHOOD HAVE ON LOW-INCOME LESBIAN MOTHERS[73]

Since the mid-1990s, political and religious conservatives have constructed two seemingly contradictory threats to the American body politic: poor, presumably heterosexual, single mothers who fail to marry and same-sex couples, presumed to be economically privileged, who seek to marry. Both were portrayed as threats to the future of American—even Western—civilization. In 1996, proponents of the Personal Responsibility and Work Opportunity Reconciliation Act (known as welfare reform) claimed a causal relationship between the failure to marry and child poverty, as well as a host of social pathologies, such as child abuse, poor school performance, and juvenile crime. These unsubstantiated causal claims garnered wide public support despite the fact that higher out-of-wedlock birth rates exist in many European countries that also have much lower child poverty rates.[74] Also in 1996, the Defense of Marriage Act (DOMA) was passed by a bipartisan majority of Congress, banning federal recognition of same-sex marriages and allowing states to refuse to recognize such marriages performed in other states.[75]

The Bush-Cheney administration is promoting heterosexual marriage and the reinsertion of fathers into single-mother-led families as a key solution to child poverty. In January 2004, it was reported that the Bush administration is seeking $1.5 billion over five years to promote heterosexual marriage through "counseling services, public awareness campaigns and marriage enrichment courses."[76] This follows a great deal of state-level experimentation with heterosexual marriage promotion as a solution to poverty. The marriage and fatherhood movements are driving forces behind all of these efforts.[77] They have advocated policies promoting heterosexual marriage and fatherhood, including privileging married couples with children in the distribution of such limited supply benefits as public housing units, requiring mutual consent for divorce, and banning access to fertility clinics by unmarried couples.[78] Such policies would disproportionately hurt African American and Latino parents, who are more likely than white non-Hispanic parents to be single or unmarried.[79] Marriage and fatherhood promotion policies aimed at poor women also assume that all poor women are heterosexual and are both capable of and desire to marry a man. In fact, many poor women are bisexual or gay.

GAY YOUTH AND CHILDREN OF GAY PARENTS

Harassment and Violence in Schools

Gay and lesbian youth are self-identifying as gay at younger ages than ever before (on average at age sixteen), which dramatically impacts their family experience.[80] Self-identification at such an early age can expose gay, lesbian, bisexual, and transgender youths to harassment and violence, especially at school, where 85 percent hear anti-gay slurs and 31 percent are physically harassed on a regular basis.[81] Many children of gay and lesbian parents also suffer anti-gay harassment and violence.[82] A 1998 study of school counselors and their perceptions of the gay and lesbian students in their schools found that many of the students targeted for harassment were those whose parents were gay or lesbian.[83] While such widespread homophobic abuse requires an immediate response from school administrators and teachers, it also creates a greater need for appropriate counseling, health education, and family support.[84]

The Impact of Anti-Gay Harassment on Young People

School harassment and violence motivated by anti-gay bias can lead to lower levels of academic performance. Such harassment and violence is the foremost contributor to the high dropout rate among gay teens. It can drive down self-esteem and correlate with a higher incidence of self-destructive behaviors, including substance abuse and unsafe sex.[85] Consequently, up to 25 percent of all homeless youth identify as gay or lesbian, and gay youth appear to be more likely to attempt suicide then their heterosexual peers.[86] These problems may be more prevalent among youth of color, who already face social prejudice because of their race or ethnicity.[87] By coming out, they also risk rejection by members of their own ethnic community and, therefore, even more isolation.[88]

Policy Interventions That Protect Gay Youth and Children of Gay Parents

Eight states and the District of Columbia have laws banning discrimination and/or harassment of students on the basis of sexual orientation. Three of these states also prohibit discrimination against students on the basis of gender identity.[89] At least four states have promulgated professional standards stating that educators cannot discriminate against students on the basis of sexual orientation.[90] At least five other states have adopted nondiscrimination and/or antiharassment regulations or ethical codes through state administrative regulation.[91] Interventions in public schools also include gay-straight alliances (GSAs)—school-based support groups for gay and straight allied youth, safe schools programs aimed at preventing homophobia and the harassment that often accompanies it, and curricula that include the role played by gay people and gay social movements in history. A growing body of both legal precedents and social science research supports the efficacy of these policy interventions.[92]

While policy innovations at the local and state level have made many schools safer for gay students and children of gay parents, several elements of the federal No Child Left Behind (NCLB) Act,[93]—abstinence-only-until-marriage promotion, parental notification laws affecting sex education, and laws prohibiting the "promotion" of homosexuality—can make it difficult to teach tolerance of students who are gay or perceived to be gay.[94] The NCLB Act's promotion of school vouchers for private and religious schools and its promotion of charter schools, single-sex education, standardized testing, and Internet filtering raises concerns for LGBT youth and children of LGBT parents. Private religious schools are usually exempted from nondiscrimination laws, making it harder for teachers to be openly gay role models and leaving gay students unprotected. (That said, because many religious schools have stricter discipline, gay students are often safer in private, religious schools; some religious schools have taken affirmative steps to make their institutions safe for and affirming of gay students.) Charter schools may offer opportunities to LGBT students, but the decentralized nature of charter school governance also poses potential threats. The NCLB

Act authorizes the use of federal funds for single-sex schools for the first time in three decades, which clearly has implications for transgender youth but could also negatively affect all students, including those who are lesbian, gay, or bisexual. NCLB Act provisions related to parental rights and the "promotion and encouragement" of sexual activity also raise concerns. Two amendments to the NCLB Act guaranteeing the ability of the Boy Scouts and U.S. military to meet and recruit at schools with nondiscrimination policies concerning sexual orientation also send a disturbing message to gay students and children of gay parents.

ELDER ISSUES

Gay and lesbian elders experience a number of particular concerns as they age. In a recent study, three in four gay elders reported not being completely open to health care workers about their sexual orientation.[95] Discrimination following disclosure of sexual orientation has been reported in nursing homes and senior centers.[96] Social Security and retirement plan regulations deny gay elders access to funds from systems they pay into throughout their working lives but cannot access due to the unequal treatment of same-sex couples.

Social Security and Pensions

Nearly two-thirds of U.S. retirees rely on Social Security for more than half of their annual income; for 15 percent of seniors, Social Security is their only source of income.[97] Social Security survivor benefits allow widows, widowers, and dependent children to put food on the table and fairly compensate them when their spouse pays into the system his or her whole life but dies before being able to enjoy these retirement savings. But gay and lesbian survivors are not eligible for these benefits, even when they have paid taxes into the system for their entire lives. The September 11 attacks illustrated the unfairness of this policy: same-sex survivors of victims were denied Social Security survivor benefits and worker's compensation survivor benefits. They also had to struggle to access funds from the victims compensation fund administered by the U.S. Department of Justice. Gay partners are also ineligible for spousal benefits, which allow a partner to earn about half of his or her life partner's Social Security payment if that rate is higher than that partner's personal benefits.

THE COST OF UNEQUAL TREATMENT UNDER SOCIAL SECURITY

Thorsten Behrens, 33, and Christopher Schiebel, 32, have been in a committed relationship for five years. They live in western Massachusetts. Thorsten has no children, but Christopher has two children from a previous marriage that they are both raising. Thorsten is the main breadwinner. In 2002, Thorsten earned a total of $44,198, and Christopher earned $4,044 in W-2 reported income and $3,645 in unemployment compensation.

Spousal benefit: Based on their current earnings, upon retirement Thorsten and Christopher's combined monthly Social Security retirement benefit would be $1,830—representing $303 per month for Christopher and $1,527 per month for Thorsten. However, if they could marry and their marriage were recognized by the Social Security Administration, Christopher would be eligible for the spousal benefit, which would allow him to earn half of Thorsten's monthly payment, or an additional $461 a month. Their combined Social Security retirement benefit would be $2,291 a month, almost 25 percent more than they would otherwise receive.

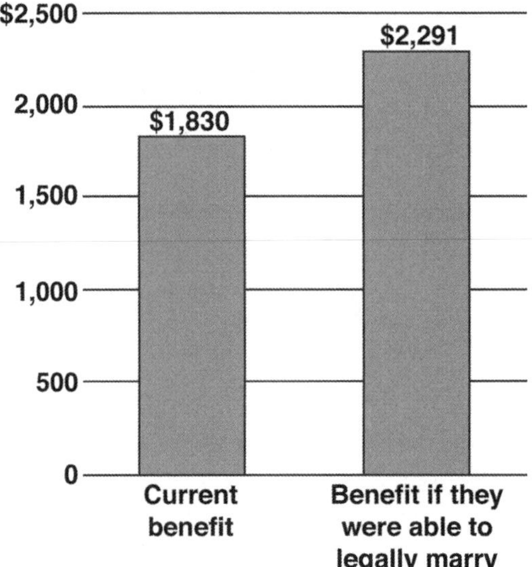

Fig. 8. Combined monthly Social Security retirement benefit for Thorsten and Christopher's family.

Survivor benefit: If Thorsten and Christopher were able to legally marry, and then Thorsten died, Christopher would be eligible for the survivor benefit upon retirement. This would mean he would receive $1,527 a month from Social Security instead of the $303 he would otherwise receive. If Thorsten and Christopher could marry and then Thorsten died, Christopher would receive more than 400% more ($1,224 more) in Social Security benefits in retirement.

Source: From T. Dougherty, *Economic Benefits of Marriage under Federal and Massachusetts Law* (New York: Policy Institute of the National Gay and Lesbian Task Force, 2004), 7.

Same-sex partners of workers with defined-benefit pensions also do not receive the same legal protections provided to married spouses. The Retirement Equity Act of 1984 created spousal rights to a worker's pension benefits while both are living and after the worker's death. Though such rights can be waived, the measure was intended to protect widows or widowers from a severe loss of income. The gay or lesbian partner of a pension plan participant cannot claim such rights, however. When a retired worker (gay or straight) dies, the remaining pension wealth can be distributed to any beneficiary. But certain tax rollover treatment for these distributions—a significant advantage—is only available to a spouse.

If a person dies after becoming vested in a pension plan but before reaching retirement age, a spouse is entitled to begin receiving benefits the year that the deceased would have started drawing on the pension, or the spouse can take a lump-sum distribution and roll the full amount over into an individual retirement account (IRA), where it maintains its tax-deferred status. A surviving same-sex partner can be a named beneficiary of the pension upon the participant's death, but the proceeds are not tax-favored. If someone with a 401(k) plan dies and the beneficiary is a married spouse, the beneficiary may roll over the total amount of the distribution into an IRA without paying income tax. But if the surviving beneficiary is a same-sex partner, the pension distribution is subject to a 20 percent federal withholding tax.[98]

Strong majorities of Americans support treating same-sex couples equally under Social Security policy (68 percent) and inheritance rights (73 percent).[99] In addition, in January 2002 the Democratic National Committee called for equal treatment of gay and lesbian couples by the Social Security Administration. All the Democratic candidates for president in 2004 supported equal treatment of gay partners under Social Security except Senator Joseph Lieberman, who said he was studying the issue. The Bush-Cheney administration, however, opposes equal treatment of same-sex couples under Social Security.

MEDICAID SPEND-DOWN

Other senior family issues include the Medicaid spend-down provision. Following the death of a spouse in a nursing home or assisted care facility, Medicaid regulations allow the surviving widow or widower of a married heterosexual couple to remain in the couple's home for the rest of his or her life without jeopardizing the right to Medicaid coverage. Upon the survivor's death, the state may then take the home to recoup the costs of terminal care. Because same-sex couples cannot marry, they can be forced into choosing between a home and life's savings or medical coverage.[100]

At least two states have taken steps to rectify this inequity. Since 2003, Vermont has spent state Medicaid dollars to allow individuals in same-sex civil unions to stay in their homes after their partners enter a nursing home or assisted care facility. In 2005, Massachusetts legislators filed a bill that would treat married same-sex spouses the same as married opposite-sex spouses under the state's Medicaid program.[101]

HEALTH CARE

In times of illness, most people rely on the support of their families. Hospitals routinely call on an incapacitated patient's next of kin to make medical decisions. Many people receive their health insurance through family members. But because of lack of recognition of their families, gay and lesbian people face unique problems when dealing with the health care system and often have to struggle to have their relationships respected.

Among the many rights to which heterosexual parents are automatically entitled but lesbian and gay partners are routinely denied are the ability to visit hospitalized loved ones; the right to make medical, legal, and financial decisions for an incapacitated partner; the right to take time from work to care for an ill partner; access to health insurance for one's partner and the partner's children; and the right to make funeral arrangements for a deceased partner. Even when same-sex partners are eligible for domestic partner health benefits, they have to report this as income and pay taxes on it. Another critical health-related policy concern is gay partners' inability to sue for wrongful death in most jurisdictions.

If a gay man or lesbian is incapacitated in the hospital, his or her closest blood relative will automatically be given the power to make decisions about their care unless a medical power-of-attorney form has been completed. If this form exists, the specified health care proxy may act on behalf of the incapacitated person and make decisions as their agent. But even if they are armed with a durable power of attorney, a health care proxy, or other legally binding documents, gay couples' familial rights are still regularly ignored by hospital staff.[102]

The lead plaintiff couple in the landmark Massachusetts marriage case,

Julie and Hillary Goodridge, experienced a nightmare after Julie gave birth to their daughter. While both mother and daughter experienced complications in the difficult birth by cesarean section, Hillary was denied entry to both neonatal intensive care and post-op, on the basis that she was "not immediate family." Hillary finally lied and said she was Julie's sister and was allowed to see her partner. In fact, the Goodridges had adopted the same last name years earlier so that, in just such an event, they could plausibly claim to be sisters.[103]

LESBIAN FAMILY DENIED HEALTH COVERAGE FOR TERMINAL CANCER

A Profile of Lisa Stewart

Lisa Stewart, a thirty-three-year-old South Carolina native, lives with her partner of ten years, Lynn, and their five-year-old daughter, Emily. In March 2000, Lisa was diagnosed with breast cancer. Up until that point, life was "about as good as it could get for us," says Lisa. They had a beautiful daughter, had just bought a second home, and were able to travel during the summers.

Unfortunately, the cancer progressed to stage four, or terminal, cancer. In dealing with her illness, Lisa became painfully aware of the nonrecognition of her relationship to Lynn, and the family struggled through many different obstacles. Lisa was unable to keep her job as a real estate appraiser because of her cancer-related disability. Not only did she lose her income, but she also lost her health insurance. As an independent contractor with a small company, she had no benefits from work. She needed to go elsewhere to find the coverage that was especially necessary as she faced the prospect of twenty-thousand-dollar-a-month chemotherapy bills. Health insurance coverage is not available to domestic partners through Lynn's job in the public school system, so Lisa pursued health coverage through the State Cancer Aid Program. In response to her application, she was told that their combined household income was too high and so Lisa was not qualified for coverage.

Lisa was in a double bind: though Lynn's income was counted against Lisa's application for state aid, Lynn's employer refused to recognize their relationship and give Lisa access to group health insurance coverage. On the advice of a financial counselor, Lisa separated her household from Lynn's and began using a different address in order to qualify for the state aid. "I'm not listed on the deed. I got rid of everything I owned," says Lisa. "I felt forced into the situation."

Because of the serious nature of the illness, the family has also had to consider end-of-life issues. Lisa, Emily's biological mother, is her only legally recognized parent. This means that Emily's relationship to Lynn is precarious. They were told that second-parent adoption has never been allowed in South Carolina. "We would have loved to do second-parent adoption," Lisa says, but they feared their case would become a "media circus." Instead, Lisa has declared Lynn to be Emily's guardian, which will protect their parent-child relationship—at least from everyone but Lisa herself. Lisa has power to revoke guardianship and says that she knows of other relationships in which that has occurred after the couple broke up. Since Emily is Lisa's legal child, she will qualify for Lisa's Social Security survivor benefits in the event of her passing, but Lynn will not.

The couple has put a great deal of care into getting their financial matters in order and writing their wills. Though they had never thought about it before Lisa's illness, she says, "I encourage everybody to make their wills very explicit." In fact, they have declared their documents binding before two attorneys. On a broader level, she wishes that her family could have been recognized and respected as many others are. She says that in a better world, "Lynn and I would be considered a couple, married or partnered, and she could have added me to her insurance."

Despite these hardships, the family has stayed involved with their community and church and Emily has been very active in local sports. Fortunately, Lisa says she has wonderful support from her community. "I have wonderful doctors who've worked through so many issues with me—not just providing medical care, but working with insurance and aid programs to get me the best treatments. We have so many wonderful family and friends that are always available to help. We've had tremendous family support from both our parents and our siblings."

Source: Adapted from Cahill, Ellen, and Tobias, *Family Policy.*

FAMILY AND MEDICAL LEAVE

The Family and Medical Leave Act (FMLA), a federal law passed in 1993, discriminates against same-sex couple families, as do all but one of the two dozen state medical leave laws. The federal FMLA provides up to twelve weeks of unpaid leave after the birth or adoption of a child, to facilitate recovery from a "serious health condition," or to care for an immediate family member who is extremely sick. But "family" is defined specifically to exclude same-sex couple families. This prevents gay men and lesbians from taking care of their partners on equal terms with their married heterosexual counterparts and exposes them to additional vulnerability in the workplace.[104]

California is the only state that provides paid family leave to employees. It allows state residents to take six weeks of paid leave from work to care for an ill relative—including a domestic partner—or after the birth, adoption, or foster placement of a child. While on leave, most workers are paid at a rate of about 55 percent of their salary. This is funded by a payroll tax that averages twenty-six dollars per year per employee.[105] Two other states, Hawaii and Vermont, provide unpaid family leave for domestic partners. Nearly two dozen other states provide some form of unpaid family and medical leave, but to spouses only, not same-sex partners.

DOMESTIC VIOLENCE

Same-sex couples are excluded from domestic violence protections in three states—Delaware, Montana, and South Carolina.[106] Domestic violence cuts across all racial, class, religious, age, and sexual orientation lines. Studies indicate that domestic violence is as prevalent in same-sex relationships as it is in opposite-sex relationships. Preliminary studies of lesbian couples found that 22 to 46 percent of lesbians have been in physically violent same-sex relationships.[107] The Gay Men's Domestic Violence Project did a survey of over two thousand men at the 1997 Boston Gay Pride event, finding that one in four gay men have experienced domestic violence.[108] A survey of twelve service organizations nationwide yielded 4,048 reported cases of LGBT domestic violence in 2000.[109] This is likely a tiny portion of the actual cases nationwide.

Domestic violence remains an underreported crime, and many victims experience barriers to accessing services. Some factors responsible for this include

- a real or perceived lack of services;
- feelings of shame or denial;
- economic dependence on the batterer;
- unresponsive law enforcement agencies;
- cultural and linguistic barriers;
- fear of loss of immigration status;
- fear of further violence;
- a desire to protect the batterer.

In the case of LGBT people, other factors compound this problem:

- a dearth of resources, services, and education on LGBT domestic violence issues;
- a fear of being "outed," or experiencing public disclosure of one's sexual orientation;
- belief in the myth that same-sex relationships cannot be abusive, therefore an inability to recognize abuse when it happens;
- fear of homophobic reactions by service providers, police, and others;
- greater risk of losing children to a third party than in opposite-sex relationships;
- fear of having to cut ties to what may be a relatively small LGBT community.[110]

Anecdotal evidence from same-sex survivors suggests that poor law enforcement responses occur more frequently with same-sex situations. The National Coalition of Anti-Violence Programs reports: "sometimes, they inappropriately arrest the victim, especially if she or he is physically larger or is perceived as 'more masculine,' than the assailant; worse yet, police often make anti-gay comments and occasionally even perpetuate anti-gay violence."[111] Additionally, survivors of same-sex abuse often confront ignorance and/or prejudice in treatment from medical professionals, domestic violence specialists, and other service providers who lack training in the unique challenges that LGBT survivors face. Gay and bisexual men, along with transgender survivors, suffer the added obstacle that many domestic violence services and shelters only offer services to battered women. Even in such places as Boston, where safe houses offer two weeks of shelter to gay, bisexual, and transgender men fleeing violence, more long-term shelters do not exist.[112] In contrast, women can access as much as eighteen months of transitional housing in Massachusetts.[113] Lesbian survivors often can enter shelters originally created for heterosexual women. However, in some instances they have been denied access to shelters, on the premise that a female partner could too easily infiltrate a women's shelter.[114]

Many domestic violence service providers see gender inequality as one of the root causes of domestic violence. Since same-sex domestic violence does not fit this framework, it has been under the radar screen of many providers.[115] LGBT people have also been reluctant to believe that domestic violence can occur in their relationships.[116] There needs to be continued education about same-sex domestic violence within both the LGBT community and among domestic violence and health care service providers.

In addition, domestic violence laws were originally written in response to a phenomenon conceived of as "wife battering." One of the primary tools available to survivors is a protective order, also known as a restraining or stay-away order. Although many laws have been rewritten to be gender neutral, there are still at least three states—Delaware, Montana, and South Carolina—in which domestic violence protective orders are unavailable to same-sex couples. In eighteen states, the laws are gender neutral but only apply to household members. This problem also exists at the federal level. For example, the Violence Against Women Act explicitly does not apply to male victims of domestic violence.

Furthermore, in many jurisdictions, family courts only decide cases of domestic violence between married couples or heterosexual couples with a child. As a result, an LGBT survivor of domestic abuse might have to pursue his or her claim in the criminal courts, which have different standards—for example, requiring an arrest to have been made.[117] A related problem is that many judges do not spend the time to discover who the batterer is in a same-sex relationship and to issue mutual restraining orders to both parties.[118] This creates a very dangerous situation where a batterer can use a restraining order as a tool to control the survivor, manipulating the situation to lead to the survivor's arrest. The lack of legal recognition of same-sex relationships poses additional obstacles for a survivor who is trying to leave a relationship. For example, if the survivor is not the legal parent of the couple's child or does not have legal possession of their home, car, or other assets, they might be more likely to tolerate the abuse and stay in the relationship.

STEPS TOWARD ADDRESSING SAME-SEX DOMESTIC VIOLENCE

Massachusetts' programs can provide a useful starting point for other regions of the country seeking to protect survivors of same-sex domestic violence. Two programs based in Boston were created specifically to meet the needs of LGBT victims of domestic violence: the Gay Men's Domestic Violence Project (GMDVP), serving gay, bisexual, and transgender men; and the Network/La Red, serving lesbians, bisexual women, and transgender individuals. They both provide hotline services, counseling, advocacy, and access to safe beds or homes. They also have spearheaded outreach and education programs geared toward the LGBT community and the general public. In addition, Fenway Community Health Center's Violence Recovery Program provides services to all LGBT victims of violence, including domestic violence. Their services for domestic violence survivors include counseling, support groups, advocacy, and referral services, but are more limited than those of the programs focused only on domestic violence. Nationally, there are less than twenty LGBT programs, most of which, like the Fenway Violence Recovery Program, were initially created to respond to anti-LGBT violence and have since expanded to include domestic violence.[119]

As with most domestic violence programs, state and federal sources of funding are essential to maintaining the programming of both the GMDVP and the Network. Their governmental funding sources include

- the Network/La Red;
- the Department of Social Services (the primary state source of funds for all domestic violence programs in Massachusetts);

- the Boston Police Department;
- the Executive Office of Public Safety (federal);
- federal funding through the Violence Against Women Act;
- the Gay Men's Domestic Violence Project;
- the Department of Social Services;
- the Department of Public Health;
- the Massachusetts Office of Victim Assistance (federal funding through the Victims of Crime Act).[120]

The gender-neutral language of much of the laws and regulations concerning domestic violence made it possible for the GMDVP to gain access to this funding. However, Massachusetts, like the other forty-nine states, does not have a shelter for men. In Massachusetts this is because the line item regarding shelter services is specific to female victims.[121] Both the GMDVP and the Network run safe homes programs, which offer up to fourteen days of shelter in volunteers' homes or in hotels or apartments. The funding for these safe homes comes from a line item intended to cover "underserved populations." However, there is no funding for full shelters for these populations. After fourteen days, the only option for some survivors, especially men, is to enter a homeless shelter.[122]

The Network says that the most underfunded portion of their programs is education and outreach.[123] The GMDVP Boston Pride Survey found 87 percent of those surveyed did not realize that domestic violence laws in Massachusetts apply to same-sex relationships, and 70–75 percent could not name any resources for gay male domestic violence victims.[124] This perception of lack of services is especially striking in Boston, which is unique in the wide range of services it does provide. Clearly, even when services exist, there is a continued need to fund education directed at the LGBT community.

ANTI-LGBT DISCRIMINATION AND ITS IMPACT ON SAME-SEX COUPLE FAMILIES

Discrimination in Employment, Housing, and Public Accommodations

Anti-LGBT discrimination affects not only individuals but also their families. Discrimination can cause loss of income, denial of health care, and mental anguish. A number of studies have documented widespread discrimination based on anti-gay or anti-transgender bias. One study reports:

> 54% of respondents in a 2001 statewide survey of lesbian, gay, and bisexual New Yorkers had experienced discrimination in employment, housing, or public accommodation since 1996, with eight percent reporting that they were fired specifically because of their sexual orientation; 27% also reported being called names such as "faggot" and "dyke" in the workplace.[125]

In 2003, almost half of respondents in a study of transgender people in San Francisco said that they had been discriminated against in employment. The respondents shared stories of anti-transgender bias affecting hiring, promotion, and termination.[126] In a similar study of transgender women in San Francisco, 38 percent reported actually being fired for being transgender.[127] Thirty-five percent of respondents in a 2003 National Gay and Lesbian Task Force survey of residents of Topeka, Kansas, reported receiving harassing letters, e-mails, or faxes at work because of their sexual orientation, and 29 percent had observed anti-gay discrimination based against individuals seeking social or government services.[128]

In a Washington, D.C., study of transgender people, only 58 percent of respondents were employed in paid positions. Twenty-nine percent reported no annual source of income, and 31 percent reported that their annual income was under ten thousand dollars. Fifteen percent reported that they lost a job due to employment discrimination.[129] Anti-gay employment discrimination was reported by 33 percent of a national sample of members of the National Gay and Lesbian Task Force; the National Latino/a Lesbian, Gay, Bisexual, and Transgender Organization; and the National Black Lesbian and Gay Leadership Forum.[130]

Housing Discrimination

Access to a place to live is an important human right, but same-sex couples and LGBT individuals are vulnerable to housing discrimination. When same-sex couples search for apartments or homes together, they may be easily identifiable as gay or lesbian. Housing discrimination based on sexual orientation is banned in the District of Columbia and sixteen states: California, Connecticut, Hawaii, Illinois, New York, New Mexico, Maryland, Massachusetts, Maine, Minnesota, New Hampshire, New Jersey, Rhode Island, Vermont,

Washington, and Wisconsin. But in many cases, LGBT families have little or no remedy when denied a home because of their sexual orientation, marital status, or gender identity/expression. In addition, same-sex couple families are unable to qualify as a "family" when applying for public housing, which decreases their likelihood of being able to access public housing. Federal fair housing laws do not protect LGBT people from discrimination.

In 1977, the Department of Housing and Urban Development (HUD) attempted to adopt an expansive definition of family that would have encompassed same-sex couples, but Congress eliminated this provision. In the 1989 *Braschi* case, a New York court ruled that a gay man whose partner died of AIDS had the right to stay in his rent-controlled apartment under state protections against the sudden eviction of family members following the death of the person on the lease. Under the Clinton administration, HUD policy was not to discriminate on the basis of sexual orientation. It is unclear whether or not that is the policy under the Bush administration. Low-income and elder LGBT people are in particular need of affordable housing and are especially vulnerable to discrimination.

The Growth of Nondiscrimination Laws at the Local and State Level

At the beginning of 2006 nearly half of all Americans, or 48 percent of the U.S. population, lived in a city, county, or state with a law banning discrimination on the basis of sexual orientation.[131] By contrast, a decade ago, in 1995, only 34 percent of Americans lived in a local jurisdiction[132] or state with a gay rights law. In early 2006, roughly one in three Americans lived in a city, county, or state that bans discrimination on the basis of gender identity or expression. In 1995, less than 4 percent of Americans lived in a local jurisdiction or state with a gender identity nondiscrimination law; in 2000, just under 5 percent did.

As of early 2006, seventeen states banned sexual orientation discrimination, and eight of these also banned gender identity discrimination in certain areas. Washington, D.C., and more than two hundred towns, cities, and counties banned sexual orientation discrimination, and more than seventy local jurisdictions banned anti-transgender discrimination. An additional eleven states that do not have statewide sexual orientation nondiscrimination laws do have executive orders that protect public sector employees against anti-gay discrimination; three of these state executive orders also ban gender identity discrimination.

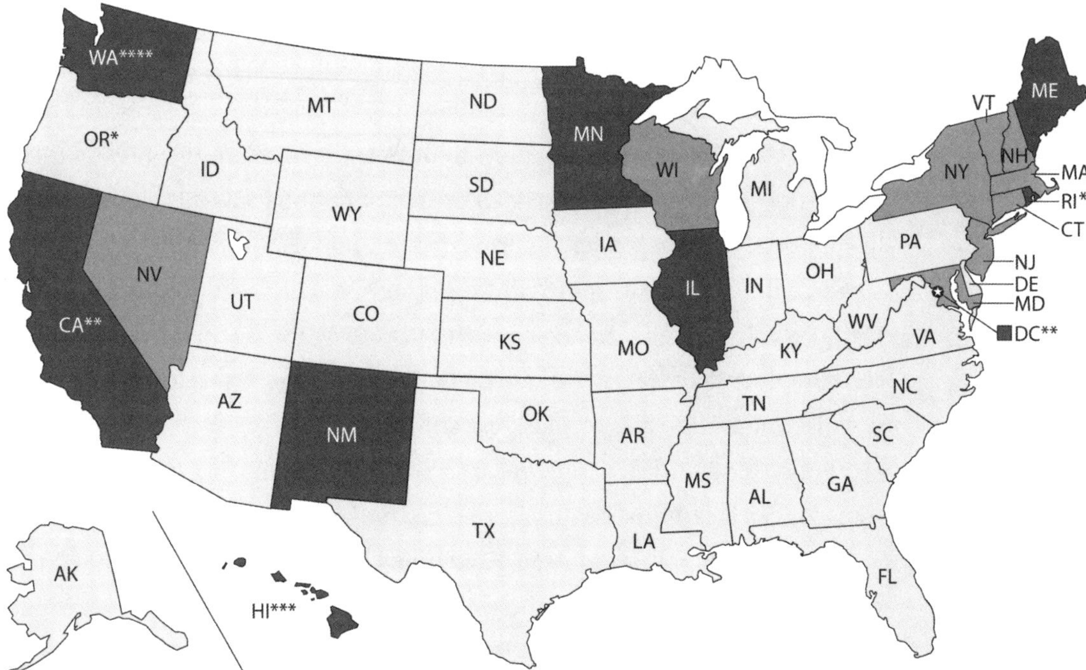

States banning discrimination based on sexual orientation and gender identity/expression (8 states and the District of Columbia)
Minnesota (1993); Rhode Island (1995, 2001)**; New Mexico (2003); California (1992, 2003)**; Hawaii (1991, 2005, 2006)***; Illinois (2005); Maine (2005); Washington (2006); District of Columbia (1997, 2005)**.

Laws banning discrimination based on sexual orientation (9 states)
Wisconsin (1982); Massachusetts (1989); Connecticut (1991); New Jersey and Vermont (1992); New Hampshire (1997); Nevada (1999); Maryland (2001); New York (2002).

*An Oregon appellate court ruled that the state law prohibiting sex discrimination in the workplace also covers sexual orientation.

**California, DC and Rhode Island first passed sexual orientation nondiscrimination laws, then later passed gender identity/expression laws.

***In 1991, Hawaii enacted a law prohibiting sexual orientation discrimination in employment. In 2005, it enacted a law prohibiting sexual orientation and gender/identity/expression discrimination in housing. In 2006, public accommodations protections were added for sexual orientation and gender/identity/expression.

****Washington State's law passed in January 2005 and will be effective June 8, 2006. However, those opposed to the law are gathering signatures to put the measure on the statewide ballot in Nov. 2006 and it may not go into effect before the election.

Note: In addition to these 17 state laws, about 100 municipalities in the 33 states without nondiscrimination laws have local nondiscrimination laws.

Fig. 9. State nondiscrimination laws in the United States as of November 2005. Reproduced courtesy of the National Gay and Lesbian Task Force.

Federal Nondiscrimination Legislation

The federal gay and lesbian civil rights bill, which would have expanded the Civil Rights Act of 1964 to include sexual orientation, was first introduced into Congress in 1975 by Bella Abzug, congresswoman from New York. This bill was comprehensive and would have outlawed discrimination in employment, housing, and public accommodations, as the Civil Rights Act did on the basis of race, color, national origin, and other characteristics. In 1994, after nearly two decades of frustration over the inability to pass the gay rights bill, activists shifted strategy and promoted the Employment Nondiscrimination Act (ENDA), a bill that only covered employment and exempted small businesses. Though ENDA just barely failed to pass the U.S.

Senate in 1996 (on a vote of forty-nine to fifty), it has never passed the House and does not appear likely to pass any time soon. In the late 1990s, the gay, lesbian, bisexual, and transgender movement split over ENDA's failure to include gender identity in its nondiscrimination language. However, today there is a consensus among all the major national LGBT rights groups in support of a transgender-inclusive federal nondiscrimination bill.

Since ENDA was introduced into Congress in 1994, a Republican majority has blocked any movement on the bill save for the unsuccessful Senate vote. Fair-minded lawmakers have passed dozens of sexual orientation nondiscrimination laws at the local and state level. Yet the lack of federal protections for LGBT people means that most victims of anti-gay or anti-transgender discrimination have no recourse in federal court.

President Bill Clinton issued Executive Order 13087 in May 1998 banning discrimination in federal civilian employment on the basis of sexual orientation. In the second presidential debate in October 2000, George W. Bush, then governor of Texas, expressed opposition to what he called "special rights" or "special protective status" for gays and lesbians, using rhetoric of the anti-gay movement. While Clinton and Vice President Al Gore supported ENDA, Bush has expressed his opposition to it. Yet he did not revoke the nondiscrimination executive order issued by President Clinton in 1998, and the order still bans sexual orientation discrimination in federal civilian employment. After a U.S. special counsel questioned whether the executive order mandated sexual orientation nondiscrimination in federal employment and after references to the law were removed from federal government Web sites, a Bush spokesperson promised that the administration would enforce the executive order against anti-gay discrimination.[133]

The Faith-Based Initiative and Discrimination in Employment and Service Provision

The faith-based initiative, issued as an executive order by President Bush in December 2002, authorizes the transfer of federal funds to religious institutions to pay for the delivery of a wide range of social services. This executive order represents a significant step toward the privatization and desecularization of the social service infrastructure in the United States. Under the faith-based initiative bill passed in the U.S. House of Representatives in 2001 (HR 7), institutions receiving such funding were explicitly allowed to discriminate on the basis of religious affiliation. While the Senate bill (S 1924) removed this explicit authorization of discrimination, its silence on the issue might have been interpreted by the Department of Justice as authorizing such discrimination. Bush issued his executive order after the Democratic-controlled Senate failed to pass the bill. Religious discrimination can serve as a proxy for discrimination based on race, gender, and sexual orientation. Under the faith-based initiative, LGBT people could be discriminated against in hiring and in the provision of services, and religious organizations could justify this as essential to maintaining the "religious character" of a program.

When he signed the executive order in late 2002, Bush issued guidelines urging compliance with local and state nondiscrimination laws that go further than federal law. Evidently, however, religious conservatives lobbied the Bush-Cheney administration to reverse course. Six months later, in between the U.S. Supreme Court's controversial decisions on affirmative action and anti-gay archaic sex laws, the Bush-Cheney White House sent a memo to Congress advocating allowing faith-based service providers to ignore local and state nondiscrimination laws that include sexual orientation or gender identity when hiring for positions paid for with federal funds.[134]

The memo, titled *Protecting the Civil Rights and Religious Liberty of Faith-Based Organizations: Why Religious Hiring Rights Must Be Preserved* and authored by Jim Towey, director of the White House Office of Faith-Based and Community Initiatives, portrays anti-gay and religion-based discrimination in hiring for positions paid for with public funds as religious liberty. The White House argues that faith-based service providers receiving public money should be able to discriminate in hiring for jobs funded by federal and state funds. It explicitly says that these providers should be able to discriminate on the basis of sexual orientation, and it portrays state and local gay rights laws as a hindrance to serving the needs of African American and Latino urban poor.

The June 2003 Bush administration memo to Congress argues that Title VII of the Civil Rights Act allows religious entities to discriminate in hiring. While such discrimination is allowed with private funds, whether or not it is legal for faith-based groups to discriminate in employment funded by state or federal dollars has not been established. Civil rights and civil liberties groups ranging from the National Association for the Advancement of Colored People to Americans United for Separation of Church and State, the American Civil Liberties Union, and People for the American Way believe that the Title VII exemption cannot constitutionally apply to jobs that are funded by the federal government. According to these groups, the Title VII exemption is constitutionally limited to privately funded positions. Indeed, although the Supreme Court has not definitively ruled on this issue, at least one federal court has held that it would be unconstitutional for a religious institution to invoke the Title VII exemption for a federally funded job.[135]

In language reminiscent of George Orwell, the Bush memo justifies its encouragement of discrimination by characterizing this policy as "safeguard[ing] the religious liberty of faith-based organizations that partner with the Federal government, so that they may respond with compassion to those in need in our country." It portrays state and local nondiscrimination laws as "uncertain regulatory waters" that are "simply too difficult and costly for many faith-based organizations to navigate." It ignores the cost of discrimination to those who are not even considered for employment or are fired because they are the "wrong" sexual orientation or religion. It asserts that forcing religious groups to hire gay people would be like forcing Planned Parenthood to hire people who are antichoice and against birth control. In fact, being gay is not a matter of ideology or belief; it is a matter of who people are. The Bush administration memo also portrays gay rights laws as a hindrance to meeting the service needs of low-income people.

> This hodgepodge of conflicting approaches has led to confusion . . . and a consequent reluctance by many faith-based groups to seek support from Federally funded programs . . . The real losers are the homeless, the addicted, and others who are denied access to a range of effective social service providers, including faith-based providers.

Rev. Eugene Rivers of Boston, an African American minister and community activist, is quoted in the memo as making a similar claim:

> Faith-based organizations must be protected from the kind of discrimination that would prevent us from hiring the people who are best equipped to fulfill our mission and do the work . . . This discrimination is a violation of the civil rights of religious groups and would effectively prevent the delivery of services to this country's black and brown urban poor.

Faith-based service providers have long played a critical role in providing services particularly to African Americans and immigrants who were often not able to access other service providers due to discrimination. But until charitable choice (a provision of the 1996 welfare reform act and a precursor to the faith-based initiative) and the faith-based initiative, religious providers had to set up separate, secular 501c3 organizations to administer public funds and could not discriminate in hiring or the delivery of services funded by public monies. President Bush is seeking to transfer up to eight billion dollars a year in federal funds to religious service providers. Allowing religious groups to discriminate in hiring for jobs funded by federal monies could open the door to widespread discrimination on the basis of race, religion, national origin, sexual orientation, gender, marital status, and other characteristics. Regulatory oversight and professional training standards are also greatly diminished.[136]

Already, under experiments with public funding of religious social service providers, people have lost or been denied social service jobs in Kentucky and Georgia. Two people were fired because they are lesbians, and one was denied a job because he is Jewish. Alicia Pedreira, a therapist supervisor employed by the state-funded Kentucky Baptist Homes for Children, was fired because it became known that she is a lesbian (after a picture of her and her lover at an AIDS fund-raiser was entered into the Kentucky State Fair). A federal judge ruled that the firing of Pedreira did not violate any laws or constitutional principles.[137] Judge Charles R. Simpson III, chief judge of the U.S. District Court in Louisville, argued, "The civil rights statutes protect religious freedom, not personal lifestyle choices."

Lambda Legal Defense and Education Fund filed suit against the United Methodist Children's Home in Decatur, Georgia, in August 2002. Lambda charged the home with using state tax dollars to discriminate in employment and to "indoctrinat[e] foster youth in religion."[138] One lesbian counselor was fired "because her sexual orientation conflicted with the Home's religious teachings,"[139] or, as the home said, "her religious beliefs were not in conformity with those required," because she condoned homosexuality.[140] A highly qualified Jewish applicant for a psychotherapist position was asked to indicate his religion, church, and four references, including one minister. During his interview he was told, "We don't hire people of your faith."[141] It is unclear whether they would also refuse to hire an individual who was Catholic or of a different Protestant denomination. The United Methodist Children's Home receives 40 percent of its budget from the state of Georgia. Lambda Legal also challenged the home's practice of forcing all the youth in its care to attend Methodist religious services and forcing lesbian and gay youth in its care to undergo "potentially dangerous intervention therapy" based on its religious opposition to homosexuality.[142]

To preserve our democracy, the separation of church and state must be maintained. The wholesale privatization and desecularization of the social service infrastructure in the United States could be devastating for the LGBT community and religious minority groups in particular. Counselors and social workers who are gay or Jewish may be unable to find employment in their field in entire states or regions of the country. Such a phenomenon threatens basic principles of diversity and cultural pluralism, church-state separation, and individual rights that are at the core of the American political system. It is anything but compassionate.

TALKING POINTS ON NONDISCRIMINATION LAWS

Q. Aren't sexual orientation nondiscrimination laws special rights?

A. No. As Rutgers University Law School professor Suzanne Goldberg notes, the concept of "special rights" is legally meaningless: "no such 'rights' exist."[143] Nondiscrimination laws simply prevent discrimination against everyone based on the enumerated characteristics, such as sexual orientation or gender identity/expression, meaning that people who are heterosexual and nontransgender are also protected by these laws.

Q. Won't these laws cause a barrage of frivolous lawsuits?

A. No. Opponents of nondiscrimination legislation make two conflicting claims: (1) discrimination based on sexual orientation does not exist, and (2) nondiscrimination laws will lead to a flood of litigation. A 2002 U.S. General Accounting Office (GAO) report on states' experience with legislation prohibiting sexual orientation discrimination shows both claims to be false.[144] The GAO report illustrates that although individuals have filed discrimination complaints, the number of complaints is relatively few compared to the total number of discrimination complaints filed on all bases. The GAO report also makes clear that there is no significant upward trend in the volume of sexual orientation discrimination cases over time (see fig. 10).[145] Although many people experience anti-gay discrimination, such claims are a proportionally small percentage of the total number of discrimination cases and do not overwhelm the legal system.

UNEQUAL TAX TREATMENT OF SAME-SEX COUPLES

Another area where gay people face discrimination is in tax laws. Same-sex couples confront significantly different tax burdens than do married couples. Specifically, same-sex couples do not enjoy the tax exemptions that married couples do with regard to gift taxes and estate taxes. Moreover, gay and lesbian partners are liable for taxes on any domestic partner benefits they receive. Finally, gay men and lesbians face obstacles in claiming their partners as dependents. There are three main areas of tax disparity of particular concern:

1. Married spouses can transfer an unlimited amount of money to each other without incurring taxes—unless their spouse is not a U.S. citizen, under which circumstances they can transfer up to $101,000 per year without being liable for gift tax. The IRS stipulates, however, that a person who transfers more than eleven thousand dollars to someone who is not his or her spouse is liable to pay a gift tax on the amount that exceeds eleven thousand dollars, unless it is designated to pay for tuition or medical expenses.
2. Whereas gift taxes apply to monetary transfers between unmarried people while they are alive, the estate tax applies to monetary transfers between unmarried people in the event that one of them dies. Spouses can inherit each other's estates tax-free. For unmarried couples, the value of the estate exceeding $675,000—after 2006, $1 million—will be taxed.
3. Most employees enjoy, tax-free, the health insurance they and their spouse or dependents receive from their employer.[146] Same-sex

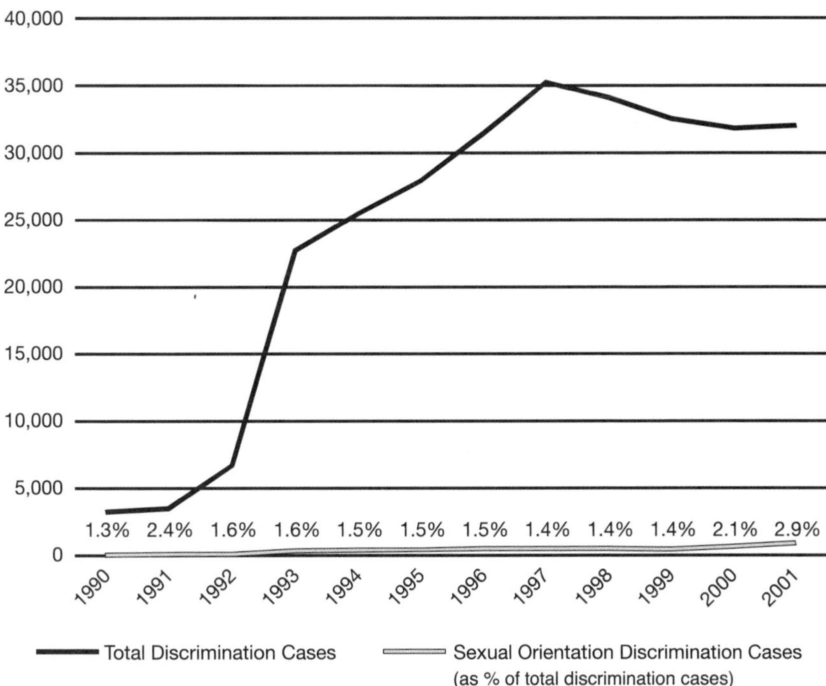

Fig. 10. Sexual orientation discrimination cases as a percentage of all discrimination cases in twelve states that prohibit sexual orientation discrimination.
From General Accounting Office, *Sexual Orientation–Based Employment Discrimination: States' Experience with Statutory Prohibitions,* GAO-02-878R (Washington, DC: General Accounting Office, 2002).

couples, however, do not qualify as spouses and normally do not qualify as dependents.[147] The value of their domestic partner benefits, such as health insurance, is taxable income, paid by the employee. This can have significant tax consequences, even to the point of making it financially detrimental for an unmarried partner to access health benefits. For instance, if the value of the health benefits is enough to bump an employee up to the next tax bracket, they could pay more for their partner's benefits than if they acquired insurance independently.

THE COST OF UNEQUAL TREATMENT UNDER FEDERAL AND STATE TAXES

Donna Triggs and Donna Moore are both 54 years old and live in Massachusetts. They met in college 36 years ago, have been in a relationship for 7 years, and rent a home together. They each have two children from previous marriages, all four of whom are adults. A medical technologist, Donna T. had an annual income of about $72,000 in 2002. Donna M., a massage therapist, earned about $25,000 in 2002. Donna M. is covered under Donna T.'s employer domestic partner health insurance.

Because in 2002 they were unable to legally marry, both Donnas are considered

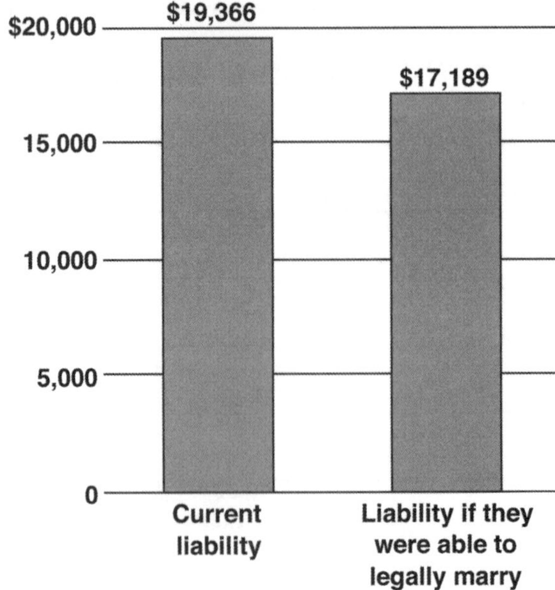

Fig. 11. Total income tax liability (2002) for Donna T. and Donna M.

single persons in Massachusetts and by the federal Internal Revenue Service (IRS). Their combined federal and state income tax liability in 2002 was $19,366. If they were able to file a joint federal and state income tax return as a married couple, Donna T. and Donna M. would incur a total federal and state income tax liability of only $17,189. Because they could not legally marry and because their marriage would not be recognized by the IRS, Donna Triggs and Donna Moore paid $2,177 more in taxes in 2002, or 13% more, than they would have if they could marry and file joint returns.

Source: T. Dougherty, *Economic Benefits of Marriage under Federal and Massachusetts Law* (New York: Policy Institute of the National Gay and Lesbian Task Force, 2004), 5–6.

CONCLUSION

LGBT people and their families are discriminated against in a broad number of policy areas, including partner recognition, parenting, and issues related to health care and death. In addition, gay youth, children of gay parents, and elders face unique obstacles in the major institutions that they count on: schools, social services, hospitals, and nursing homes. Reform is needed to address these problems and to protect LGBT families. Although there have been significant policy advances in recent years, most states have also enshrined discrimination in their law by passing anti-gay marriage laws.

One of the areas of most blatant discrimination in family policy is the lack of recognition of same-sex relationships. Even in many "gay-friendly" communities, same-sex couples can only assemble a patchwork of rights that in no way approaches the range of rights and protections granted to married heterosexual couples and their children. We will discuss issues related to partnership recognition in chapter 3.

Chapter 3

LEGAL PROTECTIONS FOR FAMILIES AND CHILDREN

THE UNITED STATES: LAGGING BEHIND ITS ALLIES AND NEIGHBORS IN PARTNER RECOGNITION

Government recognition of same-sex partner relationships has come slowly in the United States, especially when compared with other industrialized democracies. At the federal level, there have been very few affirmative steps taken, such as the Mychal Judge Act of 2002, providing a federal death benefit to any beneficiary listed in the insurance policy of a police officer or firefighter killed in the line of duty. Such limited advances are overshadowed by the 1996 Defense of Marriage Act, whereby Congress and the president defined marriage as exclusively heterosexual and declared that states did not have to recognize same-sex marriages conducted in other states.[1]

Since May 2004, Massachusetts has offered marriage to same-sex couples, as long as they reside in the commonwealth or swear that they intend to move to the commonwealth within the next three months. Vermont and Connecticut offer "civil unions,"[2] a policy that grants same-sex couples the same rights, privileges, and responsibilities as spouses under state law. A civil union is notably less comprehensive than marriage, because it offers no federal protections, and with few exceptions, it has not been recognized outside Vermont and Connecticut. California has a comprehensive domestic partnership law, securing many rights and benefits for cohabiting same-sex couples. Other states, such as Maine and New Jersey, have set up statewide domestic partner registries conferring a variety of benefits to same-sex couples. More than a dozen states and hundreds of municipalities also provide health benefits to same-sex partners of public sector employees and/or offer domestic partner registries to resident gay and lesbian couples.[3] But four in five states have passed laws restricting marriage to heterosexual couples.

THE REST OF THE WORLD: A TREND TOWARD RECOGNIZING SAME-SEX UNIONS

Internationally, there is a distinct trend toward recognizing the committed relationships of same-sex couples. Governments in Latin America and Africa, as well as in Europe and Australia, have gone significantly further than the U.S. federal government and most states in granting benefits and responsibilities to same-sex couples. On March 31, 2001, Holland became the first country to end marriage discrimination against same-sex couples. Two years later, Belgium followed suit, opening up civil marriage to gay and lesbian couples.[4] Spain became the third country to legalize same-sex marriage, in June 2005. Then, the following month, the Canadian parliament approved a bill to make same-sex marriage legal throughout the country—the culmination of an incremental process of granting marriage rights to same-sex couples in different provinces that began in 2003, after an Ontario appeals court ruled unanimously that Canada's Charter of Rights and Freedoms mandated equal access to civil marriage for gay men and lesbians. Finally, in December 2005, South Africa's highest court recognized the marriage of a lesbian couple and ruled that it is unconstitutional to deny same-sex partners marriage rights. The South African Constitutional Court ruled that parliament must extend marriage rights to same-sex couples within a year and that if parliament failed to fulfill this mandate, the laws would automatically change to recognize marriages between same-sex partners.

Several European countries offer "registered partnerships" that, with few exceptions, provide legal standing identical to marriage. The first such scheme went into effect in Denmark in 1989, and the Danish Registered Partnership Act has subsequently become a model for other countries seeking to extend greater protection to their gay and lesbian citizens. During the 1990s, Norway, Sweden, Iceland, and France were among the European countries to adopt laws recognizing same-sex relationships. Germany, Finland, Austria, and Luxembourg were among the European countries to follow suit in the early 2000s. At the end of 2005, the British government began to offer civil partnerships, a registration scheme extending a broad range of rights and protections to same-sex couples—and a status largely equivalent to marriage in all but name.[5]

Outside Europe, Brazil allows same-sex couples to inherit each other's pension and Social Security benefits; Taiwan is considering legalizing same-sex marriage; and Tasmania, one of Australia's most conservative states, has created a broad domestic partnership status.[6] Worldwide, at least fourteen countries, including South Africa, Israel, and the United Kingdom, recognize same-sex couples for the purposes of immigration. As this pattern of reform continues internationally—and especially in light of the increased economic and political globalization—the United States will soon be forced to decide what consideration it will give to the laws of sovereign nations who have extended the right to marry to their lesbian and gay citizens. The question will not be limited to tourists whose visits are easily quantifiable but will extend to same-sex couples who are employed in the service of their countries or by multinational corporations and whose jobs will force them to relocate here for long periods.

THE BENEFITS OF PARTNER RECOGNITION

Marriage is an institution that has evolved over human history and has come to provide a comprehensive package of protections for committed couples. The inability to access the institution of civil marriage prevents same-sex couples and children of gay and lesbian parents from enjoying many rights and forms of economic and emotional security that married heterosexual families take for granted. Fairness is a core value in the United States. With the increased recognition of the unjust exclusion of a class of people—LGBT people in same-sex relationships—from these protections, local and state governments have begun to take steps toward rectifying this situation. They have offered domestic partnership protections and civil unions as alternative means of recognizing same-sex relationships.

There are distinct advantages to providing formal support to the family relationships of gay and lesbian couples (and the same-sex relationships of bisexual and transgender people) who are in committed same-sex relationships:

- legal recognition enhances their ability to care for one another, particularly in the event of a health emergency or other crisis;
- formal recognition of same-sex partners and parent-child relationships enhances emotional and physical health as well as economic security of all family members;
- children of LGBT parents benefit from increased social acceptance and familial support.

Marriage has advantages as a comprehensive, default system for the couples who participate in it. However, even if marriage discrimination against same-sex couples ends, there will be individuals, couples, and families who will not want to or be able to participate in the institution of marriage. Whether because their family is not based on a committed couple unit, because they are philosophically opposed to marriage as an institution, or because they desire to have more flexibility in defining their relationships, there are individuals who need protections for their families regardless of their marital status. Even as ending marriage discrimination is an important step toward creating legal equality for families headed by same-sex couples, it is important that we acknowledge and support family diversity, including the more complex ways many LGBT individuals structure their lives, care for their children, and maintain extended family networks.

Domestic partnership or reciprocal beneficiary laws offer important alternative systems that should be pursued. In addition, policymakers should create various systems for individuals to affirmatively define their family relationships. These already exist to some extent: individuals may name guardians for their children in the event of their passing, can designate health care and legal decision makers in the event of their incapacitation, or can use a will to leave their possessions to anyone. However, these protections need to be expanded so that people can choose to name other significant individuals as their beneficiaries in different contexts. There also needs to be increased education efforts so that people who can benefit from the existing protections know how to access them.

CIVIL MARRIAGE

> . . . civil marriage is, and since pre-colonial days has been[,] precisely what its name implies: a wholly secular institution.
>
> —*Goodridge v. Dept. of Public Health*, 440 Mass. 309 (2003)

Civil marriage is a unique private and public demonstration of love and commitment that provides access to an enormous range of familial benefits and protections. In 1996, the U.S. General Accounting Office listed 1,049 ways in which marital relationships are given special treatment by the federal government.[7] In January 2004, a review by the GAO updated these findings, identifying 1,138 federal benefits associated with marriage. There are also hundreds of protections, recognitions, and obligations automatically conferred under state law.

As of mid-2006, when this book went to press, same-sex couples can marry in only one state—Massachusetts. However, same-sex couples in other states, including California, New York, New Jersey, Connecticut, Florida, Washington, and Oregon, have sued to acquire the right to marry. These cases will be decided over the coming years. In 2005, the California legislature passed legislation that would legalize same-sex marriage there; Governor Arnold Schwarzenegger vetoed the bill.[8]

Because most same-sex couples are denied access to civil marriage, they are also deprived of the benefits associated with this institution. The following list includes some of the protections and responsibilities afforded through marriage.

Health-related rights and benefits

- Access to employer-provided health care, prescription drug coverage, and retirement benefits for family members
- Access to a partner's coverage under Social Security and Medicare
- Ability to take sick or bereavement leave to care for a partner or a nonbiological or adopted child
- Ability to visit or make medical decisions for an ill or incapacitated partner

Increased financial and emotional security

- Exemption from taxation of gifts, inheritance rights, and shared health benefits
- Right to sue for wrongful death of partner
- Ability of a surviving spouse to shelter an individual retirement account and 401(k) from early taxation when the other spouse dies
- Access to pensions, workers' compensation, or Social Security death benefits and spousal benefits
- Access to the courts in case of divorce
- Ability to sponsor one's partner for immigration
- Protection of one's home under the Medicaid spend-down provision if one partner has to go to a nursing home
- Cannot be forced to testify against spouse in a court of law

Protections for children

- Streamlined stepparent adoption and couple adoption processes, creating a legal tie to both parents
- Access to health benefits, Social Security death benefits, and inheritance from both parents

- Right to maintain a relationship with nonbiological or adoptive parent in the event of the other parent's death
- Right to financial support and a continued relationship with both parents should they separate

In an attempt to achieve some measure of recognition and protection for their relationships, many same-sex couples have been forced to spend thousands of dollars drawing up legal contracts to secure their families—a financial burden that married heterosexual couples do not have to confront. Many legal protections, including the right to sue for the wrongful death of one's partner, are conferred by law and cannot be secured by drafting legal documents or by other private arrangements.

This unequal treatment particularly burdens the most vulnerable members of the LGBT community. Low-income LGBT families are often unable to afford the hefty price tag that comes with contractual arrangements and have few legal options to secure their most cherished relationships. Children are especially vulnerable, often having only limited access to health care and economic protections. They are at risk of being severed from nonbiological, nonadoptive parents if their parent-child relationship is ever challenged.

Heterosexual relatives of LGBT family members also suffer as a consequence of discriminatory marriage laws. For instance, the parents of a lesbian are denied their legal status as grandparents when the state refuses to recognize their daughter's relationship to her partner and nonbiological child. In contrast, a married man is automatically considered to be the legal parent of any child born to his wife during the course of their marriage, even if he is not the biological parent.

THE STRUGGLE FOR SAME-SEX MARRIAGE RIGHTS: AN OVERVIEW

In 1993, the Hawaii Supreme Court set off a firestorm of national debate when it ruled that it was discriminatory to deny three lesbian and gay couples the right to obtain a marriage license. The court's ruling stipulated that the state could only deny marriage licenses to same-sex couples for a compelling reason. Three years later, a trial court ruled that Hawaii was unable to find such a reason. Judge Kevin Chang, who wrote the trial court's decision, ruled that Hawaii had "failed to establish or prove that the public interest in the well-being of children and families, or the optimal development of children[,] will be adversely affected by same-sex marriages."[9] The court concluded that gay and lesbian couples must be allowed to marry under civil law. In 1998, a trial court in Alaska also ruled that civil marriage was a fundamental right that could not be denied to same-sex couples. Residents of Hawaii and Alaska reacted to these rulings by passing constitutional amendments defining marriage as a union between a man and a woman. The Hawaii legislature then created a "reciprocal beneficiary" law for same-sex and other non-married couples—defining a legal relationship associated with many fewer rights and privileges than marriage.

Fearing that legalization of lesbian and gay marriage in Hawaii would require other states to extend formal recognition to same-sex couples, conservatives in Congress responded to the Hawaii decision by introducing the so-called Defense of Marriage Act.[10] DOMA defined marriage as a union between a man and a woman. The bill thereby ensured that federal benefits would be denied to same-sex couples if, at some point in the future, they won the right to marry in any particular state. DOMA also enabled states to ignore valid marriages entered into by same-sex couples in other states. The bill overwhelmingly passed both houses of Congress in 1996. Following DOMA's passage, many state legislatures passed laws to prevent same-sex couples from receiving formal recognition.[11] In the late 1990s, dozens of states passed laws similar to the federal DOMA.

DOMA effectively circumvented the traditional role of state governments in determining who could marry, the process by which couples could marry, and the rules for divorce. Until 1996, the federal government always accepted state definitions of marriage and used them to set policy for spouses and families. Although marriage laws have traditionally varied from state to state, couples married in one state have never been required to remarry in another to have their relationship recognized and acquire the benefits associated with marriage. The "portability" of marriage has rendered it unique as a societal institution.

It is no accident that DOMA and the Personal Responsibility and Work Opportunity Reconciliation Act, or the welfare reform act, were passed and signed into law within days of each other in 1996. Both same-sex relationships and welfare "dependency" were decried as a threat to the American family and American society.[12] Politicians and pundits argued that unmarried straight people and same-sex couples create families that threaten the future of American—and even Western—civilization. During the national debate on welfare that started under the Reagan administration and continues into the present, welfare recipients have been portrayed as lazy, self-indulgent individuals whose incompetence as parents threatens America's social, cultural, and economic fabric and the "American family." A 1986 report by the Reagan administration claimed, "[T]he easy availability of welfare in all of its forms has become a powerful force for the destruction of family life through the perpetuation of a welfare culture."[13] In 1994, Robert Rector of the Heritage Foundation reported that "behavioral" poverty continued to grow "at an alarming pace." He defined behavioral poverty, as opposed to material poverty, as "a cluster of severe social pathologies including: an eroded work ethic and dependency, the lack of educational aspirations and achievement, an inability or unwillingness to control one's children, as well as increased single parenthood, illegitimacy, criminal activity, and drug and alcohol use."[14] In 1995, Mississippi governor Kirk Fordice averred, "[T]he only job training that welfare recipients need is a good alarm clock."[15]

In order to address this alleged dysfunctional and destructive "welfare culture," the welfare reform act prioritized—in addition to work—marriage, the reduction of out-of-wedlock births, the reinsertion of fathers into families led by single mothers, and the promotion of mother-father families as essential for the successful rearing of children. As Anna Marie Smith notes, the welfare reform act "places most of the blame for poverty—and indeed, for the entire reproduction of poverty—on what it regards as sexually irresponsible women." Smith concludes, "Wherever heterosexual women selfishly choose to engage in extra-marital sex or to leave their male partners (lesbians have been entirely erased from this imaginary scenario), they are engaging in behaviors that will ultimately impose unacceptable costs on the rest of society."[16] The DOMA debates were rife with similar themes, painting gays and lesbians who want to marry as sexually irresponsible, selfish, and a direct threat to civilization.

Since the federal DOMA's passage, legal scholars have continued to debate its constitutionality. Critics maintain that it intrudes on state power, thereby violating the Tenth Amendment, which guarantees all unenumerated powers to the states. They also contend that the federal DOMA violates the "equal protection" clause of the Fourteenth Amendment, by singling out a disfavored minority group—gay men and lesbians—for the sole purpose of excluding them from an important civil right. Finally, critics argue that the federal DOMA potentially violates the "full faith and credit" clause of the

Constitution, which requires states to recognize contracts, including marriages, made in other states.[17]

Experts argue that DOMA would be unable to withstand the scrutiny of the U.S. Supreme Court. But challenging the federal law's constitutionality has required at least one state to permit same-sex marriages and another state to refuse to recognize them. This has only been an option since gay and lesbian couples began to legally marry in Massachusetts in 2004.

SAME-SEX MARRIAGE IN MASSACHUSETTS

In 2001, Julie and Hillary Goodridge and six other same-sex Massachusetts couples attempted to acquire marriage licenses from their local town and city halls but were denied them. The couples then sued the state's Department of Public Health, which administers the marriage laws in Massachusetts. They argued that the state violated their constitutional rights by denying them marriage licenses.

On November 18, 2003, the Massachusetts Supreme Judicial Court ruled, by a vote of four to three, that same-sex couples have a constitutional right, under the due process and equal protection provisions of the Massachusetts Constitution, to marry the person of their choice. "The marriage ban works a deep and scarring hardship on a very real segment of the community for no rational reason," wrote Chief Justice Margaret Marshall in the court's opinion. She continued, "Limiting the protections, benefits, and obligations of civil marriage to opposite-sex couples violates the basic premises of individual liberty and equality under law protected by the Massachusetts Constitution."

The court rejected claims, made by some opposed to same-sex marriage, that allowing same-sex couples to marry would undermine the institution of marriage. The court concluded: "Extending civil marriage to same-sex couples reinforces the importance of marriage to individuals and communities. That same-sex couples are willing to embrace marriage's solemn obligations of exclusivity, mutual support, and commitment to one another is a testament to the enduring place of marriage in our laws and in the human spirit." In its decision, the court distinguished between civil and religious marriage. It argued that children as well as their parents suffered from the inability to marry; in this context, it noted the social status afforded children of married couples as compared with children of unmarried parents.

The court nevertheless stayed its judgment for 180 days "to permit the Legislature to take such action as it may deem appropriate in light of this opinion."[18] In February 2004, the court responded to a question posed by the Massachusetts State Senate, asking whether providing Vermont-style civil unions would be an adequate means of conforming the state's laws to the court's opinion. The court's ruling made it unequivocally clear that civil unions would not suffice. They would instead create, in the judges' opinion, an "unconstitutional, inferior, and discriminatory status for same-sex couples." The judges argued that enabling same-sex couples to enter civil unions rather than marriages "would have the effect of maintaining and fostering a stigma of exclusion that the Constitution prohibits" and "would deny to same-sex 'spouses' only a status that is specially recognized in society and has significant social and other advantages." "The history of our nation," wrote the judges, "has demonstrated that separate is seldom, if ever, equal."[19]

The Massachusetts legislature responded to the court's ruling by summoning a constitutional convention to debate an amendment that would define marriage as the union between one man and one woman. At the end of March 2004, the legislature approved an amendment that would prevent same-sex marriages in the state and create civil unions for gay and lesbian couples instead. But in September 2005, the Massachusetts legislature reversed its position, voting 157-39 against the amendment. Anti-gay activists are now trying to garner enough signatures to place an antigay marriage amendment on the ballot through citizen initiative in 2008.

Meanwhile, Massachusetts began issuing marriage licenses to gay and lesbian couples on May 17, 2004. Within the first half year or so, some five thousand couples married, the majority of them lesbian couples. Because of the existence of DOMA, however, Massachusetts same-sex couples who marry are currently denied access to all 1,138 federal marriage benefits.

OTHER MILESTONES IN THE STRUGGLE FOR SAME-SEX MARRIAGE RIGHTS

In February 2004, San Francisco mayor Gavin Newsom asserted that the state's constitution prohibits discrimination against same-sex couples and that the San Francisco County Clerk's Office should begin issuing them marriage licenses. Barring gay men and lesbians from marriage "denies them more than a marriage license," said the mayor, who explained, "it precludes millions of couples from obtaining health benefits, hospital visitation rights and pension privileges."[20] More than four thousand marriage licenses were issued before the California Supreme Court told officials to stop issuing the licenses in mid-March. Several months later, the California Supreme Court ruled that the marriages were "void and of no legal effect."[21]

A lawsuit in San Francisco's Superior Court is currently challenging the constitutionality of California's marriage law. California voters approved a ballot measure in 2000 stipulating that only marriages between a man and a woman can be recognized in the state. The California Supreme Court said that if this law is found unconstitutional, same-sex couples "would be free to obtain valid marriage licenses and enter into valid marriages."[22] Lawsuits on behalf of same-sex couples wanting to marry have been filed in states around the country, including New Jersey, New York, California, Connecticut, Oregon, and Washington State.

Inspired by the same-sex marriages in California, gay and lesbian couples in other states requested marriage licenses in their own jurisdictions during February and March 2004. Marriage licenses were issued to same-sex couples—only to be invalidated—in Sandoval County, New Mexico, and Asbury Park, New Jersey. Gay and lesbian couples in Ithaca and Nyack, New York, requested and were denied marriage licenses and have subsequently brought lawsuits against the state. In New Paltz, New York, Mayor Jason West solemnized the marriages of twenty-five same-sex couples who did not have a marriage license. On March 4, 2004, New York state attorney general Eliot Spitzer ruled that state law does not currently allow same-sex marriages to be recorded in the state. But he also noted that state law required legally valid same-sex marriages conducted in other states to be recognized in New York.

Officials began issuing marriage licenses to same sex couples in Multnomah County, Oregon, on March 3, 2004, and continued through April 20, 2004, when a judge ordered them to stop. The same judge said that the state's laws preventing same-sex marriage were unconstitutional and that Oregon must recognize the marriages of gay and lesbian couples that have already been performed there. A lawsuit about the legality of same-sex marriage in Oregon is currently fast-tracked for the state supreme court. In the November 2004 election, however, Oregon voters passed a constitutional amendment prohibiting same-sex marriage. The legal status of same-sex marriage in Oregon is presently unclear.

Benefits of marriage for same-sex couples

- Ends discrimination against same-sex couples, giving them access to the same rights, responsibilities, and privileges as opposite-sex couples
- Provides numerous economic and social protections to couples and children, providing a more secure environment for raising children and increasing family members' ability to care for each other effectively

Drawbacks of marriage for same-sex couples

- Does not create protections for families that are not centered around an amorous couple, such as adult siblings raising children or other extended family networks
- Does not increase protections for couples who, for personal, religious, or philosophical reasons, may find the institution of marriage objectionable and may choose not to participate
- May require couples who separate to pay thousands of dollars in legal fees for divorce

ANTI-GAY MARRIAGE LAWS AND ANTI-GAY FAMILY LAWS

The backlash to the Hawaii decision has been felt beyond the federal level. Fearing that they could be required to extend formal recognition to same-sex couples, many states have passed laws to prevent this possibility by explicitly defining marriage as limited to heterosexuals. By the end of 1996, sixteen states had laws prohibiting same-sex marriage. By the end of 2005—just nine years later—thirty-nine states had such laws; fifteen of these states went beyond banning marriage and also banned more limited forms of partner recognition.

State anti-gay marriage laws have significant implications for same-sex couples. In 2002, a Pennsylvania court used that state's Defense of Marriage Act to prevent a second-parent adoption from taking place. A higher court ultimately overturned this decision. Broader anti-gay family laws and amendments in effect in fifteen states threaten or explicitly prohibit any kind of recognition of same-sex relationships, including civil unions. These laws potentially endanger employer-provided domestic partner benefits, joint and second-parent adoptions, the recognition of same-sex couples' legal contracts, health care decision-making proxies, and any policy or document that recognizes the existence of a same-sex partnership. In some cases, they also affect unmarried, opposite-sex couples.

Nebraska passed the first broad anti-gay family measure in 2000—but the measure was struck down in federal court in May 2005 for being too restrictive. Virginia and Ohio passed laws denying any type of recognition to same-sex relationships in 2004. Voters in nine states—Louisiana, Arkansas, Georgia, Kentucky, Michigan, North Dakota, Ohio, Oklahoma, and Utah—passed sweeping constitutional amendments in November 2004, which prohibit same-sex marriage and threaten or ban more limited protections for unmarried couples. In 2005, voters in Kansas and Kentucky followed suit by passing restrictive anti-gay family amendments. These dangerous laws make same-sex partners and their nonbiological children legal strangers. Such legislation could cause a child to be torn away from a nonbiological parent because a second-parent adoption is not recognized or could cause an ill partner to be denied health care because domestic partner benefits are eliminated. They are an attempt to negate family bonds

TALKING POINTS ON MARRIAGE EQUALITY FOR SAME-SEX COUPLES

Q. When gay men and lesbians insist on the right to marry, aren't they demanding a special right?

A. No. When gay men and lesbians ask for equal access to civil marriage, they are asking to be treated equally. When a heterosexual couple marries, the couple automatically benefits from numerous policies and laws related to marriage. Committed gay and lesbian couples are regularly denied these protections and, at best, can access some of them piecemeal. This discriminates against LGBT families and hurts them—putting couples and children at risk.

On the federal level alone, there are over one thousand federal benefits associated with marriage. In addition, hundreds of state, local, and private sector rights and privileges are automatically granted to couples through the institution of marriage. Some of these include the couple's being viewed as an economic unit (for filing of taxes, inheritance purposes, and receipt of pensions or Social Security benefits in the event of one spouse's death), protections that help the couple stay together geographically (immigration rights, economic supports during a relocation process), health-related rights (insurance coverage, visitation and decision-making rights), and parental recognition (automatic parental status in relation to any child born during the marriage, simpler adoption processes).

Q. What about the fact that many religions do not allow the marriage of individuals of the same sex?

A. Same-sex couples are seeking the right to civil marriage, not religious marriage. Many religions, including Reform and Reconstructionist Judaism and Unitarianism, already sanctify same-sex marriages. Furthermore, it is standard and tear families apart, potentially causing great harm to children and partners during times of crisis.

THE FEDERAL MARRIAGE AMENDMENT

As part of a growing backlash against same-sex marriage, a group of federal legislators has begun a campaign to amend the U.S. Constitution to define marriage strictly as a union between a man and a woman. With this goal in mind, Representative Marilyn Musgrave (R-CO) introduced House Joint Resolution 56, otherwise known as the Federal Marriage Amendment, on May 21, 2003. In its original form, the resolution stipulated:

> Marriage in the United States shall consist only of the union of a man and a woman. Neither this Constitution, nor the Constitution of any State, nor State or Federal law, shall be construed to require that marital status or the legal incidents thereof be conferred upon unmarried couples or groups.

In March 2004, the second sentence of the resolution was revised slightly, and the words "nor State or Federal law" were removed. However, the effect of the amendment, if enacted, would be largely similar. By preventing the recognition of "marital status or the legal incidents thereof," hundreds of thousands of gay and lesbian couples, along with unmarried heterosexual couples, would lose vital protections—ranging from domestic partnership provisions to the ability to adopt and foster parent.

Before the amendment could be added to the Constitution, two-thirds of the House and Senate would have to approve it, then three-quarters of the states would need to ratify it. In February 2005, the resolution had 131 bipartisan cosponsors. President Bush said that he would support the measure in early 2004. An anti-gay marriage constitutional amendment was expected to be considered by Congress in June 2006, as this book went to press.

TRANSGENDER PEOPLE IN MARRIAGE

There are several different ways that transgender people enter into marriage. Sometimes, after a heterosexual couple marries, one of the

practice for states (which are bound by secular laws) to recognize marriages that some religious traditions disallow, such as second marriages after divorce. The Roman Catholic Church does not recognize divorce, yet divorce is legal in all fifty states. However, the ability of couples to divorce under secular law does not affect the right of the Catholic Church to not allow divorces by members of its congregation under church law. This distinction is critical. Just as the Catholic Church should not be allowed to dictate divorce policy to other Americans, especially to Jews and Protestants who are able to divorce within their congregations, so conservative religious groups should not be able to dictate that only opposite-sex couples can marry under secular, civil marriage laws.

Q. What about civil unions or domestic partnership benefits—don't these provide protections for gays and lesbians?

A. Civil unions and domestic partnership are not a substitute for full and equal civil marriage. Only two states, Vermont and Connecticut, allow same-sex couples to enter into civil unions. Although civil unions provide many of the same rights, benefits, and responsibilities of marriage, gay and lesbian couples in a civil union are still denied access to all of the rights and responsibilities provided to married couples by federal law. Also, it remains unclear whether the benefits and obligations associated with civil unions will be recognized in other states. If a heterosexual married couple moves from Vermont to Texas, they retain all the benefits and supports of marriage. But a lesbian couple's civil union is unlikely to be recognized in the same situation. Civil unions give gay and lesbian couples important rights and protections, but not full equality.

Domestic partner benefits are not

universally available. Even where they do exist, their comprehensiveness varies from state to state, from locality to locality, and from employer to employer. None are as substantial as the benefits associated with marriage, and none are portable. Most are limited to just a handful of benefits. Domestic partner benefits are not a substitute for civil marriage.

Q. Won't allowing lesbians and gays to marry fundamentally undermine the institution of marriage itself?

A. No. The institution of marriage is not a static one; it has changed significantly over time. Married women used to be the legal property of their husbands, and interracial marriages used to be prohibited by antimiscegenation laws. A strong institution endures by accommodating social and cultural shifts; a weak one is brittle and easily undermined. Allowing committed lesbians and gay men to marry will modify the institution of marriage, but it will not undermine it. Las Vegas fifteen-minute wedding chapels and such television shows as *Who Wants to Marry a Millionaire?* cheapen the institution of marriage. Same-sex couples who want to spend their lives together do not.

Q. Since most Americans don't support marriage for gay couples, shouldn't it remain illegal?

A. No. Although no national public opinion poll yet shows majority support for marriage equality, this is not a legitimate reason to deny equal treatment under the law. All people should be treated equally because this is just and mandated by key provisions of the U.S. Constitution and state constitutions. They should not be treated equally only when to do so is popular and enjoys majority support.

That said, much public opinion data indicates widespread support for same-sex marriage or at least a sense

spouses in the relationship subsequently "comes out" as transgender and "transitions" to living as a person of the opposite sex. Alternatively, a transgender person transitions prior to entering into a marriage with a person of a different sex. Finally, in some jurisdictions, a transgender person can legally marry a person of the same sex: this occurs when the jurisdictions themselves refuse to recognize a transgender person as a legal member of his or her reassigned sex.

Some state courts have upheld the validity of marriages involving transgender people. Both California and New Jersey have case law indicating that a transgender person's sex after transitioning will be recognized for the purpose of marriage.[23] But in most states, all of the paths to transgender marriage are susceptible to legal challenge. Transgender people in marriages must therefore live with the fear that in times of crisis, their relationship will not be recognized—an uncertainty that other married couples do not confront. Many high-profile cases have revealed the vulnerability of transgender people in marriage.

Recently, Jiffy Javenella, the legal spouse of Donita Ganzon, was denied immigration benefits because Ganzon is a postoperative transsexual. Ganzon, who was born in the Philippines, underwent sex-reassignment surgery over twenty-five years ago, transitioning from a man to a woman. The state of California recognized Ganzon's transition, granting her a new birth certificate that indicates her reassigned sex. Six years after transitioning, Ganzon became a U.S. citizen. U.S. citizens have the right to sponsor their foreign-born spouses for permanent residence. After marrying Javenella, a Filipino who had entered the country legally in 2001, Ganzon applied to the Department of Citizenship and Immigration Services (CIS) to begin this process. But in an immigration interview, Ganzon revealed that she was a postoperative transsexual. Within a month, the CIS denied Javenella permanent residence and revoked his work permit. He is now subject to deportation.

According to the Department of Homeland Security "no federal statute or regulation addresses specifically the question whether someone born a man or a woman can surgically change his or her sex." However, in a letter to Javenella, the agency cites a CIS memorandum from April 2004 noting that it will not recognize "change of sex in order for a marriage between two persons born of the same sex to be considered bona fide." The memo cites the 1996 Defense of Marriage

Act to justify its conclusions. Ganzon and Javenella have filed a suit against the CIS, accusing the agency of discrimination.[24]

To minimize the problems that can potentially arise when transgender marriages are found invalid, couples are advised to draw up legal agreements like those drafted by lesbian and gay couples, assigning certain rights and privileges to the other partner. Each partner should prepare a will, assign medical and financial powers of attorney to the other, and draft a personal relationship agreement outlining their mutual rights, responsibilities, and expectations, as well as any other issues important to the couple.[25] To avoid claims of fraud, the agreement should include a statement that the nontransgender partner is aware of the transgender partner's status as transgender. Although some states create forms, such as medical power-of-attorney forms, that can be used without charge, the cost of drawing up a legal agreement with the assistance of an attorney can be prohibitive for many low-income people.

CIVIL UNIONS

Civil unions are a limited, alternative way for gay- and lesbian-headed families to formalize their bonds and gain access to legal protections. Vermont and Connecticut are currently the only states to offer civil unions to same-sex couples. An increasing number of election officials, however, have expressed support for civil unions.[26] Even President Bush expressed support for civil unions one week before the November 2004 presidential election.[27]

Civil unions were created by the Vermont legislature in response to a ruling by the state's supreme court in December 1999. Two lesbian couples and one gay couple had filed suit, and the Vermont Supreme Court ruled that the state could not legitimately deny the "common benefits" of marriage to same-sex partners.[28] Instead of striking down the existing marriage law, however, the court commanded the legislature to determine whether those benefits should be administered by allowing same-sex partners to marry or by some parallel means. The legislature's response was "civil unions," a mechanism by which same-sex couples could receive all of the state-conferred benefits, privileges, and responsibilities of marriage.[29]

Any same-sex couple can enter a civil union so long as both individuals are eighteen or older,[30] capable of consenting, and not already in a marriage or other civil union. The parties must not be related by

that it is inevitable. Most Americans (66 percent) believe that same-sex marriage will be legalized in their lifetime.[31] Majorities in Massachusetts, New Hampshire, and New Jersey support legalizing same-sex marriage.[32] A majority of young people nationwide (58 percent) support civil marriage for same-sex couples.[33]

blood to the degree that would prevent them from marriage.[34] Procedurally, the mechanism for forming a civil union in Vermont is similar to that of marriage. The couple obtains a license from any town clerk in the state and then presents the license to a judge, assistant judge, justice of the peace, or clergy member for certification. The form is returned to the town clerk and then filed with the Office of Vital Statistics.

There is no Vermont residency requirement to form a civil union. However, civil union dissolution requires residency. Civil union certification entitles the couple to all of the approximately three hundred rights and responsibilities conferred to married couples under Vermont law. These include

- health care decision making;
- inheritance rights;
- the right to divide property at the end of a relationship;
- rules related to child custody and visitation;
- rules related to "standing" as a parent, such as the right to second-parent adoption;
- state tax benefits;
- the right of a partner or child to make burial decisions;
- guardianship;
- the right to utilize state courts formally to dissolve a relationship;
- protection under domestic violence laws;
- the ability to bring a wrongful death claim on behalf of a partner.

Significantly, civil unions grant same-sex partners the same rights, privileges, and responsibilities as married spouses under state law only. They offer no federal recognition and do not entitle lesbian and gay couples to any of the federal rights and benefits acquired through marriage.[35] Some of the benefits of marriage that a civil union cannot offer include federal tax benefits, Social Security survivor benefits, access to federal family leave to care for a partner, and the ability to sponsor a partner for immigration. In general, civil unions are not deemed portable (i.e., a Vermont couple's civil union is not recognized in New Mexico). Also, unlike heterosexual married spouses, who can divorce in any state where they reside, the only way for parties to a civil union to divorce is to establish residency in Vermont and file for divorce there. Even if there were no substantive differences in the way the law treats marriages and civil unions, the fact that a civil union remains a separate status just for gay and lesbian people represents real and powerful inequality for those who want to marry. Mary Bonauto, the attorney for the same-sex couples in *Goodridge v. Dept. of Public Health*, recently wrote:

> "Civil unions," however defined, are not an adequate remedy. By definition they are not marriage. Everyone knows that a married person has the right to be by his or her spouse's side no matter what emergency may arise. Only a legally married couple has the unique legal status marriage confers and which allows marriage to be respected by state and federal governments, other countries and third parties like banks and employers.[36]

Vermont's civil union law went into effect on July 1, 2000. Five years later, in December 2004, almost seven thousand couples from around the country had registered in a Vermont civil union.[37] Connecticut created civil unions through its state legislature in April 2005; the law took effect on October 1, 2005. In the 2004 presidential election, exit polls showed that 60 percent of the public supported either same-sex marriage or civil unions for same-sex couples. Hunter College political scientist Kenneth Sherrill notes:

> Today, the public clearly views civil unions to be a viable alternative to same-sex marriage. Some 35% of all voters in the 2004 elections supported civil unions, while another 25% supported marriage for gay couples. Thirty-four percent of Kerry voters and 36% of Bush voters supported civil unions, while 40% of Kerry voters supported same-sex marriage.[38]

In December 2004, *People* magazine asked President George W. Bush and Laura Bush about civil unions: "Is a couple joined by that kind of legal arrangement as much of a family as, say, you two are a family?" The president responded, "Of course."

Benefits of civil unions

- Creates a legal status for same-sex couples akin to marriage at the state level, with a comprehensive, parallel package of rights, benefits, and obligations
- Increases protections for same-sex couples and decreases their unequal treatment in several important areas

Drawbacks of Vermont's civil union law

- Creates a second-class status for same-sex couples, thereby perpetuating bias and infringing on their equality and dignity

- Does not make civil unions portable across states
- Makes partners living in Vermont eligible for state benefits only, not for federal benefits
- Creates an awkward situation where the parties to the civil union are considered to be spouses for state, but not federal, purposes;[39] allows continued discrimination, for example, under immigration policy, federal taxes, Social Security, and Medicaid.
- Does not include opposite-sex couples who choose not to marry

DOMESTIC PARTNERSHIPS

Domestic partnership refers to a range of policy and statutory methods for recognizing the nonmarital relationships of both same-sex and opposite-sex couples. The term *domestic partner* was coined to describe an identifiable group of loving and committed, cohabiting couples whose relationships were more akin to a marriage than to a relationship between roommates or friends. Domestic partnership benefits reflect the idea that unmarried couples and their children are families and deserve the same supports routinely provided to married couples and their children.

Domestic partnership originated in workplace settings in the early 1980s as lesbian and gay employees, along with unmarried heterosexual couples, sought to broaden workplace benefits policies and make them more inclusive. By the 1990s, hundreds of companies offered benefits to their employees' same-sex partners. Domestic partnership also became a vehicle by which state and municipal governments could provide limited recognition to unmarried couples through registries. Most city laws and policies related to domestic partnership were intended primarily to allow unmarried city workers to obtain health insurance and other benefits for their partners. However, several cities branched out to allow residents or anyone else in a nonmarital relationship to register with the city. Registries work differently in different places; while most convey little more than a symbolic recognition of the relationship, such cities as New York go beyond the employment context to ensure that city law and policy acknowledge domestic partner relationships in many ways.[40]

The domestic partnership benefits and plans that are offered to employees' families vary from workplace to workplace. They can include

TALKING POINTS ON CIVIL UNIONS

Q. Why should same-sex couples be allowed to enter into civil unions?

A. Same-sex couples and their children are denied opportunities for recognition and support that are automatically granted to the families of married heterosexuals. Civil unions are a way of protecting same-sex couples and their children.

Q. Why do the families of same-sex couples need protection? What type of protections do civil unions provide?

A. Civil unions protect families in many of the same ways marriage laws do, in the realms of health care, parenting, and securing close relationships in times of crisis, such as illness or death. When relationships are not recognized, families are vulnerable to being torn apart or to experiencing financial or emotional hardship. A child can be unjustly separated from a parent, a woman can be deemed a stranger to her incapacitated partner, a distant relative can claim inheritance rights over those of a life partner, and a child can be denied health care coverage because his legal parent is not employed. In Vermont, state laws pertaining to married couples apply equally to members of a civil union in all areas, including adoption, taxation, inheritance, and hospital visitation.

Q. Why are civil unions needed? Don't comprehensive domestic partnership policies provide many of these same benefits?

A. Domestic partnership policies vary hugely. They often only provide work-related benefits, such as health insurance coverage. Only the state of California provides comprehensive domestic partnership benefits. Short of marriage, civil unions provide the most extensive protections for same-sex couples in the United States.

- medical benefits, including dental and vision care;
- dependent life insurance;
- accidental death and dismemberment benefits;
- tuition assistance;
- long-term care;
- day care;
- flexible spending accounts;
- bereavement and sick leave;
- adoption assistance;
- relocation benefits;
- child resource and referral services;
- access to employer recreational facilities;
- participation in employee assistance programs;
- inclusion in employee discount policies.[41]

DOMESTIC PARTNERSHIP IN CALIFORNIA

The state of California provides the most extensive range of domestic partner benefits. California first established a statewide registry for domestic partners in 2000. Initially, this provided registered partners with hospital visitation rights and extended health insurance coverage for certain public sector employees.[42] These rights were expanded in 2002 to include rights for partners to

- collect employment benefits, to the same extent as spouses, when they voluntarily quit a job to relocate with their domestic partner;
- use sick leave to care for a partner or partner's child;
- file disability benefits on behalf of an incapacitated partner;
- have the cost of domestic partner health benefits excluded as taxable income for purposes of state taxation;
- make medical decisions for an incapacitated partner or act as a conservator (one who is appointed by a court to manage the estate/assets of a protected/incompetent person);
- sue for wrongful death or for infliction of emotional distress;
- adopt a partner's child using the stepparent adoption process;
- continue health coverage for surviving domestic partners and children of retired state employees;
- inherit a share of a partner's property as next of kin (or interstate heir)

if the partner dies without a will or other estate plan (as of July 1, 2003);[43]

- take up to six weeks of paid leave from work to care for a new child or sick family member if one is participating in the state-paid family leave insurance plan (as of July 1, 2004).

In January, 2005, Assembly Bill 205, the California Domestic Partner Rights and Responsibilities Act of 2003, went into effect. The new law stipulates,

> Registered domestic partners shall have the same rights, protections, and benefits, and shall be subject to the same responsibilities, obligations, and duties under [California state] law, whether they derive from statutes, administrative regulations, court rules, government policies, common law, or any other provisions or sources of law, as are granted to and imposed upon spouses.[44]

Domestic partners in California are now financially responsible for each other's living expenses and debts. They are subject to the state's community property system and have access to the courts to enforce property divisions in the event of a breakup.

A child born to one parent in the context of a registered domestic partnership in California will automatically be considered the child of the second parent. Parents adopting during the relationship will still be able to use the stepparent adoption process. They can sue for alimony and child support if their relationship ends.

While same-sex couples who decide to terminate a Vermont civil union or a Massachusetts marriage must live in the state where the relationship was originally legally recognized, those ending a California domestic partnership may live out of state. When entering a California domestic partnership, both parties agree to be bound by the state's laws should their relationship end. "A family is a family not because of gender but because of values, like commitment, trust and love," said former California governor Gray Davis upon signing Assembly Bill 205 into law.

Benefits of adopting CA-style domestic partner registry law

- Decreases the unequal treatment of and provides significant protections for same-sex couples in many important areas
- Creates a legal status for the coupled and family relationships of lesbians and gay men that will heighten the standing of their relationships in other contexts, such as the courts and administrative agencies
- Extends social affirmation to same-sex relationships, which has an effect on how family, coworkers, neighbors, and colleagues regard the relationship

Drawbacks of CA-style domestic partner registry law

- Still requires registered domestic partners to file individual, rather than joint, state income taxes
- Does not provide increased access to federal rights, such as Social Security benefits, veteran's benefits, or immigration rights
- Due to incremental approach, leads to confusion among the couples and the public regarding what rights and protections are in place over the course of time
- Not available to heterosexual unmarried couples who are under the age of sixty-two

DOMESTIC PARTNERSHIP BENEFITS ELSEWHERE

In addition to California, Maine and New Jersey have also enacted state laws giving domestic partnerships varying degrees of protections. New

Jersey law now requires that a same-sex domestic partner be treated as a dependent for purposes of administering certain retirement and health benefits. The law does not specifically require private employers to offer health insurance coverage for domestic partners, but it does require insurance companies and HMOs to offer policies that cover domestic partners. Maine law enables partners of same-sex couples to have guardianship over each other if one becomes sick or injured, to act as next of kin when making funeral arrangements, and to have inheritance rights.

Domestic partner benefits are generally employment-related. In addition to California and New Jersey, nine states—Connecticut, Illinois, Iowa, New Mexico, New York, Oregon, Rhode Island, Vermont, and Washington State—provide domestic partner health benefits to partners of public employees. Several dozen municipalities also provide these benefits to public employees.

At least 130 cities, local governments, and quasi-government agencies offer domestic partner benefits, and the majority provide these benefits to both same- and opposite-sex couples. These include Berkeley, California; Denver, Colorado; Atlanta, Georgia; Iowa City, Iowa; Brookline, Massachusetts; Takoma Park, Maryland; Ann Arbor and Kalamazoo, Michigan; Minneapolis, Minnesota; Ithaca and New York City, New York; Pittsburgh, Pennsylvania; Seattle, Washington; and Madison, Wisconsin.[45] Many other jurisdictions have considered instituting such laws.

In addition to state and local governments, thousands of private companies in all fifty states provide domestic partner benefits. These include General Motors, Ford, Citigroup Inc., Chevron Texaco, IBM, Verizon, AT&T, Boeing, Bank of America, J. P. Morgan Chase, Fannie Mae, Hewlett Packard, and Morgan Stanley. Many colleges and universities, nonprofits, and labor organizations also offer domestic partner benefits.

A small number of employers, including Bank of America and the local Catholic Charities of San Francisco, have chosen to extend benefits to any designated member of an employee's household, including a relative or friend. A broader definition of domestic partner creates more flexibility for the employee and takes into account a wider range of family relationships. It offers greater security to many more nontraditional families, enabling, for example, two single sisters who cohabitate and raise their children together to provide health insurance and other benefits for each other and their children. Unfortunately, some plans limit their scope by requiring that beneficiaries who are not spouses or intimate domestic partners are dependents according to the Internal Revenue Service's definitions.[46]

Typically, nonsalaried benefits constitute around 30 percent of a worker's compensation and include such things as health and life insurance, tuition benefits, and retirement benefits.[47] Domestic partner benefits may therefore be considered an issue of equal pay for equal work. Unfortunately, however, domestic partners are economically discriminated against, as their benefits are taxed as income whereas spousal benefits are not.

EQUAL BENEFITS ORDINANCES

An equal benefits ordinance (EBO) or a contractor law usually requires private companies doing business with a city government to provide domestic partners of employees with the same benefits as spouses of employees. San Francisco was the first city to implement such a law, in 1997.[48] San Francisco supervisor Michael Yaki discussed the rationale behind the ordinance: "In terms of us giving out our public dollars, we don't want to give them to people to discriminate. It's as simple as that."[49] According to a 1999 report, the law was directly responsible for the decisions of more than two thousand employers to offer domestic partner benefits. The law also had the effect of increasing—more than tenfold—the number of insurance companies in California offering domestic partnership benefits. The law withstood two legal challenges,[50] and other cities and counties have subsequently implemented similar laws. Other jurisdictions with EBOs include Seattle and Tumwater, Washington.[51] The state of California has passed a groundbreaking state-level law enabling employees of businesses with state contracts to get benefits for their domestic partners on virtually the same terms as married couples.

RECIPROCAL BENEFICIARIES

The term *reciprocal beneficiaries* has been adopted by two states, Hawaii and Vermont, as a means of creating a legal status for people who are involved in close relationships but cannot legally marry. Hawaii's reciprocal beneficiary law, in its original form, provided very extensive coverage: reciprocal beneficiary status was extended to certain blood relations, such as a widowed mother and her unmarried son, as well as to same-sex partners. By contrast, Vermont's reciprocal beneficiary law provides relatively little coverage. Also, the Vermont law does not extend to same-sex couples, as they have the option of entering into civil unions.

Hawaii

The concept of reciprocal beneficiary status grew out of the Hawaii legislature's attempt to derail *Baehr v. Lewin*, the court case that seemed to be on a clear path toward ending marriage discrimination against same-sex couples.[52] When the legislature put a constitutional amendment before the voters "to reserve marriage to opposite-sex couples," they simultaneously passed a law creating the concept of reciprocal beneficiaries. This law established a registry for those couples that qualified for the new status, and it extended as many as sixty benefits to those who registered.[53]

Reciprocal beneficiaries are defined as individuals in a close relationship who are legally prohibited from marrying one another. They must be at least eighteen years old, unmarried, and not in another reciprocal beneficiary relationship. They need not live together. In the four-year period between July 1997, when the law went into effect, and August 2001, the health department recorded 592 registrations for reciprocal beneficiary status, with twenty-seven terminations.[54]

Initially, health and life insurance and retirement benefits were available to registered beneficiaries of state employees. But the Hawaii legislature refused to renew portions of the law that expired in June 1999.[55] Currently, the reciprocal beneficiaries law provides much more limited rights, including workers' compensation, inheritance without a will, protection under domestic violence laws, and standing to sue for wrongful death of a partner.[56] Reciprocal beneficiaries have not been granted tax privileges under state law, rights to property distribution and support upon termination of the relationship, or parenting privileges, such as joint adoption.

Vermont

Tucked in at the very end of Vermont's groundbreaking civil union law is an adaptation of the equally groundbreaking Hawaii reciprocal beneficiary law. Though much narrower in scope than the Hawaii law, the Vermont provision recognizes that certain family privileges and benefits should be available to individuals who are committed to supporting one another but are unable to marry. The Vermont law also represents an attempt to respond to the volatility associated with the state's supreme court decision that same-sex couples have an equal right to the benefits of marriage under the state constitution.[57]

While Vermont's reciprocal beneficiaries policy does not apply to couples who are able to enter into either civil unions or marriages, it does provide a possible framework for other jurisdictions contemplating extending some form of recognition to same-sex couples. To register as reciprocal beneficiaries in Vermont, two people must be related by blood or adoption to the degree that bars them from marriage or civil union. Entering into a marriage or civil union automatically terminates the reciprocal beneficiaries relationship. For instance, a person cannot be simultaneously in a civil union with their partner and in a reciprocal beneficiary relationship with their sibling.

Under Vermont law, the rights of reciprocal beneficiaries are limited primarily to the health care context. Reciprocal beneficiaries can visit each other in the hospital and make medical decisions for each other. They can also dispose of a cobeneficiary's remains and make anatomical gifts.

TREATMENT OF SAME-SEX UNIONS IN THE EVENT OF A BREAKUP

Marriage and civil unions are structured to enable the courts to oversee the dissolution of relationships. The goal, in part, is to ensure the equitable division of property when a couple separates. With the exception of Vermont, California, and now Massachusetts, no state has adopted comprehensive legal provisions to govern the division of property between separating unmarried couples. Disputing unmarried partners have typically had to base their claims of financial and personal obligation upon actual, verbal, or de facto contractual arrangements. But since contract law is usually applied in the realm of business and property, its translation to the world of human relationships and emotions is imperfect. Historically, courts have been reluctant to enforce contractual agreements between unmarried people in a sexual or intimate relationship, although this situation has begun to change in recent years.

Many same-sex couples with the financial means to do so have hired lawyers to draft contractual agreements governing the terms of their financial relationship while they remain together and regulating the division of their property in the event of separation. When a same-sex couple has entered a written contract of this sort, even conservative courts have upheld them as long as the contract strictly relates to the couple's finances and not to their personal relationship.[58] Most couples, however, do not have formal, written contracts governing their separation and property agreements. Since the California Supreme Court opened the door to recognizing verbal and de facto agreements between nonmarital opposite-sex partners in the case of *Marvin v. Marvin*,[59] some courts have gradually started to enforce oral agreements between same-sex partners.[60] If, however, a nonmarital partner cannot prove even an oral agreement but, rather, must rely solely on the existence of a cohabiting relationship and an implicit agreement to share finances, courts generally refuse to apply other legal theories to same-sex couples at the end of a relationship.[61] Courts have been divided when confronted with parenting agreements written to reflect the intentions of a separating couple. Some courts have treated these agreements as irrelevant,[62] while others have seen these agreements as evidence that the biological or adoptive parent wanted their partner to have a parentlike relationship to the child.[63]

IMMIGRATION POLICY AND BINATIONAL SAME-SEX RELATIONSHIPS

Unlike binational heterosexual couples, binational same-sex couples face substantial hurdles to building a life together in the United States. Heterosexual partners involved in binational relationships can simply marry, achieve immigration status, and enjoy the benefits this status provides—including the legal right for the foreign partner to find employment in the United States. The current prohibition barring U.S. citizens from sponsoring their same-sex partners for immigration purposes places an enormous burden on couples in binational relationships, causing them to live in constant fear that the foreign partner will be deported. In some instances, this can mean deportation to a country where LGBT people are repressed by the government or live at great risk of persecution. Moreover, because the foreign partner in a same-sex relationship is often unable to secure employment in the United States, these couples often live under tremendous economic pressure. Without economic resources, even the few avenues available to some couples to stay together legally through work and other visas become inaccessible as they are unable to pay the necessary legal fees.

To remedy this situation, in 2000, Congressman Jerrold Nadler introduced the Permanent Partners Immigration Act. This bill would amend numerous sections of the Immigration and Nationality Act—

Advantages of relying on contractual agreements

- Allows flexibility for individual couples to create their own distinct terms for governing their relationships

Disadvantages of relying on contractual agreements

- Does not address rights and protections that cannot be acquired through contract, including the right to sue for wrongful death in the event of a loved one's death, the right to file taxes jointly, and the right of a stepparent to adopt
- Tends to favor the partner with most power and resources in the relationship
- Inevitably results in inconsistent rulings because the law is still unformed, causing many deserving partners great financial hardship
- Not feasible for many unmarried partners who lack the financial resources to seek legal representation to assist with the drafting or enforcement of contractual agreements

TABLE 2. Ways to Protect Same-Sex Relationships: A Comparison

Relationship	Portability	Federal law	Availability	Benefits provided
Marriage	Portable—i.e., those married in one state are recognized as married in every other state.	Federal protections conferred by 1,138 federal laws and policies, such as Social Security, family medical leave, federal taxation, and immigration policy	Available in all states, unless a couple is same-sex. Massachusetts allows resident same-sex couples to marry since May 17, 2004.	The broadest array of federal and state benefits, including Social Security benefits, inheritance, Medicaid spend-down protections, the right to take family leave under federal law, the right to file federal taxes jointly, the right to sponsor a partner for immigration, and many others
Civil unions	Unclear to what extent are portable—i.e., those who have entered into a civil union in Vermont or Connecticut most likely lose some or all the benefits of their status when they enter another state. To date, civil unions have not been recognized by other states.	No federal rights, responsibilities or protections	Available only in Vermont and Connecticut and only to same-sex couples	Provides access to all state benefits in Vermont and Connecticut
Domestic partnerships	Most commonly not portable	No federal protections	Available in many states and cities; provisions vary widely. California, New Jersey, and Maine offer the most comprehensive protections.	Benefits can include health care, hospital visitation, and the right to meet with your nonbiological child's teacher.

Source: Adapted from National Gay and Lesbian Task Force Web site, http://www.thetaskforce.org/downloads/MarriageDifferences.pdf (accessed May 15, 2006).

the federal law that governs immigration to the United States—to allow U.S. citizens in same-sex relationships to sponsor their partners for permanent residence. According to Nadler, "The bill is simply a matter of common sense and fairness," as it is inappropriate for "the government to tear apart committed and loving couples."[64] Senator Patrick Leahy introduced companion legislation in the U.S. Senate on July 31, 2003.

FORCED TO MOVE TO CANADA TO STAY TOGETHER
A Profile of Charles Zhang and Wayne Griffin

Charles Zhang met Wayne Griffin over the Internet in 1998. Charles was very impressed that the New Hampshire native fluently communicated using "Ping Yin," Chinese words written with English letters. Wayne had spent several years in China as a missionary and a teacher. They decided to meet up in New York City, where Charles, a native of the Chinese province Hainan, was living under an H1-B work visa. Charles was excited to find a friend who understood his culture and language, and when they met, he says, "It didn't take me very long to realize this was the person with whom I wanted to spend my time and share my life."

Wayne decided to leave his home and family in New Hampshire to move to New York. He found a job as a training manager on Wall Street, and in February 1999, the couple moved in together. "We were so overjoyed by our relationship that we spent weeks painting and decorating our new home," says Wayne. "We thought life from then on would be 'happily ever after.'"

The couple was determined to stay together and expected to be able to do so because Charles's boss had sponsored him for a green card. Unfortunately, he also began adding more and more responsibilities to Charles's already overwhelming workload. The situation was becoming unsustainable, as Charles was supposed to be managing two separate and unrelated departments: shipping and credit. Each day, he considered quitting but stayed on in the hopes the situation would work out. He then discovered from an attorney that the amount he was getting paid was just one-half to a third of what his job title required and so his green card application was unlikely to be approved.

The sole route Charles and Wayne had to staying in the United States together was quickly becoming infeasible. "I realized it was almost impossible to go on like that," Charles says. When Charles initially came to the United States, he did not come to stay long term. "I used to be a college teacher in China and I had a good life, good income, and respect," says Charles. "The only reason I decided to stay was I felt I was more free as a gay person. After I met Wayne I became more determined to stay in the States. I wanted to live with him."

They were quickly feeling more and more hopeless. They wrote hundreds of letters to congresspeople and senators but got no response. In the summer of 1999, Wayne and Charles saw a flyer from the Lesbian and Gay Immigration Rights Task Force. The couple contacted the group about their predicament, and the group suggested they pursue moving to Canada. After looking into it, the couple decided that Charles, who had more education and so would be more likely to qualify under Canada's point system, should apply first. The couple then contacted a lawyer who had previously worked for Canadian immigration. She recommended that Wayne also apply and that they send a letter explaining their relationship.

In April of 2000, Charles finally quit his job and returned to school, even though they had not yet heard about their applications. In August they received letters inviting them for interviews at the end of October. Charles and Wayne took great care in preparing for their interviews, practicing answers to various questions and dressing appropriately. Their lawyer said they should have no problems. Everyone was very optimistic. Unfortunately, the couple was interviewed by an infamously difficult immigration agent. She quickly told Charles that he did not have the appropriate job qualifications, even before he had described the work he had done. Wayne's interview was even more brief. "That was the darkest day of our lives," says Charles. "We became numb. We didn't know what to do." Fortunately, their lawyer—who was shocked by their treatment—recommended they write an account of their experience that she forwarded to the Consulate General. Their applications were approved two weeks later.

Wayne quit his job and the couple moved to Toronto in February of 2001. Though they are pleased to have legal status that allows them to stay together without fear of expiring visas and deportation, the transition has not been easy for them. Both of them have made significant sacrifices, not the least of which was moving away from Wayne's family and starting from scratch in rebuilding their careers. After over a year and a half of frustration in the employment arena in Toronto, Charles and Wayne have decided to start a photography and video business together.

Discrimination has been a significant impediment for the couple. "I hate to say this," says Charles, "but it is probably true that because I'm Asian, it's been much harder for me to find a job—even survival jobs at hotels and coffee shops. Wayne and I would both walk in together and Wayne was the only one to ever get called back. At job fairs, people would talk to Wayne, giving him suggestions. I never got anything." Charles only had one informational interview in his field. It was going very well until the interviewer asked Charles if his wife was working. "I was honest with him," Charles says, telling the interviewer of his relationship with Wayne. "His face changed right then and that was the end of it." Of their situation, Wayne says, "It feels very strange to have to leave a country that is supposed to be a leader in human rights . . . The last time I did my taxes, I felt a lot of anger. I was forced to pay for a government that would rather have me leave than help me to keep my family together. When I think about trying to work with my own country to obtain rights that I should have, I feel that it would be more useful to try and push a mountain into the sea with my bare hands."

Source: Adapted from S. Cahill, M. Ellen, and S. Tobias, *Family Policy: Issues Affecting Gay, Lesbian, Bisexual, and Transgender Families* (New York: Policy Institute of the National Gay and Lesbian Task Force, 2002).

Chapter 4

THE INTELLECTUAL HISTORY OF FAMILY
A Contested Discourse within the LGBT Movement

The debate about whether to allow same-sex couples to marry has emerged as a major political issue in the United States, as evidenced by the rhetoric surrounding the 2004 election campaign and the ongoing attention paid to same-sex marriage in the mass media. Pundits frequently proclaim that if lesbians and gay men win the right to marry, gays will have won the "culture wars." But such assertions are grossly inattentive to the debates that have dominated discourse in the LGBT community itself over the last thirty years. For many in this community, the current centrality of gay marriage to LGBT politics is both unexpected and undesirable. Indeed, that the issue of gay marriage now dominates the community's policy agenda indicates to some that gays have lost, rather than won, the culture wars. Other community members argue that winning the right to gay marriage will not constitute a victory in the culture wars. The eradication of homophobia requires pervasive social transformation. Entrenched hostility to gay men and lesbians will not be obliterated through legal change and institutional access alone.

In this chapter, we will discuss the ways in which marriage has always been a controversial, contested terrain for gay men and lesbians. Among the intellectual and political currents we will address are

- the 1970s emphasis that gay liberation will only be achieved as a by-product of women's liberation and the eradication of gender roles;
- the development of a "queer" politics that validates sexual diversity while challenging heteronormative institutions;
- the reenvisioning of family through the recognition of functional relationships;
- the emergence of conservative voices in the LGBT movement;
- the pursuit of formal equality through strategies based on civil rights.

These intellectual currents, which shaped the dominant discourse in the LGBT community from the 1970s through the 1990s, are neither chronologically nor discursively discrete. But separating them out is useful—and in fact necessary—for understanding many of the current responses to marriage by the LGBT community. Throughout this chapter, we will discuss some of the dominant intercommunity critiques of these intellectual and political currents. In chapter 6, we will discuss contemporary scholarly writing about same-sex marriage.

WOMEN'S LIBERATION AND GAY LIBERATION

When, in February 2004, San Francisco City Hall threw open its doors and throngs of gay and lesbian couples rushed in to marry, it came as a shock to many. During the 1970s and early 1980s, in the heyday of gay liberation, marriage was the last thing on many lesbian and gay activists' minds.[1] Lesbian scholar Paula Ettelbrick strenuously argued, "marriage runs contrary to two of the primary goals of the lesbian and gay movement: the affirmation of gay identity and culture and the validation of many forms of relationships."[2] Furthermore, sexual revolution aimed to create sexual freedom, and marriage was antithetical to this goal.

Many activists in the gay and lesbian liberation movement derived their conclusions about the undesirability of marriage from second-wave radical feminism. Paramount among radical feminist arguments was the assertion that we live in a patriarchal world—a society thoroughly structured by male dominance. Patriarchy represents the world as divided into two distinct sexes. In this dichotomized universe, the female is defined by the absence of typical male qualities: he is autonomous, while she is dependent; he is competitive, while she is nurturant; he is identified with the public sphere of citizenship, while she is identified with the private sphere of domesticity; he is associated with the positive, while she is associated with the negative. Radical feminists assert that these gender roles subordinate women while eroticizing inequality and male dominance. Likewise, gender roles oppress both lesbians, who resist "the female sex role of sexual passivity and the servicing of men," and gay men, who challenge "everything that masculinity typically connotes, including sex with women."[3]

Marriage reproduces both patriarchy and the bifurcated gender roles that characterize it; hence, it is a personal relationship with profound political implications. The structural pervasiveness of male power means that the liberal dichotomy between a political, public sphere and an apolitical private sphere is a false one; there is no clearly demarcated boundary between the personal and the political. The power dynamics underlying marriage reveal the fallacy of the liberal distinction. Scholar Carole Pateman observes that the persistence of male dominance means that women cannot decide to enter marriages as "free" and "equal" individuals. Moreover, marriages themselves are circumscribed by the state in ways that diminish individual freedom, since only two people of the opposite sex can marry. The state then assigns these partners the ascriptive roles of husband and wife. Indeed, marriage is a distinct and distinctively gendered form of contract. As Pateman notes, it entails the performative act of saying "I do," but thereafter it "can still be invalidated unless another act is performed . . . *the sex act.*" Pateman continues, "Not until a husband has exercised his conjugal right is the marriage complete."[4] Marriage therefore reinforces men's freedom and women's subordination.

Gay liberationists shared the radical feminist critique of marriage as a gendered institution. Lesbian legal scholar Nancy Polikoff maintained that marriage by lesbians and gay men would be unlikely to undermine stereotypical gender roles and would merely serve to valorize the institution of traditional marriage. "The desire to marry in the lesbian and gay community," she wrote, constitutes "an effort to fit into an inherently problematic institution that betrays the promise of both lesbian and gay liberation and radical feminism."[5] Like radical feminists, gay liberationists also objected to the role of the state in circumscribing sexual relationships. Michael Bronski argued:

> the feminist critique of marriage, signed onto fully by the Gay Liberation Front, made clear that the state had no business telling us what we could do with our bodies (especially with regard to reproduction), what we could do in bed, or with whom we could do it. We understood that what the state allowed, or sanctioned, was in the state's interests, and not ours.[6]

Central to the feminist critique of marriage was an understanding of freedom that went beyond liberal boundaries. For radical feminists, freedom differs fundamentally from formal equality: "We believe that to be equal where there is not universal justice, or where there is not universal freedom is, quite simply, to be the same as the oppressor . . . [T]here is no *freedom* or *justice* in exchanging the female role for the male role. There is, no doubt about it, equality."[7] Rather, freedom entails a much more substantial conception of justice and a social transformation that begins with the elimination of gender roles.

Gay liberationists shared this enlarged conception of freedom with radical feminists. Paula Ettelbrick, for instance, emphasized:

> the fight for justice has as its goal the realignment of power imbalances among individuals and classes . . . A pure "rights" analysis often fails to incorporate a broader understanding of the underlying inequities that operate to deny justice to a fuller range of people and groups . . . [M]aking legal marriage for lesbian and gay couples a priority would set an agenda of gaining rights for a few, but would do nothing to correct the power imbalances between those who are married (whether gay or straight) and those who are not. Thus, justice would not be gained.[8]

Justice was therefore seen as a much richer phenomenon than equality, one deeply tied to the transformation of power structures within society.

As we will see in the rest of this chapter, the radical feminist problematization of gender roles, critique of marriage, and vision of justice are contested and rearticulated throughout the debate over partnership recognition in the LGBT community. For instance, in her discussion of resistance to same-sex marriage in twenty-first-century North America, legal scholar Josephine Ross draws directly on the radical feminist analysis of gender roles.

> The ideal of marriage as straight helps men feel masculine and women feminine. As in much homophobia, discrimination in marriage is based on fear that gays undermine the male/female, masculine/feminine paradigm . . . By preventing gay couples from calling their relations marriages, insecure heterosexuals may feel their own claim to masculinity or femininity enhanced. Hence, the use of gender to determine who can marry and who cannot serves the uses that discrimination always does, of making others feel better . . . The fight against gay marriage is best understood as a desperate attempt to keep the gender line from further eroding, to preserve at least some demarcations between what it means to be a man and what it means to be a woman.[9]

As we will also see later in this chapter, a repudiation of formal equality remains central to the contemporary LGBT critique of marriage. Radical feminist ideas are therefore, in many ways, foundational for the discourse on partnership recognition within the LGBT community.

With any foundational discourse, critiques from within are inevitable. Radical feminism has been challenged for being falsely universalistic and implying that women everywhere experience gender oppression in similar terms. The black lesbians who created the Combahee River Collective, for instance, stressed the importance of their commonality with, rather than their oppression by, black men. Gay and lesbian critics have also challenged the essentialism associated with the radical feminist analysis of marriage. Nan Hunter, for instance, argues that while "some feminist critiques of marriage posit an unalterable and forever oppressive institution, implicitly assuming that the gendered terms can never change," same-sex marriage could potentially "destabilize the gendered definition of marriage for everyone."[10] Marriage is socially constructed and therefore should be seen as a patriarchal tool rather than an entity that is inherently patriarchal in character. Indeed, the structure of marriage changed radically in the late twentieth century, after, as Hunter puts it, "two decades of feminist litigation efforts . . . established virtual equality in formal legal doctrine" about marriage.[11] Hunter argues that if same-sex couples—individuals who share the same status in the world as male or female—gain the right to marry, these relationships could create "the model in law for an egalitarian kind of interpersonal relation, outside the gendered terms of power, for many marriages."[12] For Hunter, then, marriage is a historically contingent institution that need not necessarily be a mechanism for the perpetuation of male dominance.

QUEER POLITICS AND THE VALIDATION OF SEXUAL DIVERSITY

In the 1980s and early 1990s, the movement for gay liberation sought greater inclusion—explicitly incorporating first bisexuals and then transgender people. Correlated with this, the movement began vigorously to celebrate sexual freedom. As one queer theorist put it, "complete freedom of expression for gay sexuality is the keystone of gay freedom, for it is homosexual activity that makes gay people different."[13] For queers, conventional mores were seen as undesirable mechanisms to regulate sexuality and inhibit sexual pleasure. Queers countered these repressive tendencies by teaching that "any self-esteem worth having must not be purchased by a disavowal of sex; it must include esteem for one's sexual relations and pleasures, no matter how despised by others."[14]

While radical feminists and early activists in the gay liberation movement had focused on the problems emanating from patriarchy, queer theorists focused on challenging heteronormativity—the dominant, heterosexual-prioritizing norms dictating how society should be organized. They built on the radical feminist critique of gender roles but with a postmodern twist, seeking to destabilize identity categories based on sexual orientation, sex, and gender. Queer theory "calls into question even such apparently unproblematic terms as 'man' and 'woman'" by showing that a "natural" conception of sexuality is "impossible."[15] Accordingly, queer theorists have sought to recognize and validate a wide "diversity of sexual and intimate relations as worthy of respect and protection."[16] The goal was to break down the boundaries between sexual minorities and build an inclusive movement of sexual minorities for social change.

For queer theorists, the state is a particularly problematic institution. The state has typically categorized some types of consensual sex as "good" and others as "bad," creating a stark dichotomy between "deserving" insiders (those willing to conform to heterosexual norms) and "reprehensible" outsiders (queer resisters to conformity). Queer theorists therefore strive to resist such hierarchical tendencies, insisting that "any vision of sexual justice begin by considering the unrecognized dignity of these outcasts, the ways of living they represent, and the hierarchies of abjection that make them secondary, invisible or deviant."[17]

As a hierarchical, state-sanctioned institution, marriage is the object of much criticism by queer theorists. Marriage is quintessentially a divisive mechanism, enabling the state to distinguish between certain types of consensual sexual relationships that should be rewarded and deemed worthy of protection, on the one hand, and others that are deemed less valuable and potentially punishable, on the other. Lesbian and gay relationships fall into the latter category, along with the sexual relationships of nonmarried adults, especially those who are single parents. Michael Warner writes that marriage thereby "sanctifies some couples at the expense of others." Warner continues:

> It is selective legitimacy. This is a necessary implication of the institution, and not just the result of bad motives . . . To a couple that gets married, marriage just looks ennobling . . . But stand outside it for a second and you see the implication: if you don't have it, you and your relations are less worthy . . . The enobling and the demeaning go together. Marriage does one only by virtue of the other. Marriage, in short, discriminates.[18]

For advocates of queer politics, then, marriage constitutes an exclusionary form of moral regulation that reifies an unjust dichotomy between those the state deems to be worthy of support and those it denigrates. Most queers therefore argue that as an institution, marriage should be shunned. Judith Butler, for example, maintains:

> [T]o demand and receive recognition according to norms that legitimate marriage and delegitimate forms of sexual alliance outside of marriage, or to norms that are articulated in a critical relation to marriage, is to displace the site of delegitimation from one part of the queer community to another or, rather, to transform a collective delegitimation into a selective one. Such a practice is difficult, if not impossible, to reconcile with a radically democratic, sexually progressive movement.[19]

Queer advocates not only regard marriage as exclusionary, divisive, and antidemocratic; they also emphasize that given the institution's privileged status, it is entirely inappropriate to talk of marriage as a "free choice." It is at best a contextually coerced choice, given the prolific array of benefits that accrue to a married couple but are denied to the unmarried. Some argue that it is inappropriate to regard marriage as an exclusively personal decision taken by two committed, long-term partners. When people marry, they actively participate in consolidating hierarchy and reinforcing state power in a way that has consequences for the unmarried. Warner argues:

> As long as people marry, the state will continue to regulate the sexual lives of those who do not marry. It will continue to refuse to recognize our intimate relations, including cohabiting partnerships, as having the same rights or validity as a married couple. It will criminalize our consensual sex.[20]

Queer theorists also argue that supporting marriage would be assimilationist. In other words, it would be a way for LGBT people to minimize, rather than to emphasize, the differences between themselves and heterosexuals. Queer theorists maintain that by marrying, lesbian and gay couples would be endorsing an institution that has historically been associated with heterosexuality. They would be privileging their identity as spouses over their other identities, including their LGBT identities. Marriage might therefore be viewed as an attempt by same-sex couples to forge an alliance with the "mainstream" rather than with the "deviants" at the margins of society—including those LGBT individuals who resist conforming to dominant social norms and expectations. In particular, married lesbian and gay couples might privilege the marital norm of monogamy over the queer ethic of sexual freedom.

But some scholars point out that same-sex marriage can be understood in more ambiguous terms. Same-sex marriage may actually constitute a challenge to heteronormativity rather than an act of assimilation. For instance, as Kenji Yoshino notes, same-sex marriage may be understood as an alliance between LGBT individuals—literally—rather than an alliance with the wider, heterosexual community. Same-sex marriage is also a means of publicly demonstrating both the existence of emotional ties between same-sex couples and the existence of same-sex relationships in which gay or lesbian sex is presumably an important component. Furthermore, same-sex marriage undermines the heteronormative conception of marriage based on ascribed gender roles. Finally, many activists within the LGBT community are agitating for same-sex marriage; hence, supporting it is tantamount to participating in gay rights activism and thus to resisting, rather than accepting, the status quo.[21]

Both the assimilationist argument against same-sex marriage and the counterargument just outlined are susceptible to criticism by those maintaining that queer theory validates some differences at the expense of others and that queer politics is similarly divisive. Scholar Cathy Cohen notes, for instance, that like other people of color, she feels "distance and uneasiness" in relation to the term *queer*.[22] Queer theory and politics are conceived around a dichotomy between queers and straights. Accordingly, queer theorists often fail to address the fact that most people have intersectional identities—in other words, that "numerous systems of oppression interact to regulate and police [them]."[23] These systems include race, class, and gender. Because of this oversight, queer politics fails to recognize that power distributions do not correlate with the gay/straight binary. For instance, they overlook the fact that "'nonnormative' procreation patterns and family structures of people who are labeled heterosexual have . . . been used to regulate and exclude *them*."[24] On this reading, arguments for or against same-sex marriage that do not address how "identities of race, class, and/or gender either enhance or mute the marginalization of queers, on the one hand, and the power of heterosexuals, on the other,"[25] are fundamentally noncompelling.

THE REENVISIONING OF FAMILY THROUGH THE RECOGNITION OF FUNCTIONAL RELATIONSHIPS

Drawing on both feminist and queer insights, LGBT activists began to move toward defining family expansively in terms of functional relationships, rather than through marriage or blood ties. This led to attempts to develop a legal structure that recognized same-sex relationships for what they were: familial ones. The model for these laws, however, was distinctly not the heterosexual one of marriage. Rather, activists and legal scholars attempted to create mechanisms for legal recognition that started from the reality of LGBT lives.

Two main goals dominated lesbian and gay family law during the 1980s. First, gay and lesbian legal scholars sought to broaden the scope of legal protections for families, ensuring that legal protections could be created for nonmarried families without biological ties. These protections were designed to reflect the way in which caregiving relationships often functioned within lesbian and gay families. In other words, the goal was to ensure that "insofar as government controls the benefits and legal rights of family, function, not morality, should govern family definitions and legal access to such benefits."[26] Second, gay and lesbian lawyers recognized that "good family policy must distribute family benefits more democratically, not just to those who can or choose to marry, or who are biological parents, but also to those functioning in the role of family."[27]

In promoting these goals, lesbian and gay legal scholars stressed that their priority was to "value equally all family forms."[28] Providing benefits only to narrowly circumscribed families—such as two-parent, heterosexual families—discriminates against all others and therefore contravenes any public policy aimed at supporting the well-being of family as lived, as opposed to family as represented in dominant social norms. Moreover, the two-parent-plus-children model is often at odds with gay and lesbian families' creative parenting relationships, which frequently allocate a parenting role to more than two individuals. A functional approach to family recognition is sufficiently flexible to support these relationships and others that do not fit the dominant normative model.

As a result of the functional approach to family recognition, law and policy began to recognize relationships that were not based on blood or marriage, in three vital ways: through domestic partnership agreements (more closely discussed in chap. 3), through the acknowledgment of coparent status for nonmarried partners (discussed in chap. 2), and through second-parent adoption (discussed in chap. 2). Many advocates of this approach rightly view it as a successful way of extending support to families and thereby expanding both the definition of family and the appreciation of divergent family forms.

But the functional approach to family recognition has not been without its critics. For instance, despite the goals of many legal scholars, neither law nor policy has adapted to recognize relationships that transcend a pairing of two adults and (sometimes) their dependent children.[29] In many ways, functional relationships in law and policy therefore resemble a "thin" form of marriage. In other words, they reflect coupled relationships that are less subject to state control and definition but that accrue fewer state-sanctioned benefits. Under such circumstances, some critics argue that supporting domestic partnerships and other functional relationships without also "degendering" marriage by enabling gay men and lesbians to participate in that institution "creates a second-class status rather than an alternative" to marriage.[30]

Furthermore, critics argue that state recognition of functional relationships splits the LGBT community, legitimizing some of its members at the expense of others. Lesbian legal scholar Julie Shapiro, for instance, notes that second-parent status is of "no use to lesbians raising children born into their partner's previous heterosexual relationship, where the father remains a legal parent to the child," since such status provides no protection to the relationship between nonlegal parent and child in these situations. In addition, notes Shapiro, lesbians with "a history of drug or alcohol abuse, a criminal record, or an unconventional lifestyle" are frequently unable to qualify for second-parent adoptions. "In serving the needs of some but not all nonlegal mothers," Shapiro concludes, "second-parent adoptions reinforce the idea that there are two distinct categories of lesbians raising children: 'real' lesbian mothers, who may be able to adopt if they are fortunate, and those other lesbians, whose status as women raising children is diminished."[31]

Indeed, state recognition of functional relationships splits the LGBT community in other ways, too. Domestic partnership and second-parent adoption have associated financial costs. Domestic partner benefits, for instance, are frequently taxed, whereas spousal benefits are tax-exempt. Similarly, second-parent adoption is only available to those who can afford expensive lawyers fees. One commentator notes:

> Queer parents are not *only* educated, comfortable, employed, dual-income, guppy (gay upwardly mobile, professional) couples. We are also people who live in cars with our kids, and people who live in rural areas in economically stressed regions with little to look forward to in the way of work or education . . . We are families on welfare, living in public housing. We

> are incarcerated, we are homeless. We are people whose desire to parent is every bit as strong as the middle-class candidate, but we lack . . . the funds to cover legal counsel (a basic requirement in a society where our children can still be taken away from us based on our sexual orientation).[32]

Many within the LGBT community cannot afford to purchase protection for their families. Marriage would therefore be a much less expensive and significantly more accessible way to acquire familial benefits and protections for low-income LGBT families.

Finally, the functionalist approach elicits criticism from those within the LGBT community who simply want to be married. Lawyer Evan Wolfson has observed: "when it comes to the marriage issue, the gay community—men *and* women—has been far ahead of the 'leaders' . . . They have made the personal political; they know what they want, and it includes equal marriage rights."[33] For those sharing this perspective, state recognition of functional relationships will always be an inadequate solution; marriage is the goal. This is why dozens of same-sex couples have sued for the right to marry since 1971.

CONSERVATIVE VOICES IN THE LGBT MOVEMENT

Reacting in part to the ravages of the AIDS epidemic, such prominent gay social conservatives as Andrew Sullivan and William Eskridge began to write about marriage as a means to reject queer values, promote monogamy in gay relationships, and stabilize gay life. In a 1989 essay, for instance, commentator Andrew Sullivan acknowledges the early radicalism of the gay liberation movement. He argues, however, that a fundamental change has taken place in the self-perception of the gay and lesbian community: "a need to rebel has quietly ceded to a desire to belong. To be gay and to be bourgeois no longer seems such an absurd proposition. Certainly since AIDS, to be gay and to be responsible has become a necessity." Marriage, Sullivan believes, "is conservative in the best sense of the word." It will likely make gay men less promiscuous, while married gay couples will provide stable role models for gay youth. Sullivan argues that gay marriage promotes "social cohesion, emotional security, and economic prudence," thereby extending family values to gay and lesbian households. To conservatives, he offers a challenge: "why not coax gays into traditional values rather than rain incoherently against them?"[34]

Similarly, law scholar William Eskridge remarks that the rebellious, anti-assimilationist strand dominating gay activism is the socially constructed product of context. "We are gender rebels because that role has been thrust upon us by oppressive dividing practices, including legal discriminations like the exclusion from marriage," he writes, continuing, "If those dividing practices were to collapse, we might tend to meld back into society's mainstream, which does not inevitably strike me as baleful."[35] Eskridge anticipates that constant confrontation with an anti-gay environment served to radicalize his generation of activists. The next generation, however, will likely encounter far less hostility and therefore be significantly less inclined to disengage from the mainstream.

Eskridge gives little credence to arguments, derived from radical feminism, suggesting that gay men and lesbians should shun marriage because it is a fundamentally oppressive institution. These arguments essentialize marriage, he maintains. Marriage does not necessarily cause Western women's subordination, which, Eskridge claims, "may be more deeply related to social attitudes about gender differences than to the formal construct of marriage per se." If this is the case, says Eskridge, advocating on behalf of same-sex marriage "does not buy into a rotten institution; it only buys into an institution that is changing, as women's roles and status are changing in our society."[36]

Eskridge also attacks the queer theorists' claims that gay marriage would divide the gay community into married "insiders" and unmarried "outsiders," with the insiders most likely to be privileged gay white men and the outsiders most likely to be women, people of color, and the less affluent. Eskridge argues that "there is no evidence—such as polls, surveys, or theoretical models—suggesting that the marriage option would be disproportionately exercised by rich gay men than by men and women of color, lesbians, or less affluent bisexuals and homosexuals." Furthermore, marriage is not likely to change the existing hierarchies within the lesbian and gay community. "The gay man is already more likely to be an insider," Eskridge asserts, adding, "Allowing him to marry another man will not change that."[37]

Other LGBT scholars, however, make compelling criticisms of conservative approaches to same-sex marriage. They point out, for instance, that Eskridge does not adequately address issues of race and poverty. Thus, Darren Leonard Hutchinson emphasizes that it is most unlikely that people of color and other marginalized groups would "meld back into the mainstream" if restrictions on civil marriage and other legal prohibitions were lifted. "[P]oor gays and lesbians and gays and lesbians of color, unlike the white and affluent, are excluded from society before they ever discover their sexual orientation," he maintains, concluding, "Therefore, they cannot meld back into the mainstream—they have never been part of it."[38]

Indeed, Hutchinson argues that there are good reasons to anticipate that women, people of color, and the less affluent would be less likely to marry than affluent white men. The marginalized status of people who are oppressed on multiple dimensions—through a combination of race, sexuality, gender, or class—is not likely to be significantly enhanced by gaining marriage rights. Members of these groups are likely to experience continued oppression regardless of access to civil marriage, and they consequently may also be less inclined to marry if the option were available to them. Marriage, in other words, would not be "the only reform that truly matters"[39] for members of these groups. Furthermore, Hutchinson notes that anthropological evidence also suggests that the nuclear family is less prominent in communities of color and that heterosexuals of color—especially African Americans and Latinos—are less likely to marry than heterosexual whites. It is at least reasonable, therefore, to assume that gay men and lesbians of color who grew up in unmarried families and who share a similar economic background will in turn give less priority to marriage.[40]

Critics have noted how inherently conservative arguments have seeped into the current advocacy for gay marriage—differentiating between "worthy" gay men and lesbians, who are "virtually normal" and desirous of marriage, and "less worthy" others. Lisa Duggan, for instance, notes that a recent pamphlet by a major LGBT advocacy organization uses conservative rhetoric to make a case for gay marriage, claiming: "Denying marriage rights to lesbian and gay couples keeps them in a state of permanent adolescence . . . Both legally and socially, married couples are held in greater esteem than unmarried couples because of the commitment they have made in a serious, public, legally enforceable manner."[41]

Duggan argues that there are grave implications of advocating for gay marriage in these conservative terms, especially for a movement that seeks social justice. Such language, she says, "insults and marginalizes unmarried people, while promoting marriage in much the same terms as the welfare reformers use to stigmatize single-parent households, divorce and 'out of wedlock' births." Moreover, by emphasizing the supremacy of marriage rather than disentangling the religious, economic, symbolic, and kinship aspects of marriage, LGBT community leaders reinforce a traditional hierarchy that privileges marriage above all other relationships. Duggan argues that they also fail to democratize the distribution of benefits by advocating for a "flexible menu of choices for forms of household and partnership recognition open to all citizens, depending on specific and varying needs."[42]

As an alternative to the conservative approach to marriage promotion that derives from within the LGBT community, Duggan recommends the philosophical position articulated by Kay Whitlock of the American Friends Service Committee. Whitlock stresses:

> We cannot speak about equal civil marriage rights and the discrimination that currently exists without also speaking of the twin evil of coercive marriage policies promoted with federal dollars . . . For us, it is critical that the LGBT movement work for equal civil marriage rights in ways that do not further reinforce the idea that if a couple is married, they are more worthy of rights and recognition than people involved in intimate relationships who are not married . . . We do not want to convey the message that marriage is what all queer people should aspire to. We also do not want the discussion of marriage to overwhelm and suppress discussion about a broader definition of human rights and basic benefits that ought to accompany those rights.[43]

Critics of gay conservatism therefore argue that the pursuit of same-sex marriage should not obscure the more progressive goals of the movement for LGBT equality.

THE CIVIL RIGHTS STRATEGY OF COMBATING DISCRIMINATION

The gay conservative focus on marriage is closely tied to the prioritization of marriage as a policy goal for the LGBT movement. Tom Stoddard, former director of Lambda Legal Defense and Education Fund argued that "marriage is . . . the political issue that most fully tests the dedication of people who are not gay to full equality for gay people, and also the issue most likely to lead ultimately to a world free from discrimination against lesbians and gay men."[44] Similarly, lawyer Evan Wolfson, who played a leading role in the Hawaii same-sex marriage case *Baehr v. Lewin*, maintains that "marriage is the central legal and social issue of our society."[45]

By 1993, the LGBT movement had definitively adopted a civil rights strategy aimed at ending discrimination on the basis of sexual orientation. Being denied the right to marry, according to these arguments, constitutes inequality before the law. On this paradigm, marriage becomes an institution that should be accessible to all—gay and straight alike. Legislation becomes the main vehicle for achieving this end.

The civil rights approach derives, in large part, from the liberal theory of personhood. Liberalism claims that everyone is equal from a moral point of view and therefore that people should be treated similarly by law and government. In other words, everyone is due equal respect. The implication of moral equality from a legal perspective is that unless a rational case can be made to justify differentiating between different people or groups, the law should treat everyone the same. Liberalism also claims that people are equally rational and capable of discerning their own conception of the good life. From a legal perspective, they therefore acquire a right to negative liberty, or a right to privacy that would enable them to pursue their chosen ends without government interference.

From this reading of law and personhood, LGBT lawyers and activists argue that gay men and lesbians deserve the same access to marriage as their heterosexual counterparts. Marriage is a basic constitutional right that cannot legitimately be denied in the absence of a compelling interest by the state. Furthermore, gay men and lesbians encounter discrimination when they are granted the right to marry opposite-sex individuals but denied the right to marry a same-sex partner. As Wolfson puts it, "the denial of one's ability to choose a same-sex spouse violates substantive constitutional guarantees such as the right to privacy, the right of personal liberty, and the fundamental right to marry as such."[46]

The civil rights perspective is much in evidence in ongoing court struggles for same-sex marriage. Plaintiffs in recent lawsuits have sued their states to gain the right to marry based on the due process and equal protection clauses of their respective state constitutions. For instance, the complaint filed in *Hernandez v. Robles*, a New York case, argues:

> The right to marry is one of the deeply personal liberty and privacy interests protected by the due process clause of the New York State Constitution, Art. I, section 6. The exclusion of Plaintiffs and other same-sex couples from legal marriage violates this fundamental right. The right

> to equal protection of the laws under the New York State Constitution, Art. I, section 11, also prohibits the State's discriminatory marriage scheme, which, by drawing impermissible distinctions based on sexual orientation and sex, denies all same-sex couples access to this extraordinarily significant legal institution.[47]

The Massachusetts judges who ruled in favor of same-sex marriage in that state also recognized the importance of due process and equal protection for lesbian and gay families.

There have been definite advantages for the LGBT movement pursuing a strategy of legal advocacy based on civil rights. Urvashi Vaid notes:

> Through its emphasis on the equality of all human beings, the civil rights framework gave us what we most needed, some hope that we would one day be accepted by society as fully as we accepted ourselves . . . [T]he adaptation of the minority group model to our experience worked: we achieved some legal and legislative recognition that people ought not to be stigmatized because of their sexual orientation. We came to realize that gay and lesbian people shared a common legacy of discrimination, harassment, violence and rejection, as well as common aspirations of justice, fairness and human dignity.[48]

Yet a civil rights-based approach has its limitations. As Vaid explains, "civil rights are principally mechanisms to gain access" to civil society; they are not a "means to implement fundamental social change."[49]

Critics of the civil rights strategy recognize that it can at best enable the LGBT community to attain formal equality with their heterosexual counterparts. Although the achievement of formal equality will unquestionably be beneficial, it is also the case, as Hutchinson argues, that "extreme poverty, subtle and systemic discrimination, and other current effects of historical subordination limit the benefits that a formal equality framework can deliver to oppressed classes." The focus on same-sex marriage as a policy goal for LGBT advocates bespeaks the movement's prioritization of and commitment to formal equality—rather than to substantive equality or material redistribution. However, as Hutchinson notes, "[LGBT people] who face structural barriers to social resources (e.g., institutionalized racism and poverty) require much broader social reform, including policies that eradicate the pervasive material conditions of inequality."[50]

CONCLUSION

As the discussion in this chapter has shown, the debate about partnership recognition in the LGBT community has always been and remains a fiercely contested terrain. Advocates and scholars have consistently argued over the role of marriage, as well as over the conceptions of freedom, equality, and justice that the movement should prioritize. Against this intellectual backdrop, chapter 5 will describe the way in which anti-gay legislators and Republicans have successfully made marriage for same-sex couples a wedge issue in U.S. politics.

Chapter 5

RECENT POLITICAL HISTORY
The Struggle for Partner Recognition and the Right-Wing Backlash

THE MOBILIZATION OF ANTI-GAY BIAS IN SERVICE OF A POLITICAL AGENDA

Anti-gay bias and its correlate, heterocentrism (or heterosexism), are central to American culture and have an aspect of tradition that cannot be denied. The United States is not unique; anti-gay bias and homophobia are central to cultures across the globe. But while one must acknowledge the connection between anti-gay beliefs and traditional culture, it is also important to understand that anti-gay bias is something that anti-gay movements produce, amplify, mobilize, and deploy for specific political purposes.

The gay marriage issue is central in contemporary U.S. politics largely because anti-gay activists of the religious right have deployed it since the early 1970s as a divisive social issue. They have been especially vigorous and successful in this endeavor for most of the last decade. In consequence, forty states have banned state recognition of same-sex marriages, and Congress passed a ban on federal recognition, the Defense of Marriage Act, in 1996. More recently, anti-gay activists and members of Congress have also threatened to use the Federal Marriage Amendment to short-circuit state efforts to legalize gay marriage. As discussed in chapter 3, this amendment would ban same-sex marriage and prohibit courts from granting more limited forms of recognition, such as hospital visitation rights, domestic partner health benefits, and allowances for second-parent adoption.

The majority opposition to marriage equality for same-sex couples—manifested in opinion polls as well as in anti-gay family legislation—must therefore be understood not only as the expression of traditional anti-gay and heterosexist values but also as the product of a political movement among the conservative and reactionary, theocratic religious right, which has long opposed any form of legal protection or legal equality for gay people. Today, this movement spends hundreds of millions of dollars a year to convince voters and elected officials to oppose any policies that provide for the needs of gay men and lesbians. In some cases, anti-gay groups promote policies that exclude or stigmatize gay people even as they decline to acknowledge their existence. The anti-gay project of the religious right—or, more accurately, the Christian right—is central to its broader theocratic agenda of banning abortion, opposing sex education, ending no-fault divorce, and promoting religion and a particular form of religious orthodoxy in a wide range of policy arenas.

This chapter examines the recent political history of the struggle for marriage equality by same-sex couples and the backlash evoked by such advances as the Massachusetts high court ruling of 2003 legalizing marriage for gay couples. It examines the Massachusetts-based Coalition for Marriage, a network of national and local religious right groups that seeks to ban not only marriage but any form of partner recognition for gay couples in Massachusetts. The Coalition for Marriage has sought to convince the Massachusetts legislature to undercut the Massachusetts Supreme Judicial Court's ruling and adopt an antimarriage amendment that would be placed on the ballot for popular vote. Finally, this chapter examines the role that the debate about marriage played in other states in 2004 and in the 2004 presidential election.

THE ANTI-GAY MARRIAGE MOVEMENT: MASSACHUSETTS AS A CASE STUDY

The terms *religious right* and *Christian right* are frequently used but less frequently defined. Didi Herman defines the Christian right as "a broad coalition of profamily organizations (e.g., Focus on the Family, Concerned Women for America, Traditional Values Coalition) that have come together to struggle for their socio-political vision in the public sphere." She continues, "These organizations, and their activist leaders, are predominantly committed to a conservative, largely premillennial, Protestant Christianity."[1] John Green defines the Christian right as "a social movement concentrated among Evangelical Protestants and dedicated to restoring 'traditional values' in public policy." He notes that "[o]pposition to gay rights was one of the original pillars of the Christian Right."[2] In Massachusetts, Michigan, and elsewhere, leaders of the Roman Catholic Church are increasingly joining anti-gay coalitions led by evangelical Protestants.[3] Since the mid-1970s, anti-gay organizing, especially attempts to repeal or preemptively ban sexual orientation nondiscrimination laws, has been a central focus and strategy of these Christian right groups.[4]

Abortion remained the central domestic policy issue for the religious right into the 1980s. Also in the 1980s, an increasing number of cities, counties, and states passed sexual orientation nondiscrimination laws (also called gay rights laws). The gay and lesbian community responded vigorously to the AIDS epidemic and anti-gay violence, developing strength within the Democratic Party and a corresponding anti-gay reaction within the Republican Party. The promotion of safe schools initiatives and gay-straight alliances to support gay youth, public funding of "homoerotic" art, and other developments evoked a new surge in anti-gay activism in the late 1980s and early 1990s.[5] Anti-gay organizing appeals to anti-gay sentiment, which is deeply rooted in American culture.[6] According to Jean Hardisty, a leading scholar of the Christian right, anti-gay organizing supports "the right's movement building," helps build "internal movement cohesion," and allows right-wingers "to rally the movement, raise money and win recruits."[7] But anti-gay politics is not solely cynically instrumental; it also reflects a "sincere belief that homosexuality is an abomination because it is a sin against God."[8] Appeals to anti-gay sentiment have been quite successful in terms of fundraising. As a result, the Christian right is able to wield significant political influence in support of its agenda.

Because it was the first state to legalize marriage for gay couples, Massachusetts emerged in the mid-2000s as a key site of political struggle between the gay rights movement and the Christian right. Among the national groups active in the anti-gay movement in Massachusetts are Concerned Women for America, Focus on the Family, the Family Research Council (originally formed as a lobbying group for Focus on the Family), and the Traditional Values Coalition. Local groups include the Black Ministerial Alliance of Greater Boston, the Massachusetts Catholic Conference (representing the commonwealth's four Roman Catholic archdioceses), the Massachusetts State Council of the Knights of Columbus, the Bay State Republican Council, and the Catholic Action League of Massachusetts. The Massachusetts Family Institute, a leading opponent of marriage and other legal protections for gay couples, is a state affiliate of Focus on the Family. All of these groups are members of the Coalition for Marriage, a network of anti-gay groups opposing legal protections for gay couples in Massachusetts.

OPPOSITION TO SEXUAL ORIENTATION NONDISCRIMINATION LAWS

In addition to opposing any form of partner recognition for same-sex couples, all fifteen member organizations of the Coalition for Marriage also oppose sexual orientation nondiscrimination laws. This includes opposing the law passed by the Massachusetts legislature and signed into law in 1989. At that point, Massachusetts was only the second state to pass a gay rights law. Today, seventeen states have such laws.

The coalition opposes these laws because its members "do not believe that a person's sexual behavior is comparable to other protected categories such as race or sex—characteristics that are inborn, involuntary, immutable, innocuous and/or in the Constitution."[9] Lou Sheldon, chairman of the Traditional Values Coalition, which is a member of the Coalition for Marriage, wrote in a February 2003 report to coalition members:

> We are not tolerant of behaviors that destroy individuals, families and our culture. Individuals may be free to pursue such behaviors as sodomy, but we will not and cannot tolerate these behaviors . . . In short, we believe in intolerance to those things that are evil; and we believe that we should discriminate against those behaviors which are dangerous to individuals and to society.[10]

The Bay State Republican Council "oppose[s] efforts to include sexual orientation as a category for preferential treatment status under civil rights statutes."[11]

Gay rights laws enjoy bipartisan support from U.S. voters. In a study of public opinion conducted during the 2000 presidential election, 56 percent of Republicans, 70 percent of Independents, and 75 percent of Democrats supported sexual orientation nondiscrimination laws.[12] According to a 2003 Gallup poll, nearly nine in ten Americans support the principle of sexual orientation nondiscrimination, if not the laws required to enforce this practice.[13]

Nonetheless, most of the national anti-gay groups have made an industry out of opposing legal equality for gay and lesbian people. Over the past three decades, they have launched more than one hundred anti-gay ballot initiatives and referenda to repeal or prevent sexual orientation nondiscrimination laws, safe schools programs that support gay youth, same-sex partner recognition, and, most recently, same-sex marriage. During these campaigns, they deploy defamatory tactics to attack gay and lesbian people and gay rights legislation. For example, in 1978, anti-gay groups sought to ban gay people from teaching in California, and in the mid-1980s, two California referenda sought the internment of people with AIDS.[14] In fact, Lou Sheldon, now head of the Traditional Values Coalition, led the 1978 anti-teacher campaign and supported the AIDS internment initiatives.[15]

OPPOSITION TO SAME-SEX PARTNER RECOGNITION THROUGH DOMESTIC PARTNERSHIP AND CIVIL UNIONS

The Coalition for Marriage also "opposes[s] the creation of civil unions or domestic partnerships."[16] When Massachusetts acting governor Jane Swift extended limited domestic partner benefits to some state employees, the Massachusetts Family Institute denounced this as "special rights for a particular group," claiming:

> These are not equal rights since the decision is only for homosexual couples . . . Our nation, as well as this commonwealth, was founded on equal rights as asserted through our founding documents. Allowing special rights for a particular group denies these principles and has damaging and far reaching consequences.[17]

Of course, in 2001, when Governor Swift extended these benefits, gay couples were not allowed to marry under Massachusetts law.

The Massachusetts Family Institute ridicules domestic partner health insurance—offered to employees in long-term, committed relationships—as "sex partner subsidies to homosexual employees."[18] This characterization of same-sex couples as mere "sex partners" is deeply offensive, especially to life partners who have been together for decades. The Bay State Republican Council "oppose[s] granting homosexuals special privileges, including marriage, domestic partnership benefits, and child custody or adoption."[19] But allowing gay and lesbian people to protect their families through having joint legal custody of their children or through the right to be considered as adoptive parents does not constitute "special privileges." Rather, it is simply equal treatment under the law.

OPPOSITION TO JUDICIAL REVIEW AND THE COURTS' ROLE IN THE U.S. DEMOCRACY

Anti-gay groups often imply that their proposals would allow domestic partnerships, which provide some of the benefits of marriage to gay couples, and civil unions, which can provide a separate form of equality at the level of state policy but none of the federal benefits of marriage. Yet these same groups oppose domestic partnership and civil unions. The Coalition for Marriage argues that the people and the legislatures should have the right to decide on rights for same-sex couples, but when the Boston City Council passed a domestic partnership law, coalition organizations sued and successfully got the domestic partnership program struck down.

In the wake of the Massachusetts Supreme Judicial Court ruling in *Goodridge v. Dept. of Public Health*, many groups of the religious right have cried "judicial tyranny," portraying legislatures as more democratic than courts. For example, the Catholic Action League (a member of the Coalition for Marriage) called for the Massachusetts legislature to impeach and convict for "abuse of office" the four justices who voted for marriage equality for same-sex couples, so the governor could appoint new justices "who will respect their oath of office."[20] Yet when they disagree with a legislative action, Christian right groups have no qualms about challenging such laws through the courts. Such was the case with the American Center for Law and Justice, founded by the Christian Coalition's Rev. Pat Robertson, which filed a lawsuit on behalf of the Catholic Action League of Massachusetts to strike down Boston's municipal domestic partnership policy in 1998–99.[21] The Center for Marriage Law and the Alliance Defense Fund, two other members of the Coalition for Marriage, filed a similar lawsuit against domestic partnership benefits in Portland, Maine.[22]

OPPOSITION TO SAFE SCHOOLS PROGRAMS USING FALSE CLAIMS THAT GAY PEOPLE ARE PEDOPHILES

The safe schools program in Massachusetts is a national model for making schools safe for gay and lesbian youth, the children of gay and lesbian parents, and those who are perceived to be gay, bisexual, or gender variant. It was adopted because of the harassment and violence that these youth face in school, which leads to higher dropout rates and a higher risk of suicide.[23] Groups in the Coalition for Marriage oppose this program. The Family Research Council argues that gay and lesbian youth are not any more likely to be harassed in school and that reports of gay teen suicides are exaggerated,[24] and the Web site of the Massachusetts Family Institute includes a link to an article titled "The Gay Youth Suicide Myth," by Peter LaBarbera, an advocate of conversion therapy.[25]

During the 2004 campaign to ban same-sex marriage in Oregon, activists of the religious right claimed that legalizing marriage for gay couples would lead to teaching young children about gay sex. Anti-gay activists who claimed, falsely, that such efforts were underway in Massachusetts implied that the efforts followed the high court decision in favor of marriage. In fact, it was in the early 1990s that Massachusetts Republican governor William Weld launched the first statewide safe schools initiative aimed at combating suicide and other problems facing gay and lesbian youth. This initiative did not involve teaching young children about sex; it instead allowed high school students to create gay-straight alliances and involved other interventions to make schools affirming places for gay and questioning youth and for children of lesbian and gay parents.

The Family Research Council,[26] Peter LaBarbera, the Traditional Values Coalition, and others have long argued that gay people seek to abuse children. The Traditional Values Coalition's report "Homosexuals Recruit Public School Children" claims that "homosexual militants" have an ongoing "campaign to legalize sex with children" and are "pushing for aggressive recruitment programs in public schools." The report maintains that "[s]ex with children—even grammar school kids—is a primary goal of homosexual activists." It warns: "As homosexuals continue to make inroads into public schools, more children will be molested and indoctrinated into the world of homosexuality. Many of them will die in that world."[27]

In fact, gay activists do not seek to legalize sex with children of grammar school age. All the major gay rights organizations support age-of-consent laws that treat heterosexual sex and homosexual sex equally. Gay people oppose child sexual abuse and support laws that help prevent and punish such abuse.

The claim that homosexuals are more likely to molest children has been definitively refuted by peer-reviewed social science research. A study in the *Journal of the American Medical Association* noted that 90 percent of pedophiles are men and that 98 percent of these individuals are heterosexual.[28] In fact, the limited research indicates that gay men and lesbians are less likely than heterosexuals to sexually abuse children. Two studies that examined the sexual orientation of convicted child molesters found that less than 1 percent of molesters in one study and 0 percent in the other were gay or lesbian.[29]

OPPOSITION TO PARENTING IN GAY AND LESBIAN FAMILIES

Many of the national and local anti-gay groups oppose parenting by gay people, claiming that such parenting harms children. Focus on the Family claims that "same-sex parenting situations make it impossible for a child to live with both biological parents, thus increasing their risk of abuse."[30] In a full-page advertisement placed in the *Boston Globe* on January 23, 2004, Focus on the Family implied that gay marriage would lead to gay parenting in the future, ignoring that it would protect existing lesbian and gay families raising children.

> Same-sex marriage advocates and the Massachusetts Supreme Judicial Court are asking our state and nation to enter a massive, untested social experiment with coming generations of children. We must ask one simple question: Is the same-sex 'family' good for children?

Given that, according to the 2000 U.S. Census, at least eight thousand children are being raised by two lesbian or two gay parents in Massachusetts,[31] parenting by same-sex couples is not some "massive, untested social experiment." It's the lived reality for thousands of Massachusetts residents. That lesbian couples are more likely to be raising children than gay male couples and have more to gain from the family protections offered by marriage may explain why nearly two-thirds of the same-sex couples who married in Massachusetts during the first year of legal gay marriage were lesbian couples.

Maggie Gallagher, an anti-gay marriage activist and syndicated columnist whose commentary is posted on the Web site of the Massachusetts Family Institute, testified at two U.S. congressional hearings against same-sex marriage following the introduction of the Federal Marriage Amendment.[32] She also testified against same-sex marriage in front of the Massachusetts legislature (her testimony is posted on the Massachusetts Family Institute's Web site).[33] In summer 2003, as the Christian right was whipping up sentiment against gay marriage, Gallagher wrote that legalizing same-sex marriage "would mean the law was neutral as to whether children had mothers and fathers" and that "(m)otherless and fatherless families would be deemed just fine."[34] Such claims go against a large body of social science research, which confirms that children raised by gay or lesbian parents are not disadvantaged relative to their peers.[35]

Boston's Catholic archbishop Sean O'Malley warned in 2003 that legalizing gay marriage "would worsen the breakdown of the American family and exacerbate the problems of poverty, child abuse, and human suffering already wrought by 'widespread cohabitation and galloping divorce rates.'"[36] Earlier in the same year, the Vatican issued a statement accusing gay and lesbian parents of "doing violence" to their children by virtue of being gay.[37] Again, there are no data to support claims that an increase in gay and lesbian parenting will lead to greater "poverty, child abuse, and human suffering." U.S. Catholics are still reeling from the child sex abuse epidemic involving at least 4 percent of all Catholic priests in the United States and 7 percent of priests in the Boston archdiocese. Almost eleven thousand children were allegedly sexually abused by 4,392 priests in the United States from 1950 to 2002.[38] One reporter noted, "Abuse victims and their advocates said the [Boston] archdiocese's report understated the problem and reflected only part of the cases of sexual abuse."[39] This systemic and widespread abuse ruined many lives. Many have described the Catholic hierarchy's practice of covering up the abuse and shuffling abusive priests from parish to parish, without warning to the parishioners, as criminally negligent. Patrick McSorley, one of Father John Geoghan's 150 victims and an outspoken critic of the church hierarchy's handling of the problem, killed himself in February 2004 at age twenty-nine. It is unfounded and reckless for leaders of the Catholic Church, especially of the Boston Archdiocese, to charge that parenting in gay and lesbian families will cause an increase in child abuse and human suffering and do violence to children.

If one takes the claims of Focus on the Family, Maggie Gallagher, and the Catholic Church hierarchy to their logical conclusion, one must ask what is the appropriate policy conclusion—to take children away from gay and lesbian parents? Already there are many thousands, if not millions, of children being raised by gay, lesbian, and bisexual parents. Legislators and members of the media should ask these anti-gay activists if they think the state should step in and take these children away from their parents.

OPPOSITION TO BENEFITS AND SERVICES FOR SAME-SEX PARTNERS OF VICTIMS OF THE SEPTEMBER 11 TERRORIST ATTACKS

Several national anti-gay groups opposing marriage equality in Massachusetts and across the United States sought to prevent gay survivors of those killed in the terrorist attacks on the United States on September 11, 2001, from getting benefits and services from the September 11 Victim Compensation Fund and the American Red Cross. Just a month after three thousand people were killed in the worst terrorist attacks in U.S. history—attacks that involved the simultaneous hijacking of four airplanes—Robert Knight of Concerned Women for America's Culture and Family Institute accused "homosexual activists" of "trying to hijack the moral capital of marriage and apply it to their own relationships," which he characterized as "counterfeit marriage."[40]

In the wake of September 11, New York Republican governor George Pataki issued an executive order instructing the State Crime Victims Board to grant same-sex partners of the September 11 attacks the same benefits as married spouses of victims. Pataki, New York City mayor Rudolph Giuliani, and New York state's attorney general Elliot Spitzer wrote President Bush, urging that gay and lesbian partners of victims be eligible for the federal fund administered by the U.S. Department of Justice. Focus on the Family's James Dobson said, "Pataki diluted the definition of 'family' by giving gay partners the same access to terrorist relief benefits that married couples have."[41] Focus on the Family also criticized Pataki's actions as advancing the "gay agenda."[42] After the American Red Cross decided to provide services to gay surviving partners of September 11 victims, Concerned Women for America criticized the group's "broad and inclusive definition of family."[43] Forty-five members of Congress wrote Attorney General John Ashcroft, urging the federal government to adopt a policy similar to that promoted by Governor Pataki in New York State. Concerned Women for America's Culture and Family Institute criticized the letter, claiming that lawmakers and "homosexual activists" were exploiting the "tragedy to ask Ashcroft to pave way for 'domestic partner' benefits."[44]

Lou Sheldon of the Traditional Values Coalition accused gay activists of "taking advantage" of the national tragedy to promote their agenda. Sheldon urged that relief assistance be "given on the basis and priority of one man and one woman in a marital relationship."[45] Such a policy would have also left out unmarried opposite-sex partners of September 11 victims. "We don't devalue the loss of these innocent people," Sheldon insisted, explaining, "But we think this is not the time to institutionalize such 'partnerships' and put them on the same level as marriage."[46] Peter Sprigg of the Family Research Council also accused gay and lesbian people of "taking advantage of the grief and compassion that Americans do feel." He concluded, "To redefine the family based on our grief over the losses that people may have experienced as a result of the terror attacks would be bad law and bad policy."[47]

Perhaps as a result of these objections, the initial interim regulations issued by the Department of Justice in December 2001 and the final regulations issued in March 2002 did not explicitly recognize same-sex partners. They instead left it up to states to determine who is eligible for victim's compensation under the federal fund.[48] However, most states do not provide any legal recognition to same-sex partners, even those in committed, long-term or lifelong relationships.

EXTREME CLAIMS

Comparing Advances in Civil Rights for Gay and Lesbian People to Terrorism

Several leading anti-gay groups have compared gay rights advances to terrorism. Lou Sheldon of the Traditional Values Coalition compared the June 2003 U.S. Supreme Court ruling striking down sodomy laws to the September 11 terrorist attacks. He compared either gays or the Supreme Court to the terrorists who struck that day.

> This is a major wake-up call. This is a 9/11, major wake-up call that the enemy is at our doorsteps. This decision will open a floodgate. This will redirect the stream of what is morally right and what is morally wrong into a deviant kind of behavior. There is no way that homosexuality can be seen other than [as] a social disorder.[49]

Concerned Women for America warned in a September 2003 press release that same-sex marriage "pose[s] a new threat to US border security." The release called a legally married Canadian same-sex couple trying to enter the United States as a married couple "the latest pair of 'domestic terrorists.'"[50] Former Boston mayor and U.S. ambassador to the Vatican Raymond Flynn, now a professional Christian right/anti-gay activist, reacted to the Massachusetts high court ruling by calling the issue of gay marriage "a ticking time bomb in America for the last several months that has exploded in Massachusetts." He claimed, "The voice of the American people is about to be heard."[51] Family Research Council president Tony Perkins also used the analogy of a time bomb when he criticized President Bush for not going far enough in his 2004 State of the Union address.

> Sixty-four days ago the Massachusetts State Supreme Court tossed a cultural time bomb into the public square when they mandated the Legislature to create homosexual marriages. Disappointingly, in his State of the Union address, President Bush promised to help the families of America—after the bomb goes off and the damage is done.[52]

GAYS + DEMOCRATS = A DOMESTIC AL-QAEDA

The Massachusetts Family Institute posts a lot of right-wing commentary on its Web site, including a column by Ann Coulter titled "Massachusetts Supreme Court Abolishes Capitalism!" and a piece by Dennis Prager titled "San Francisco and Islamists: Fighting the Same Enemy."[53] Prager compares "secular extremism" to "religious extremism," arguing: "One enemy is led from abroad. The other is directed from home." Prager continues: "The war over same-sex marriage and the war against Islamic totalitarianism are actually two fronts in the same war—a war for the preservation of the unique creation known as Judeo-Christian civilization." Claiming that "the Left" is ignoring the threat of anti-American terrorism from groups active in the Muslim world, Prager says this is because "the Left is preoccupied first with destroying America's distinctive values." He continues, "So, if the Islamists are fellow anti-Americans, the Left figures it can worry about them later." Warning that legalizing same-sex marriage represents "the beginning of the end of Judeo-Christian civilization," Prager concludes: "This civilization is now fighting for its life—as much here as abroad. Join the fight, or it will be gone as fast as you can say 'Democrat.'"[54]

CLAIMS OF ANTI-CATHOLICISM

The Massachusetts Knights of Columbus posts a letter on its Web site from former Boston Mayor Ray Flynn, now president of Your Catholic Voice. Flynn warns: "your Church and your family are under attack . . . [A]nti-Catholicism is alive and well here in Massachusetts! Anti-Catholicism is, tragically, still an acceptable form of prejudice in America today."[55] Despite Flynn's alarmism, legalization of same-sex marriage—which is recognized in many Protestant and Jewish faith traditions—is no more anti-Catholic than is the legalization of divorce for heterosexuals. "We are part of a pluralistic society and in no way pretend to force our religious preferences on other people," Catholic archbishop Sean O'Malley said at "The Summit of October to Save Marriage," organized by the Massachusetts Family Institute in Wayland, Massachusetts, in October 2003.[56] But in fact that is exactly what O'Malley is trying to do. Pointing this out and challenging it is not a manifestation of anti-Catholicism. Charges of anti-Catholicism have particular resonance in Massachusetts, one of the most Catholic states in the country, where anti-Catholic bias interacted with anti-immigrant nativism in the 1800s and early 1900s.

AN INORDINATE FOCUS ON HOMOSEXUALITY

Although many of the national anti-gay groups purport to advocate a "pro-family" agenda, they pay much less attention to many pressing family problems. Three of the national religious right groups have Web sites that allow users to search all of the documents available on the site. Searches using a few keywords yielded revealing results.[57]

The Family Research Council, a group that has $5 million in revenue a year and claims it "shapes public debate and formulates public policy that values human life and upholds the institutions of marriage and the family," had 203 documents on its Web site containing the term *homosexual* but only 37 with *poverty*, 26 with *domestic violence*, 18 with *health insurance*, and 2 with *child support*. Concerned Women for America, a "public policy women's organization" with $12 million in revenue a year, had 602 documents on its Web site that contained the term *homosexual* but only 97 with *health care*, 80 with *poverty*, 70 with *divorce*, and six containing *child support*. The Concerned Women for America Web site had only 71 documents containing the term *rape*, 19 with *domestic violence*, and none with *pay equity*. This is especially striking given a June 2003 survey of over three thousand women conducted over two years by Princeton Survey Research Associates, which revealed that the top concerns of American women were domestic violence/sexual assault and equal pay for equal work.[58] Focus on the Family, a religious right behemoth with $126 million in revenue a year and more than one thousand employees, had the word *divorce* in 841 documents, *homosexual* in 740 documents, *poverty* in 212 documents, *domestic violence* in 85 documents, *health insurance* in only 36 documents, and *child support* in a mere 20 documents.

A BROADER REACTIONARY AGENDA

Many anti-gay, Christian right groups claim to represent the people against "judicial tyranny." But in fact, many leading groups advocate a reactionary political agenda that is not supported by a majority of Americans. For example, many of these organizations also oppose affirmative action, reproductive choice, immigration, teaching evolution in schools, the failed Equal Rights Amendment that would have banned sex discrimination (passed by Congress in 1979 and ratified by thirty-five states before the seven-year ratification period expired), and military combat service by women.

Dr. Ron Crews, president of the Massachusetts Family Institute since 2001, served as a Republican state representative in Georgia from 1992 to 1998, when his bid for reelection failed because of his hard-right views. He blamed his loss on "homosexual activists who moved into my district just to be able to vote against me." Crews sponsored the Georgia Defense of Marriage Act when it passed in 1996, and he sought legislation allowing "covenant marriage," which would have made divorce more difficult by requiring spouses to enter counseling, prove adultery or abuse, or live apart for two years before being allowed to divorce.[59] He was a leader in the fight to ban late-term abortions and also lobbied the Georgia Department of Education to teach creationism in the classroom, without success.[60] Following his defeat for reelection in 1998, Crews served as legislative director for the Georgia Christian Coalition.

OPPOSITION TO NO-FAULT DIVORCE: ADVOCATING THE REQUIREMENT OF MUTUAL CONSENT FOR DIVORCE

The Family Research Council promotes an end to no-fault divorce and advocates the requirement of mutual consent for divorce, as well as "covenant marriage" laws now in effect in Louisiana, Arizona, and Arkansas.[61] Covenant marriages are much harder to enter into and harder to dissolve. When Tony Perkins, now head of the Family Research Council, was a Republican state representative in Louisiana, he drafted the first covenant marriage law, passed in 1997. A Family Research Council document states:

> after consulting with . . . a group of pastors in his district . . . he drafted a bill that only allowed for divorce in what they saw as the biblically licit cases of adultery and abandonment. Perkins said he wanted to start with a high standard, the biblical ideal for marriage, because he knew that he would have to compromise in the legislative process.[62]

It is important to note that Perkins's bill does not list spousal abuse as a "biblically licit" reason for divorce.

The Family Research Council praises "state marriage promotion efforts," including "restricting no-fault divorce." Arguing that "abandoning fault divorce was a huge mistake," Brigit Maher of the council endorses "legislation to restrict no-fault divorce, which require[s] mutual consent, longer waiting periods, or classes for divorcing parents before a divorce can be obtained."[63] Concerned Women for America's Jan LaRue also denounces no-fault divorce as a reason why many people support marriage equality for gay couples.

> The biggest problem we have in getting people, especially younger ones, to understand why marriage is devalued by the existence of a counterfeit is that much of the public does not value marriage at all. Adultery is no big deal. No-fault divorce is tolerated. Absentee fathers and mothers devalue marriage.[64]

While it is not clear if the Massachusetts Family Institute supports an end to no-fault divorce, its Web site contains links to the national groups just noted that do. The institute's Massachusetts Marriage and Family Report 2002 calls on "public policy opinion leaders" to "encourage policies that discourage divorce without counseling."[65]

OPPOSITION TO FEMINISM

Phyllis Schlafly is one of several conservative leaders and pundits whose "timely commentary" is posted on the Massachusetts Family Institute's Web site. She helped defeat the Equal Rights Amendment in the mid-1980s. A book titled *Feminist Fantasies*—linked at the bottom of Schlafly's essay "Will Massachusetts Abolish Marriage?"—claims:

> No assault has been more ferocious than feminism's 40-year war against women, and no battlefield leader has been more courageous than Schlafly. In a new book of dispatches from the front, feminism's most potent foe exposes the delusions and hypocrisy behind a movement that has cheated millions of women out of their happiness, health, and security.[66]

Schlafly's Eagle Forum works closely with Concerned Women for America and other members of the Coalition for Marriage through the closely named Coalition to Protect Marriage and through other coalitions. The Coalition to Protect Marriage sponsored Marriage Protection Week in October 2003. Archbishop Sean O'Malley spoke at a Massachusetts event on October 2,

2003, that was organized by the Massachusetts Family Institute and the Coalition to Protect Marriage.[67]

National anti-gay groups advocate many reactionary policies. The Traditional Values Coalition, Focus on the Family, Concerned Women for America, and Phyllis Schlafly's Eagle Forum oppose reproductive choice, the teaching of evolution in public schools, and comprehensive sex education. They also promote prayer in public schools.[68] The Family Research Council supports a school prayer amendment to the U.S. Constitution and would like to abolish the Department of Education.[69] Concerned Women for America also seeks the abolition of the Department of Education.[70] Phyllis Schlafly opposes statehood for the District of Columbia and Puerto Rico (predominantly African American and Latino jurisdictions), supports making English the official language of the United States, and opposes the combat service of women. She brags about her leading role in defeating the Equal Rights Amendment.[71] She also opposes President Bush's immigration reform proposal, singling out Mexican immigrants in particular for her vitriol.[72]

OUTSPENDING GAY RIGHTS GROUPS BY AT LEAST A SIX-TO-ONE MARGIN

Anti-gay groups portray gay people and gay activists as politically powerful, well-funded elites. For example, Andrea Sheldon, executive director of the Traditional Values Coalition, slammed President Clinton for speaking at a Human Rights Campaign dinner in 1997, denouncing "an American President kissing up to the wealthiest extremists of the left."[73] The Family Research Council recently wrote: "The Human Rights Campaign and the other groups in the homosexual lobby have very deep pockets. Big corporations, elite foundations, and Hollywood celebrities underwrite the homosexual lobby with tens of millions of dollars every year."[74]

In fact, the financial resources of the nine member organizations of the Massachusetts-based Coalition for Marriage for which income data are available dwarf the revenues of national and local gay rights advocacy organizations by a margin of at least six to one ($168 million compared to just $25 million).[75] These groups range from Focus on the Family, with $126 million in revenue in 2002, to the Massachusetts State Council of the Knights of Columbus, with $593,512 in revenue in 2002. It is important to note that the Massachusetts Family Institute, with just over $400,000

TABLE 3. Annual Income of Coalition for Marriage Member Organizations versus Members of MassEquality

Coalition for Marriage members for which income data is publicly available (9)		
Focus on the Family	www.family.org	$126,251,827
Alliance Defense Fund	www.alliancedefensefund.org	$15,998,907
Black Ministerial Alliance of Greater Boston	www.bmaboston.org	$1,291,742
Concerned Women for America	www.cwfa.org	$11,999,881
Family Research Council	www.frc.org	$9,730,169
Massachusetts Family Institute	www.mafamily.org	$408,858
Morality in Media Massachusetts	www.moralmedia.net	$1,247,956
Massachusetts State Council, Knights of Columbus	www.massachusettsstatekofc.org	$593,512
Traditional Values Coalition	www.traditionalvalues.org	$581,783[a]
Total		$168,104,635
National and local members of MassEquality, the Massachusetts marriage equality coalition		
Human Rights Campaign/HRC Foundation	www.hrc.org	$17,334,997
National Gay and Lesbian Task Force/NGLTF Foundation	www.thetaskforce.org	$5,121,163[b]
Gay and Lesbian Advocates and Defenders	www.glad.org	$1,500,000[c]
Freedom to Marry Coalition of Massachusetts	www.equalmarriage.org	$200,000[d]
Massachusetts Gay and Lesbian Political Caucus	www.mglpc.org	$100,000[e]
Freedom to Marry Foundation	www.equalmarriage.org	$50,000[f]
Greater Boston Parents and Friends of Lesbians and Gays	www.pflag.org	$98,000[g]
Bay State Democrats	www.baystatestonewalldems.org	5,000[h]
Gay and Lesbian Labor Activist Network	(N/A)	$3,000[i]
Jewish Alliance for Law and Social Action	www.jewishalliance.org	$125,000[j]
Religious Coalition for the Freedom to Marry	www.rcfm.org	$15,000[k]
Citizens for Participation in Political Action	www.cppax.org	(N/A)
National Organization for Women, Massachusetts Chapter	www.massnow.org	$46,000[l]
Western Massachusetts LGBT Political Alliance	www.wmassalliance.org	$8,000[m]
National Log Cabin Republicans	www.logcabin.org	$1,000,000
ACLU of Massachusetts	www.aclu-mass.org	$950,000[n]
Bisexual Resource Center	www.biresource.org	$20,000[o]
LGBT Aging Project	www.lgbtagingproject.org	(N/A)
Total		$26,576,160

Note: Information retrieved from http://www.guidestar.org (IRS Forms 990) on October 1, 2004, unless otherwise noted.

[a] The revenue listed is for fiscal year 2001 of the Traditional Values Coalition Education and Legal Institute only. Financial data on the broader Traditional Values Coalition is unavailable.

[b] Fiscal year 2002–3 audited financial statements.

[c] 2003 income.

[d] Conversation with Josh Friedes, legislative director, March 4, 2004.

[e] Conversation with Arline Isaacson, board cochair, March 4, 2004.

[f] Ibid.

[g] Conversation with Gretchen Frasier, board president, March 5, 2004.

[h] Conversation with Steve Driscoll, board cochair, March 5, 2004.

[i] Conversation with Harneen Chernow, board cochair, March 4, 2004.

[j] Conversation with Sheila Decter, director, March 4, 2004.

[k] Conversation with Marty Rouse, director, MassEquality, March 4, 2004.

[l] Conversation with Patricia Sanders, director, March 8, 2004.

[m] Conversation with Stacy Roth, executive director, March 8, 2004.

[n] Conversation with Carol Rose, executive director, March 8, 2004.

[o] Conversation with Sheeri Kritzer, treasurer, March 8, 2004.

in revenue in 2002, is a member of the Family Policy Councils of Focus on the Family, which had $126 million in annual revenue at its disposal to use in Massachusetts. The Coalition for Marriage organizations for which data were not available also have enormous resources and clout, including the Massachusetts Catholic Conference, the Catholic Action League of Massachusetts, the Center for Marriage Law, and the Traditional Values Coali-

TABLE 4. Annual Income of Thirteen Marriage Protection Week Sponsors versus the Thirteen Largest National Gay Rights Advocacy Organizations

Thirteen Sponsors of Marriage Protection Week for which income data is publicly available		
Focus on the Family	www.family.org	$126,251,827
Prison Fellowship	www.pfm.org	$46,310,285
American Family Association	www.afa.net	$14,072,427
Concerned Women For America	www.cwfa.org	$11,999,881
Family Research Council	www.frc.org	$9,730,169
Free Congress Foundation	www.freecongress.org	$2,680,004[a]
National Coalition for the Protection of Children and Families	www.nationalcoalition.org	$1,577,827
Eagle Forum	www.eagleforum.org	$1,569,697[b]
Americans United for Life	www.unitedforlife.org	$1,118,102[b]
American Values	www.ouramericanvalues.org	$870,141
Traditional Values Coalition	www.traditionalvalues.org	$581,783[b]
American Cause	www.theamericancause.org	$415,003[b]
Citizens for Community Values	www.ccv.org	$89,338[b]
Total		$217,266,484
Thirteen largest national gay rights advocacy organizations		
Human Rights Campaign/HRC Foundation	www.hrc.org	$17,334,997[b]
Lambda Legal Defense and Education Fund, Inc.	www.lambdalegal.org	$9,509,686
Gay and Lesbian Alliance Against Defamation, Inc.	www.glaad.org	$5,300,000
National Gay and Lesbian Task Force/ NGLTF Foundation	www.thetaskforce.org	$5,121,163[c]
Gay, Lesbian, and Straight Education Network	www.glsen.org	$3,325,203
LLEGO (National Latino/a Lesbian and Gay Organization)	www.llego.org	$2,500,000
Parents and Friends of Lesbians and Gay Men	www.pflag.org	$2,363,005[b]
Victory Fund/Foundation	www.victoryfund.org	$2,000,000
Servicemember's Legal Defense Network	www.sldn.org	$1,800,000
National Center for Lesbian Rights	www.nclrights.org	$1,414,120[b]
International Gay and Lesbian Human Rights Commission	www.iglhrc.org	$1,357,355
Freedom to Marry Collaborative	www.freedomtomarry.org	$1,100,000[d]
National Youth Advocacy Coalition	www.nyacyouth.org	$1,021,907
Total		$54,147,436

Note: Information retrieved from http://www.guidestar.org (IRS Forms 990), unless otherwise noted.
[a]2000 revenues.
[b]2001 revenues.
[c]Fiscal year 2002–3 audited financial statement.
[d]2003 approved budget.
Source: Adapted from S. Cahill et al., *"Marriage Protection Week" Sponsors: Are They Really Interested in "Building Strong and Healthy Marriages?"* (New York: Policy Institute of the National Gay and Lesbian Task Force, 2003).

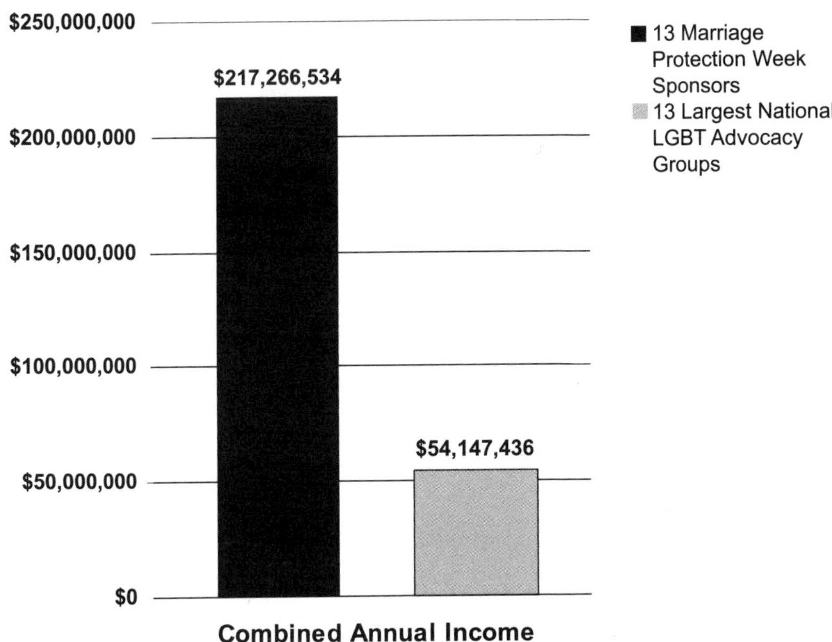

Fig. 12. Annual income analysis of thirteen Marriage Protection Week sponsors versus the thirteen largest national gay rights advocacy organizations.
Reproduced from S. Cahill, J. Cianciotto, and R. Colvin, *"Marriage Protection Week" Sponsors: Are They Really Interested in "Building Strong and Healthy Marriages?"* (New York: Policy Institute of the National Gay and Lesbian Task Force, 2003), 5–6.

tion outside its Education and Legal Institute. If the revenue and assets of these groups were added to the $168 million they report, gay and pro-gay groups would be at an even more extreme disadvantage than the six-to-one ratio we can definitively state.

As evidence of their significant resources, the Family Research Council launched a $2 million advertisement campaign on February 27, 2004, to thank President Bush for his support of the Federal Marriage Amendment. The council purchased full-page advertisements in several major U.S. newspapers, including the *New York Times*, the *Washington Post*, and *USA Today*.[76] This campaign used more resources than the entire 2003 operating budget of Gay and Lesbian Advocates and Defenders, the group that litigated *Goodridge v. Dept. of Public Health*.

MEMBER ORGANIZATIONS OF THE COALITION FOR MARRIAGE[77]

Alliance Defense Fund

The Alliance Defense Fund is a national group that, according to its mission statement, "provides the resources that will keep the door open for the spread of the Gospel through the legal defense and advocacy of religious freedom, the sanctity of human life, and traditional family values."

Bay State Republican Council

The Bay State Republican Council is a grassroots group formed in 2001 that promotes the election of Republican candidates in local, state, and federal elections.

Black Ministerial Alliance of Greater Boston

The Black Ministerial Alliance is a forty-year-old organization representing eighty African American churches in the Boston area.

Catholic Action League of Massachusetts

The Catholic Action League of Massachusetts is an advocacy and public policy group.

Center for Marriage Law

The Center for Marriage Law is affiliated with the Columbus School of Law at the Catholic University of America in Washington, D.C., and is dedicated, according to its Web site, to strengthening "the institution of marriage and to affirm[ing] the definition of marriage as the union of one man and one woman."

Concerned Women for America

Concerned Women for America is a religious advocacy group based in Washington, D.C., and dedicated, according to its mission statement, to protecting and promoting "biblical values among all citizens." It has played a leading role in dozens of anti-gay ballot campaigns.

Family Policy Councils of the United States

The Family Policy Councils are a loosely affiliated coalition of state groups under Focus on the Family, such as the Massachusetts Family Institute.

Family Research Council

The Family Research Council, a spin-off from Focus on the Family, is a Christian advocacy group based in Washington, D.C. It has been active in dozens of anti-gay ballot campaigns.

Focus on the Family

Focus on the Family is a national, Colorado-based Christian advocacy and media group whose mission is "to cooperate with the Holy Spirit in disseminating the Gospel of Jesus Christ to as many people as possible." It has been active in dozens of anti-gay ballot campaigns. It is the largest Christian right, anti-gay group, with an annual budget of $125 million and more than one thousand employees.

Massachusetts Catholic Conference

The Massachusetts Catholic Conference is the lobbying and public policy arm of the four Roman Catholic dioceses of Massachusetts.

Massachusetts Citizens for Life

The Massachusetts Citizens for Life is an advocacy group opposed to legal abortion, human cloning, and euthanasia.

Massachusetts Family Institute

The Massachusetts Family Institute, the state affiliate of the Colorado-based Focus on the Family, has coordinated the fight in Massachusetts to amend the state's constitution to define marriage as the union of one man and one woman.

Massachusetts State Council, Knights of Columbus

The Knights of Columbus is a Roman Catholic fraternal group.

Morality in Media Massachusetts

Morality in Media promotes "decency in the media" and "strongly upholds traditional family values and Judeo-Christian precepts." It is an affiliate of the Christian Coalition.[78]

Traditional Values Coalition

The Traditional Values Coalition is a national organization made up of forty-three thousand churches. The coalition is rabidly anti-gay and heavily focused on anti-gay politics. Nine of its "Top Ten Reports" on its Web site are fully or partly about homosexuality; the tenth is about transgender issues. Seven of the ten reports have the word *homosexual* in their title. The coalition has also been active in dozens of anti-gay ballot campaigns.

RECENT HISTORICAL CONTEXT: THE EMERGENCE OF MARRIAGE AS A CENTRAL POLITICAL ISSUE IN THE 1990s[79]

In June 2003, in *Lawrence v. Texas*, the U.S. Supreme Court struck down archaic laws in thirteen states banning private, consensual sexual intimacy. (The impact of archaic sex laws in two additional states, Massachusetts and

Michigan, was in dispute at the time of the ruling.) Widely known as "sodomy laws," nine of these thirteen laws banned certain practices regardless of whether the couple engaging in them was heterosexual or homosexual.[80] In the other four states, the laws banned certain sexual practices only for homosexual couples. But even in the nine states where laws targeted both opposite-sex and same-sex couples, the laws were in practice disproportionately deployed against gay couples.

The majority ruled that sodomy laws violated the Constitution's privacy provision; the court did not directly address the issue of state recognition of same-sex marriages. However, both gay rights proponents and opponents interpreted the majority's decision as hinting at future support for marriage equality. Justice Anthony Kennedy, writing for the majority, ruled that the state cannot single out gay people for harassment and discriminatory treatment simply because of "moral disapproval" of homosexuality. Kennedy wrote of "respect" for gay couples and warned that "the state cannot demean their existence." The court also described gay relationships as a "personal bond" involving much more than just sex. Kennedy said that reducing gay couples to "sex partners," as anti-gay organizations and defenders of sodomy laws often do, is offensive in the same way that describing a husband and wife as nothing more than sex partners would be offensive. However, Kennedy noted that the case against the Texas sodomy law "does not involve whether the government must give formal recognition to any relationship homosexual persons seek to enter." In her concurrence, Justice Sandra Day O'Connor agreed that the "traditional institution of marriage" was not at issue.[81]

Despite these majority caveats, Justice Antonin Scalia angrily argued just the opposite in his dissent, in which he was joined by Chief Justice Rehnquist: "Today's opinion dismantles the structure of constitutional law that has permitted a distinction to be made between heterosexual and homosexual unions, insofar as formal recognition in marriage is concerned."[82] Anti-gay activists and politicians vocally agreed. Quickly, the *Lawrence* decision became portrayed in the mainstream media as a precursor to legalization of gay marriage. Republican senator Rick Santorum of Pennsylvania warned that "the greatest near-term consequence of the *Lawrence v. Texas* anti-sodomy ruling could be the legalization of homosexual marriage."[83] Rev. Jerry Falwell warned, "it's a capitulation to the gay and lesbian agenda whose ultimate goal is the legalization of same-sex marriages."[84]

Gay rights activists also found implications in *Lawrence* for marriage equality. Of legalized same-sex marriage, Lambda Legal Defense and Education Fund's Patricia Logue, cocounsel in the *Lawrence* case, said, "I think it's inevitable now," adding, "In what time frame, we don't know."[85] *Lawrence* lead attorney Ruth Harlow, also with Lambda, said, "The ruling makes it much harder for society to continue banning gay marriages."[86]

The *Lawrence* decision and court rulings in Canada and Massachusetts in favor of marriage equality (discussed in chap. 3) were, of course, welcomed by advocates for equal rights for LGBT people. They were also denounced by anti-gay politicians and organizations, including the leading groups of the religious right. Conservatives and would-be theocrats joined together to mobilize resentment and reaction against the *Lawrence* and *Goodridge* rulings, prime examples, in their view, of judicial tyranny and liberal judicial activism. They promoted dozens of state anti-gay family laws and amendments, as well as two federal initiatives: the anti-gay Federal Marriage Amendment and the Marriage Protection Act, a bill that would strip federal courts of the power to rule on the issue of same-sex marriage. Such efforts are just the latest round of a concerted, decade-long campaign to ban marriage for same-sex couples in state and federal law. The broader anti-gay movement has been around almost as long as the modern gay rights movement: the first anti-gay ballot measure repealed a sexual orientation nondiscrimination law in Boulder, Colorado, in 1974.

The first ballot measure to target marriage for same-sex couples was proposed in Idaho in 1994. The Idaho initiative would have banned marriage for gay couples as well as many other legal protections, such as sexual orientation nondiscrimination laws. While the anti-gay movement has promoted anti-gay ballot measures as an organizing and fund-raising strategy for three decades, it was not until the mid-1990s that it started promoting anti-gay marriage and other anti-family ballot questions.

Hostility toward gays was a central theme of the Republican Convention in August 1992. Pat Buchanan denounced "the amoral idea that gay and lesbian couples should have the same standing in law as married men and women." He also ridiculed Clinton's support for gay equality to a receptive crowd, many of whom held signs reading "Family Values Forever, Gay Rights Never." Buchanan advocated a "cultural war" against secular humanism and those advocating tolerance for various differences. At least six other speakers spoke against gay people, gay rights laws, and same-sex marriage. Vice President Dan Quayle alluded to gays in his acceptance speech: "Americans try to raise their children to understand right and wrong, only to be told that every so-called 'lifestyle' is morally equivalent. That is wrong."[87] Finally, Republican National Committee chairman Rich Bond explained to the press: "We are America. These other people are not America."[88]

The Republicans' strategy failed, however. A *New York Times* poll right after the convention found that only 23 percent of voters considered homosexuality an important election issue.[89] Bill Clinton's mantra "It's the economy, stupid" was a better indicator of the sentiment of voters still trying to escape the depths of a recession. Campaign aides resisted the desire of many in the Republican Party to make Clinton's support for lifting the military ban a campaign issue, fearing further backlash like that evoked by the rhetorical excesses of the Houston convention.[90] Clinton won the 1992 presidential election partly due to the fund-raising support and votes of a newly energized gay voting bloc. Three in four gays voted Democratic, and only 14 percent voted for incumbent president George Herbert Walker Bush.[91]

THE 1996 ELECTION AND THE FEDERAL DEFENSE OF MARRIAGE ACT[92]

After the Hawaii Supreme Court ruled in 1993 that it was impermissible under the state constitution to deny three lesbian and gay couples the right to obtain a marriage license, anti-gay activists and politicians made gay marriage a central issue in the 1996 presidential campaign. Just before the Iowa caucuses, the first primary election event, they held a rally denouncing same-sex marriage. Nearly every Republican candidate attended and signed a pledge to "defend" heterosexual marriage against the threat allegedly posed by the three same-sex couples in Hawaii who had sued the state for the right to marry.

The developments in Hawaii and the Republican presidential candidates' anti-gay rhetoric quickly transformed mainstream state and national politics. Gay marriage emerged as a central wedge issue in the campaign. Throughout 1996, newspapers and talk radio hosts railed against gay marriage—even such liberal editorial boards as that of the *Boston Globe.* Six in ten Americans polled expressed disapproval of same-sex marriage.[93]

It was against this backdrop that Congress passed the 1996 Defense of Marriage Act, which barred federal recognition of same-sex marriages and allowed states to refuse to recognize same-sex marriages from other states. After it passed Congress, President Clinton not only signed the legislation but bragged about doing so, in advertisements run on Christian radio stations. Clinton's expression of opposition to lesbian and gay marriage and his decision to sign the Defense of Marriage Act into law in October 1996 prevented gay marriage from becoming a major campaign issue in the final weeks of the 1996 presidential campaign.

A total of fifteen state legislatures passed anti-gay marriage statutes by the end of 1996.[94] Another fifteen states adopted anti-gay marriage statutes in 1997 and 1998.[95] Hawaii and Alaska also passed anti-marriage constitutional amendments in 1998, reversing earlier state court victories for marriage equality.

VERMONT'S HIGH COURT RULING AND THE 2000 ELECTION CAMPAIGN[96]

Throughout the primary race for the 2000 nomination, which started in mid-1999, all ten of the Republican candidates opposed any form of legal protection for gay people, such as nondiscrimination laws. Echoing the 1996 anti-marriage rally on the eve of the Iowa caucuses, six of the Republican candidates signed an anti-gay pledge on the eve of the Iowa straw poll in August 1999, pledging to oppose domestic partner benefits, education to fight anti-gay harassment and violence in the schools, adoption by gay people, and other issues.[97]

In December 1999, the marriage issue arose again in the wake of the Vermont Supreme Court's ruling that the state must provide to same-sex couples every benefit and protection it provides to married heterosexual couples. Democratic candidates Bill Bradley and Al Gore, who sought the gay community's vote, applauded the decision, while the Republican candidates denounced it. Christian right activist Gary Bauer called the ruling "worse than terrorism."[98]

Throughout 2000, Governor George W. Bush of Texas continued to articulate anti-gay positions when asked. In South Carolina, he told a Christian radio station that if elected president, he probably would not appoint gays to his administration, because "[a]n openly known homosexual is somebody who probably wouldn't share my philosophy."[99] As governor, Bush defended Texas's sodomy law as "a symbolic gesture of traditional values,"[100] opposed sex education, and sought to tax condoms as a vice.[101] Throughout 1999 and 2000, Bush spoke out against gay adoption, same-sex marriage, hate crimes legislation, nondiscrimination laws, and sex education.

Despite this, the Log Cabin Republicans reportedly spent five hundred thousand dollars campaigning for Bush's election in 2000.

Vice Presidential nominee Dick Cheney pleasantly surprised many when he said in a debate with Democratic senator Joseph Lieberman that same-sex partners should be able to enter into relationships and that states should be able to decide whether or not to recognize such relationships.[102] However, such states' rights, usually a core tenet of conservative philosophy, were restricted by the federal Defense of Marriage Act, which Cheney and Bush support.

Despite Bush and Cheney's bottom-line adherence to anti-gay policy positions, the 2000 Republican Convention set a markedly different tone from its predecessors. In general, speakers eschewed anti-gay rhetoric, although anti-gay language was kept in the Republican Party platform. This language opposed marriage and other forms of partner recognition for gay couples, gays in military service, and sexual orientation nondiscrimination laws.

MARRIAGE AND THE 2004 ELECTION

The 2004 Democratic Presidential Candidates: The Most Pro-Gay Field Ever[103]

The ten Democratic presidential candidates who ran in 2003 and 2004 were by far the most pro-gay field of candidates ever. All of the Democrats supported most of the key issues of concern to LGBT people: sexual orientation nondiscrimination laws, HIV/AIDS prevention and treatment, lifting the ban on gays in the military, hate crimes laws, domestic partnerships, and gay-supportive education policy.[104] The few differences among the candidates regarded marriage and civil unions.

Three of the ten candidates—former U.S. senator and ambassador Carol Moseley Braun (IL), Congressman Dennis Kucinich (OH), and the Rev. Al Sharpton—supported full marriage equality for same-sex couples. The other seven candidates did not unequivocally support marriage equality. Five of these—Senator John Edwards (NC), Representative Dick Gephardt (MO), Senator John Kerry (MA), Senator Joseph Lieberman (CT), and Senator Bob Graham (FL)—repeatedly expressed their opposition to marriage for same-sex couples. At the same time, most spoke out against the Federal Marriage Amendment, which Rep. Marilyn Musgrave (R-CO) had introduced to amend the U.S. Constitution to define marriage as between a man and a woman and to prevent legislatures or courts from mandating more limited benefits, such as civil unions or domestic partnerships (see chap. 3). They also made supportive comments in the wake of the Massachusetts court ruling. Democratic nominees Kerry and Edwards both spoke out against the Federal Marriage Amendment; when it came up for a vote in July 2004, just before the Democratic National Convention, they skipped the vote but said they would have voted against it had they been present.

The other two candidates, retired general Wesley Clark and former Vermont governor Howard Dean, did not say they opposed marriage for gay couples. However, on numerous occasions, when asked if they support marriage, they answered that they support civil unions. They also expressed support for the recent Massachusetts ruling in favor of marriage equality, saying it reflected concern for "rights" (Clark) and "equality" (Dean) for all Americans, regardless of sexual orientation.[105]

Bush on Marriage Equality[106]

For much of 2003 and into early 2004, Bush sent mixed messages about the Federal Marriage Amendment. For example, in July 2003, Bush said of the amendment: "I don't know if it's necessary yet . . . [W]hat I do support is a notion that marriage is between a man and a woman."[107] However, later that month, Bush announced his intention to introduce legislation that would go beyond the restrictions expressed by the Defense of Marriage Act and further codify the ban on same-sex marriage.[108]

In October 2003, Bush endorsed Marriage Protection Week, a series of anti-gay marriage events sponsored by the leading national Christian right groups.[109] Bush repeatedly denounced the November 2003 Massachusetts Supreme Judicial Court ruling legalizing marriage for same-sex couples[110]—for example, in his January 2004 State of the Union address.[111] On February 4, 2004, the Massachusetts Supreme Judicial Court ruled that civil unions would not provide equality to same-sex couples, and it reaffirmed the right of gay couples to marry under the Massachusetts Constitution's equality and due process guarantees. Bush called the ruling "deeply troubling" and reiterated his statement from his State of the Union address.[112] Later that month, he called gay marriages in San Francisco "troubling."[113] Finally, in late February 2004, Bush officially endorsed an anti-gay marriage amendment, calling on Congress to quickly pass such a measure.

Bush on More Limited Forms of Partner Recognition

In 2000, President Bush said, "In the private sector [domestic partner benefits] are perfectly fine." On the governmental level, he said, the decision should be left up to cities and states.[114] However, as governor of Texas, Bush took no initiative to offer domestic partner benefits to state employees or to create a domestic partner registry for Texas residents. Bush has not indicated whether or not he supports domestic partner benefits for same-sex partners of federal employees. Such a bill was introduced into the Republican-controlled Congress in 2003, cosponsored by conservative Democratic senator Joseph Lieberman (D-CT), but Bush has not done anything to help move it toward passage.[115]

When White House press secretary Scott McClellan was asked how the president feels about the "concept of civil unions as an alternative to gay marriage," McClellan responded that Bush supports the Defense of Marriage Act, which "states that other states don't have to recognize the civil unions or same-sex marriages of other states." He then concluded, "So his position is very clear in support of that."[116] Texas, which Bush used to lead as governor, does not offer civil unions to same-sex couples. Bush endorsed Marriage Protection Week in October 2003, during which elected officials were asked to sign a pledge opposing not only marriage but also domestic partnership and civil unions for gay couples. Yet a week before the November 2004 election, Bush said he supported the right of states to offer civil unions for same-sex couples, and that he disagreed with the GOP platform's opposition to civil unions. This monumental flip-flop reversed Bush's earlier endorsement of Marriage Protection Week and the federal amendment, both of which sought to ban civil unions. The media failed to note this glaring inconsistency, and Bush came across as moderate and reasonable on gay issues.

In the 2000 debate with Senator Joseph Lieberman, Vice President Dick Cheney defended the right of gay couples to protect their relationships and defended states' rights to devise whatever form of partner recognition they might choose. However, in early 2004, Cheney reversed this position and endorsed President Bush's call for a constitutional amendment banning same-sex marriage, which would prevent such court rulings as the one in Vermont that prompted the state legislature to create civil unions. In August 2004, Cheney yet again reversed himself, saying that he personally thought individual states should be able to grant whatever recognition they deemed appropriate to same-sex couples. He said that he personally disagreed with the president's support for the Federal Marriage Amendment. Strikingly, in a campaign in which Senator Kerry was harshly denounced as a "flip-flopper," no mainstream media outlet or pundit pointed out the inconsistency of both Bush's and Cheney's positions on same-sex partner recognition.

The 2004 Republican and Democratic Platforms on Marriage and Same-Sex Couples

While there are many key issues on which the two major U.S. political parties disagree, their attitudes toward policy issues affecting lesbian and gay people represent one of the most striking areas of disagreement. Since 1980, the two parties have headed in sharply divergent directions in terms of platform language regarding gay issues. This is in large part because gays became an integral part of the Democratic Party base, while anti-gay activists of the religious right became ascendant in the Republican Party, particularly following the creation of the Christian Coalition after Rev. Pat Robertson's failed run for the presidency in 1988.

The 2004 Republican and Democratic platforms differed sharply on gay issues, including whether to offer legal protections to lesbian and gay couples. The Republican platform opposed any benefits for same-sex couples; supported the Federal Marriage Amendment and the court-stripping Marriage Protection Act; and claimed that being raised by heterosexual, married parents was essential to the "well-being" of children. It also denounced "judges with activist backgrounds in the hard-left" who "threaten America's dearest institutions and our very way of life."[117] While the Democratic Party platform did not take an explicit position on the issue of marriage for same-sex couples, it did call for "full inclusion of gay and lesbian families in the life of our nation" and for "equal responsibilities, benefits, and protections for these families." The Democrats denounced "President Bush's divisive effort to politicize the Constitution by pursuing a 'Federal Marriage Amendment'" and said states should be able to "define" marriage, as they had for two centuries.[118]

ANTI-GAY MARRIAGE AMENDMENTS TO STATE CONSTITUTIONS

On November 2, 2004, eleven states passed anti-gay marriage amendments, eight of which also threaten more limited partner benefits for both gay and straight couples. Margins of victory ranged from Mississippi's overwhelming approval of an amendment by 82 to 18 percent to Oregon's more narrow margin of 57 to 43 percent. Voters in Missouri and Louisiana also approved anti-marriage amendments in August and September 2004.

According to 2000 U.S. Census data on families of same-sex and unmarried opposite-sex couples, at least 2.2 million residents in thirteen states are likely to lose the right to provide legal protections for their families as a result of the passage of antifamily state constitutional amendments there in 2004.[119] Nine of the thirteen state amendments go beyond banning marriage and also ban or threaten any form of partner recognition, such as domestic partner health insurance, civil unions, inheritance rights, and second-parent adoption. This means that thousands of same-sex partners and opposite-sex unmarried partners may be stripped of their domestic partner benefits, including health coverage. Some states now have both an anti-marriage law and an amendment. As this book went to press, at least two dozen states were considering anti-gay family amendments between 2006 and 2008.

CONCLUSION

Marriage equality for same-sex couples is a central wedge issue in U.S. politics largely because anti-gay activists and Republican Party leaders sought to make it one. The 2004 election was the fourth presidential election in which gay rights controversies became central. Although three prominent 2003 court cases—*Lawrence v. Texas*, *Goodridge v. Dept. of Public Health*, and the Ontario ruling that Canadian same-sex couples should have the right to marry under the nation's charter of rights—helped galvanize LGBT people to pursue the goal of marriage equality, this occurred against a backdrop of over thirty years of vigorous anti-gay activism by the right.

The U.S. Constitution guarantees "equal protection of the laws" for all Americans—not just for heterosexual Americans. There are many basic rights that, if put up for a popular vote, would not win majority support. Many of the most basic freedoms critical to our political system—church-state separation, *Miranda* rights, freedom of the press—would not necessarily win majority approval in many parts of the country. Putting basic rights up for a majority vote is neither moral nor in the best traditions of this country. Denying loving and committed couples equal legal protections for their relationships and their children is not moral.

The reaction against marriage equality for same-sex couples will continue for the foreseeable future, but already about five thousand lesbian and gay couples have married in Massachusetts, and the sky has not fallen there. Activists are preparing for a likely ballot fight to protect the right to marry in Massachusetts and will continue to fight against antifamily amendments across the country. Meanwhile, given the centrality of gay rights controversies in the 2004 election and the three previous presidential contests, it is likely that marriage and other legal controversies will remain a central fault line in U.S. politics for years to come.

Chapter 6

CONCLUSION

In the wake of the 2004 presidential election, the passage of thirteen anti-gay marriage amendments that year, and the enormous backlash against gay families that continues into the 2006 and 2008 election cycles, it is pertinent to consider the extent to which the pursuit of same-sex marriage is currently reflective of the LGBT community's political priorities. Earlier in this book, we discussed the intellectual history of partnership recognition in the LGBT community, noting the resistance of many LGBT scholars and advocates toward same-sex marriage. In this chapter, we will show that these arguments have persisted. Data on the priorities of LGBT African Americans and Asians indicates that although members of these communities support marriage rights, the pursuit of marriage equality also competes with other policy priorities. There are many signs, however, that the push for marriage equality enjoys growing support at the grassroots level. The degree of activism in support of marriage equality by LGBT people of all racial and ethnic backgrounds remains high.

VOICES FROM THE ACADEMY

In chapter 4, we discussed the way in which LGBT scholars in the 1970s through the 1990s drew on radical feminist thought and queer theory to develop a functionalist approach to family recognition. Although the functionalist approach has largely been superseded by an approach emphasizing lesbian and gay civil rights (especially within legal and advocacy circles), many LGBT academics continue to emphasize problematic aspects of same-sex marriage, both as a construct and as a policy priority.

While advocates of the civil rights approach have framed the marriage issue as one that is related to the pursuit of LGBT equality, contemporary academic critics argue that the anti-egalitarian and, indeed, anti-democratic impulses are prevalent in the pursuit of same-sex marriage rights. For instance, Nancy Polikoff, an early feminist critic of same-sex marriage, continues to challenge the rationale behind the state's giving precedence to marriage over other relationships. She does not believe "that the good of marriage is so profound and basic to a well-functioning society that law and policy . . . [should] single out marriage for 'special rights' unavailable to other emotionally and economically interdependent units."[1] Giving "special rights" and substantial benefits to married couples both creates and reinforces social hierarchy—the antithesis of equality.

Polikoff recommends the rationale behind the Law Commission of Canada's 2001 report *Beyond Conjugality*. In a major reappraisal of the relationship between state and society, the commission recommended legal changes to recognize and support all care-based, interdependent personal relationships between adults. Underlying the commission's reasoning are the liberal principles of autonomy and equality. As Polikoff explains, the principle of autonomy stipulates that "the freedom to choose whether and with whom to form close personal relationships is a fundamental value in free and democratic societies," and since neither marriage nor other types of conjugal relationships accurately reveal the qualities of "personal adult relationships that are relevant to particular legislative objectives," the state in a democratic society should not promote some relationships at the expense of others. It follows from this that the principle of equality requires government to, as Polikoff puts it, "respect and promote equality between different kinds of relationships" as well as within relationships. Polikoff maintains that if these principles are followed, the democratic state must support a variety of different family forms.[2]

For Polikoff, taking democracy seriously means abolishing marriage. She recommends that lesbians and gay men take seriously the analysis of Martha Fineman, a feminist legal scholar who recommends replacing legal marriage with a system that confers legal support and recognition upon relationships between children and their caregivers. In such a system, there would be "complete equality between adult, coupled heterosexual and homosexual relationships," since neither of these relationship types would receive state recognition. Furthermore, there would be "equality in the protection afforded a lesbian or gay parent providing primary care to a child and that afforded a heterosexual parent providing primary care to a child." Both of these relationships would be recognized as "performing the public good of the caretaking of inevitable dependents."[3]

Like Polikoff, Judith Stacey also regards marriage as profoundly antithetical to "democratic equal regard." She expresses concern that "pro-marriage advocates rarely confront the undemocratic, zero-sum consequences of their agenda." Stacey argues:

> The more eggs and raiments our society chooses to place in the family baskets of the married, the hungrier and shabbier will be the lives of the vast numbers of adults and dependents who, whether by fate, misfortune, or volition, will remain outside the gates. In my view, this is an unacceptably steep and undemocratic social price for whatever marginal increases in marital stability might be achieved for those admitted to the charmed circle.[4]

Building on early, functionalist approaches, Stacey challenges policymakers and legal theorists to create a system of registered kinship. Her goal is "to further democratize, pluralize, and de-center marriage, rather than to eliminate it." She maintains that a system of registered kinship would "build upon a discernible social trend toward legalizing diverse forms of marital and non-marital unions."[5] Unlike domestic partnerships, registered kinship agreements would not require that all the relevant parties cohabit, nor would it restrict eligibility to couples. Rather, they would require self-specified kinship groups to negotiate the terms of their individual agreements and the distribution of rights and duties therein. These relationships would then be recognized and supported by the state.

Not everyone within the LGBT scholarly community shares this antipathy for same-sex marriage rights. Lesbian feminist Cheshire Calhoun argues that marriage and the family should be central, rather than peripheral, to LGBT politics. Calhoun argues that without the right to marry, or the culturally ascribed authority to define what constitutes marriage or family, LGBT individuals are denied a "unique citizenship status."[6] Heterosexism displaces the LGBT community from the public sphere by denying its members self-representation and forcing them to conform to heterosexual norms. Calhoun maintains that through restrictions on same-sex marriage, child custody, and adoptions, LGBT people are also denied access to "a legitimate and protected private sphere, and control over the character of future generations."[7] "When lesbians and gays are constructed as outlaws to the family and are told they cannot marry, they are being told that they are not capable of doing the work of citizens," writes Calhoun, adding, "Lesbians and gays will not be fully equal until the law recognizes same-sex marriages and equally protects lesbian and gay family life."[8]

DATA ON LGBT COMMUNITY PRIORITIES

While many—but not all—academics continue to challenge the LGBT movement's prioritization of same-sex marriage, polling data tells a more nuanced story. For instance, in a community-wide poll conducted by the National Gay and Lesbian Task Force at Gay Pride Celebrations in New York, Washington, D.C., and Los Angeles in June 2003, 1,471 people were asked what they thought were the three most important issues facing the LGBT community. Partnership recognition was the top priority of Gay Pride attendees, with 32 percent saying that this issue mattered to them. The second most important issue was nondiscrimination, prioritized by 25 percent of respondents. HIV/AIDS prevention and treatment tied for third priority with inclusive hate crimes laws; both these issues were picked by 9.5 percent of respondents.[9] The sample of people being polled was 65 percent white non-Hispanic, 10 percent black, 13 percent Latino/Hispanic, 5 percent Asian, 1 percent Native American, and 6 percent "other." Marriage and other forms of partner recognition were a priority across racial and ethnic lines.

Other recent polls conducted in the LGBT community, however, reveal greater ambiguity about the importance of partnership recognition relative to other issues. Marriage/partnership recognition was the fifth priority in a recent survey of LGBT Asian Pacific Americans (APAs) in the United States.[10] Asian American LGBT people were predominantly concerned with immigration (40 percent), as well as with hate violence/harassment and media representation (both at 39 percent). Yet since the category of "immigration" may be interpreted to include immigration-related partner protections for binational couples—a benefit of marriage—it may be that there is actually much more support for marriage equality in the APA LGBT community than an initial reading of this data suggests.

This survey's results also show a discernible gender gap. Over half (52 percent) of the women surveyed said that the most important issue facing APA LGBT people was hate violence and harassment, while only 31 percent of men and 17 percent of transgender respondents said the same. Immigration was also a top concern of women, with 38 percent indicating this was a priority. Marriage/domestic partnership came in third place for women, with 30 percent emphasizing its importance.

In keeping with a trend documented in previous surveys by the National Gay and Lesbian Task Force, HIV/AIDS ranked higher on the list of con-

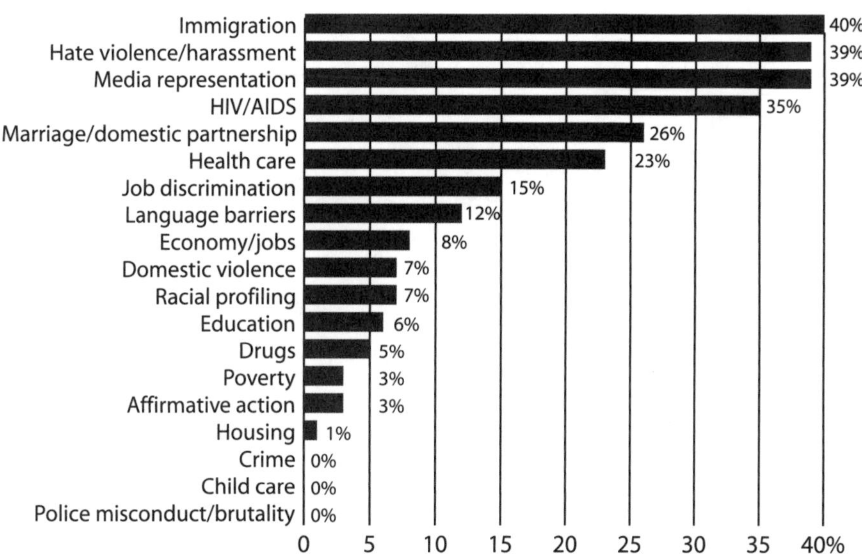

Fig. 13. Most important issues facing LGBT Asian Pacific Americans in the United States. Reproduced from A. Dang and M. Hu, Asian Pacific American Lesbian, Gay, Bisexual and Transgender People: A Community Portrait (New York: Policy Institute of National Gay and Lesbian Task Force, 2005), 25.

cerns among men than among women. Similar percentages of men said that their top concerns were media representation (48 percent), HIV/AIDS (45 percent), and immigration (43 percent). By contrast, 24 percent of APA men thought marriage/domestic partnership was a priority.

Polls of the African American LGBT community in many ways confirm the ambiguities of the APA LGBT community. For instance, the National Gay and Lesbian Task Force's Black Pride Survey sampled nearly three thousand black LGBT people at Black Gay Pride celebrations around the United States in the summer of 2000. Respondents were asked to identify the top three issues facing black LGBT people. HIV/AIDS and hate crime violence were the top two issues. Marriage/domestic partnership was the third most important issue facing black LGBT people. Marriage and domestic partnership were of particular concern to female respondents, who placed the issue into the top three. Men and transgender respondents were less concerned with marriage and domestic partnership than were women.[11]

As with LGBT Asian Pacific Americans, marriage/domestic partnership was not the most important issue for people responding to the Black Pride Survey. A gender dichotomy is evident in the black community, too. While many other issues superseded partnership recognition as a priority for black gay and bisexual men, black lesbians and bisexual women gave a relatively higher priority to marriage/domestic partnership. This may be because black lesbian couples parent at almost the same rate as black married couples and therefore potentially have more to gain from the protections offered by partnership recognition, as we discussed in chapter 2.

BEYOND THE POLLS

While academics tell one story and polls tell another, advocates in the field reveal different perspectives. For instance, Dean Spade, director of the Sylvia Rivera Law Project—an organization that works to guarantee that all people are free to determine their gender identity and expression—has suggested that the push for marriage rights may reflect the goals of a gay white elite rather than of the least privileged members of the LGBT community. He argues that the movement's current focus on same-sex marriage shortchanges other issues, including transgender discrimination and hate crimes.[12] Meanwhile, Glenn Magpantay, a lawyer who works on Asian American civil rights, notes that although the organizations he is affiliated with have endorsed same-sex marriage, they do not see it as a priority. "Our fear is that other issues more important to us including immigration will be slighted," he said, adding, "As it is, gay Asians feel overlooked and marginalized within the LGBT community."[13]

Tensions also persist in the African American LGBT community about "the white queer political machine's appropriation of the language of the black civil rights movement" in public discourse about marriage. "I don't ever want to see a white gay man stand before a camera again and equate his struggle to the black civil rights movement," says Jasmyne Cannick, a prominent African American lesbian and board member of the National Black Justice Coalition.[14] Irene Monroe, another board member of the coalition, reports that although many activists in the African American LGBT community believe that the struggle for same-sex marriage is a civil rights issue, they are concerned that LGBT communities of color have been shut out of the framing process surrounding the marriage debate. "The dominant white queer languaging of this debate at best muffles the voices of these communities and at worst mutes them," she writes. Monroe explains,

> In other words, in leaving out the voices of LGBTQ (lesbian, gay, bisexual, transgender, and queer) communities of color and classes, the same-sex marriage debate is being hijacked by a white upper-class queer universality that not only renders these marginalized queer communities invisible, but—as it is presently framed—also renders them speechless.[15]

The National Black Justice Coalition is focusing its advocacy on fairness for African-American LGBT families—incorporating a focus not only on same-sex marriage but also on such issues as unemployment, adoption, and HIV/AIDS.[16]

A Latina lesbian who works in advocacy and represents LLEGO, the National Latina/o Lesbian, Gay, Bisexual, and Transgender Organization, has a different perspective. Imelda Aguirre writes:

> The major issues that Latina lesbians face primarily revolve around family. For example, lesbians of color are more likely to have children than white lesbians; therefore, parenting rights are a major issue for us. Because bi-national couples and their families face the real threat of deportation and separation, immigration is also high on our political agenda. Since the right to marry legally will alleviate both these problems, marriage equality is of extreme importance to us.[17]

AT THE GRASSROOTS

While many academics and advocates have questioned the focus on marriage equality and argued that efforts to achieve access to civil marriage are either intrinsically problematic or supplant other, more critical issues, the push for marriage equality seems to enjoy increasing support among grassroots community members. The marriage struggle has evoked a wave of activism not seen since the days of ACT UP and Queer Nation organizations in the late 1980s and early 1990s. Thousands of LGBT and allied activists have lobbied, protested, knocked on doors, and rallied to educate the public and elected officials about the need for equal marriage rights. Activists cut across racial and ethnic lines—as do plaintiffs in the same-sex marriage lawsuits throughout the country. Despite the lesbian feminist, antimarriage stance that dominated the LGBT movement during the 1970s and 1980s, the majority of same-sex couples who have married in Massachusetts are lesbians. Victoria Brownworth writes:

> It doesn't matter what you think about same-sex marriage—whether you think marriage is a patriarchal institution queers should eschew or you think we should all tie the knot—queers deserve access to the privilege of marriage. If straight people can get married on a whim, lesbians should be able to get married after 52 years of being partnered. It's called equality.[18]

THE STRUGGLE OVER MARRIAGE EQUALITY AND THE BROADER CONTEXT OF LGBT FAMILY POLICY

The debate over whether or not same-sex couples should be able to access the benefits and protections of marriage emerged within the LGBT community in the late 1980s. However, gay and lesbian couples in the United States have been suing for the right to marry since 1971. Marriage for gay couples emerged as a national political issue during the 1992 presidential campaign. Following gay couples' successes in the Hawaii courts starting in 1993, religious conservative activists and politicians seized on the issue, making it a central domestic issue during the 1996 presidential campaign. Dozens of state legislatures passed anti-gay marriage laws, as did Congress. By the mid-2000s, forty states had passed such laws; several passed both an anti-gay marriage law and other laws or state constitutional amendments banning other forms of partner protection for same-sex couples. Anti-gay marriage politics have emerged as central in the 2000 Republican presidential primary and in the 2004 primaries and general election. It is likely that anti-gay marriage laws and ballot questions will continue to advance in states across the country through the latter half of the decade.

Within the context of debating gay couples' right to legally marry, many false claims have been made about gay and lesbian parenting, nondiscrimination laws, and other issues. This is because those groups driving opposition to marriage also oppose any form of legal equality for same-sex couples and LGBT people, including nondiscrimination laws and safe schools programs. Several of the half dozen anti-gay parenting laws currently on the books were passed in the context of debates over civil unions in 2000 and marriage in 2003–4. Other states have also considered anti-gay parenting legislation but not passed such laws. Anti-gay marriage activists make false and inflammatory claims that hurt all LGBT people, even if they do not result in the passage of anti-gay policies. Also, in supporting the anti-gay politics of the anti-gay marriage movement, voters also indirectly support the broader reactionary agenda of the Christian right in this country, such as its efforts to collapse the separation of church and state.

A majority of American voters in 2004 supported either civil unions (35 percent) or marriage (25 percent) for same-sex couples. Yet in most states and at the national level, there is majority opposition to marriage equality. Still, the level of popular support for marriage equality has grown significantly since the question was first asked in the late 1980s.

Massachusetts' highest court ruled in 2004 that denying gay couples the right to marry violates that state's constitutional guarantees of equality and due process. It is our view that the Massachusetts court was correct and that the denial of marriage rights to gay couples in most of the United States violates these provisions not only in state constitutions but in the U.S. Constitution as well. We believe that all people deserve what the Constitution terms as the "equal protection of the laws," not just those who are members of majority groups or those groups that can win a popularity contest. In our view, anti-gay ballot questions—in which the rights of a stigmatized minority are granted or withheld by a majority vote in a secret ballot—represent the majority tyranny about which founding father James Madison warned.[19] The Bill of Rights, the separation of powers, and an independent judiciary were created in large part to prevent such abuses. Therefore, anti-gay ballot campaigns are fundamentally un-American.

Access to civil marriage has the potential to benefit many LGBT families. By granting gay and lesbian couples full legal equality, states can send a message that LGBT people are full citizens, deserving of the same treatment by our government "of the people, by the people, for the people." Gay men and lesbians who married would be able to acquire a degree of recognition and economic security that is currently unavailable to them. They would no longer confront massive discrimination over issues ranging from hospital visitation rights to Social Security survivors benefits. Binational couples would be able to utilize immigration benefits to sponsor their spouses for permanent residency or citizenship. The situation of LGBT families with children would improve tremendously, as the children would be guaranteed a legal relationship with both of their parents—during their parent's marriage as well as in the event of a breakup. In the event of the death of their biological parent, children in these families would be guaranteed a right to maintain a relationship with their surviving parent.

Access to the benefits of civil marriage would be particularly advantageous for low-income families. As we noted in chapter 4, low-income LGBT couples are frequently unable to afford to piece together legal protections for their families—protections ranging from second-parent adoption to domestic partner health benefits. Other LGBT parents living in states that do not currently permit second-parent adoption would also find access to marriage tremendously helpful as a means to enhance their family's security.

Most same-sex couples raising children are lesbian couples, and a disproportionate percentage of these are lesbian couples of color. Due to the racial demographics of income, wealth, and poverty in the United States, black and Latino same-sex couples are more likely to be poor and less likely to own the home they live in. This is also likely to be true of Native American same-sex couples. In fact, people of color, low-income people, and immigrants within the LGBT community, particularly those raising children, have the most to gain from the ability to access the institution of civil marriage. As such, the fight for marriage equality is not just a matter of basic human rights; it also represents, in the United States at least, a matter of racial, economic, and social justice.

It is also entirely feasible that many more LGBT families would benefit if public policies concerning the family were divorced from marriage. If the state offered support to all caring relationships rather than to married families alone, lesbians and gay men would benefit—as would single-parent households and other families structured in ways that diverge from heteronormativity. Under such circumstances, for instance, lesbian and gay couples—whose marital status currently prevents them from jointly adopting children in most states—could conceivably embark on joint adoption regardless of their marital status and know that they would receive state recognition and support for doing so. Lesbian and gay households where more than two adults hold parenting roles could also find state support for their families.

Yet in the current political context, in which Massachusetts same-sex couples have already won marriage rights and in which same-sex couples in other states are suing for the right to marry, it is hard to imagine the LGBT movement forsaking the policy goal of marriage—especially when the right wing uses the issue of marriage to incite homophobia for political purposes. For the sake of those within the LGBT community who aspire toward marriage equality, same-sex marriage must remain on the movement's political agenda. For the sake of our whole community, we must counter the rhetoric of the Right and demonstrate the inherent dignity and worth of LGBT families.

At the same time, pursuing same-sex marriage as a policy goal does not preclude the movement from working toward a more far-reaching vision, one that entails transforming society's oppressive structures to bring about a more equitable distribution of power, rights, and benefits. For a progressively focused LGBT politics, a focus on same-sex marriage cannot be the whole story or even the end of the story. Access to the institution of civil marriage will not end anti-gay bias, which is deeply rooted in American culture as well as in cultures across the globe. It will not end anti-LGBT discrimination or hate violence. As many of the arguments in this book have made clear, while same-sex marriage rights will create a measure of formal equality for many LGBT people, structural inequalities will nevertheless continue to disempower many of the LGBT community's most marginalized members and detrimentally affect their lives. "We've done nothing to talk about my right to walk down the street," says a black gay man, adding, "Gay marriage does none of that."[20]

We need to make it safe for every LGBT person to walk down the street. Protecting our families entails more than marriage rights. It involves grappling with hard issues ranging from domestic violence prevention to welfare reform and a renewed commitment to eradicating racial disparities in poverty and wealth. It means actively forging coalitions with members of other nonnormative, marginalized communities to challenge the oppressive structures that affect us all. The voices of the LGBT community speak to a wide range of priorities and reiterate the imperative to fight on all fronts for social and economic justice. Even when we have won the right to marry, this important and utterly necessary work will barely have begun.

NOTES

CHAPTER 1

1. This account is based on a speech given by Larry Courtney on August 25, 2002, in Provincetown, Massachusetts, where Courtney received a National Gay and Lesbian Task Force 2002 national leadership award.

2. *DOMA Debate*, 104th Cong., 2d Sess., *Congressional Record* 143, no. 103 (July 12, 1996): H 7480.

3. Quoted in C. Colton and R. Davidson, "Gay and Lesbian Issues in the Congressional Arena," in *The Politics of Gay Rights*, ed. C. Rimmerman, K. Wald, and C. Wilcox (Chicago: University of Chicago Press, 2000), 362.

4. *DOMA Debate*, 104th Cong., *Congressional Record* (July 12, 1996).

5. We believe that the best descriptive term for the issue at play here is *marriage equality for same-sex couples*. However, we will often use the terms *gay marriage* and *same-sex marriage* as shorthand. While internal community surveys indicate that most people in same-sex relationships would identify themselves as gay or lesbian or some other term for homosexual, many are bisexual in orientation and would identify as such. Bisexuals are also found in opposite-sex relationships.

6. T. Emery, "Lesbian Couple Wins Landmark Ruling by State's Highest Court," *Boston Globe*, November 18, 2003.

CHAPTER 2

A version of parts of the analysis in this chapter first appeared in S. Cahill, *Same-Sex Marriage in the United States: Focus on the Facts* (Lanham, MD: Lexington, 2004), 43–64.

1. Mellman Group, *Mass Mutual American Family Values Study: Results of Focus Group and Survey Research 1* (Washington, DC: Mellman Group, 1989), available from the Mellman Group, Inc., 1054 31st St. NW, Suite 530, Washington, DC 20007.

2. U.S. Census Bureau, *Profile of General Demographic Characteristics, 2000* (Washington, DC: U.S. Census Bureau, 2001), http://www.census.gov/Press-Release/www/2001/tables/dp_us_2000.PDF (accessed June 5, 2004).

3. U.S. Census Bureau, "Table FG6: One-Parent Family Groups with Own Children under 18, by Marital Status, and Race and Hispanic Origin of the Reference Person, March 2000," (Washington, DC: U.S. Census Bureau, 2001), http://www.census.gov/population/socdemo/hh-fam/p20-537/2000/tabFG6.pdf (accessed June 25, 2005).

4. J. Stacey, "Family Values Forever: In the Marriage Movement, Conservatives and Centrists Find a Home Together," *Nation*, July 9, 2001; U.S. Census Bureau, *Profile of General Demographic Characteristics, 2000.*

5. J. Bradford, K. Barrett, and J. Honnold, *The 2000 Census and Same-Sex Households: A User's Guide* (New York: Policy Institute of the National Gay and Lesbian Task Force; Richmond: Survey and Evaluation Research Laboratory of Virginia Commonwealth University; Boston: Fenway Institute, 2002), 1.

6. L. Peplau and L. Spalding, "The Close Relationships of Lesbians, Gay Men, and Bisexuals," in *Psychological Perspectives on Lesbian, Gay, and Bisexual Experiences*, ed. L. Garnets and D. Kimmel, 2nd ed. (New York: Columbia University Press, 2003), 449–74.

7. G. Herek, "Myths about Sexual Orientation: A Lawyer's Guide to Social Science Research," *Law and Sexuality: A Review of Lesbian and Gay Legal Issues* 1 (1991): 133–72; A. Bell and M. Weinberg, *Homosexualities: A Study of Diversity among Men and Women* (New York: Simon and Schuster, 1978); K. Jay and A. Young, *The Gay Report* (New York:

Summit, 1977). Herek cites a national poll ("Results of Poll," *San Francisco Examiner*, June 6, 1989) in which 64 percent of lesbians reported they were in relationships and 60 percent of gay men were reported partnered. Bell and Weinberg found a range of 70 to 72 percent of lesbians in relationships and 51 to 58 percent of gay men partnered. Jay and Young reported 80 percent of lesbians and 46 percent of gay men partnered. Although the individuals in these studies are all considered gay or lesbian, some would likely identify as bisexual or are bisexual based on their sexual behavior and/or attraction.

8. Gottman Institute, *12-Year Study of Gay and Lesbian Couples* (Seattle: Gottman Institute, 2004), http://www.gottman.com/research/projects/gaylesbian (accessed June 25, 2005).

9. Bradford, Barrett, and Honnold, *The 2000 Census.*

10. Ibid.

11. For a summary of estimates of the gay, lesbian, and bisexual population in the United States, see S. Cahill, K. South, and J. Spade, *Outing Age: Public Policy Issues Affecting Gay, Lesbian, Bisexual, and Transgender Elders* (New York: Policy Institute of the National Gay and Lesbian Task Force, 2000), 7–8, 82–83.

12. Individuals in same-sex relationships may identify as gay, lesbian, bisexual, or some other term for homosexual or bisexual. Male-male couples and female-female couples are widely viewed as "gay" or "lesbian" couples. The terms *gay and lesbian* and *same-sex* are used interchangeably here.

13. Bradford, Barrett, and Honnold, *The 2000 Census.*

14. A. Dang and S. Frazer, *Black Same-Sex Households in the United States: A Report from the 2000 Census* (New York: Policy Institute of the National Gay and Lesbian Task Force, 2004).

15. C. Patterson, "Lesbian Mothers, Gay Fathers, and Their Children," in *Lesbian, Gay, and Bisexual Identities over the Lifespan*, ed. A. D'Augelli and C. Patterson (New York: Oxford University Press, 1995), 262 (two million); V. Casper and S. Schultz, *Gay Parents/Straight Schools: Building Communication and Trust* (New York: Teachers College Press, 1999), 4 (eight million).

16. Some individuals in these couples would identify themselves not as gay or lesbian but by some other term for homosexual. Others would identify as bisexual. Still others would not want to be categorized. But the critical point is that these individuals are in an amorous, long-term, committed, partnered same-sex relationship widely viewed as a "gay or lesbian" relationship.

17. T. Simmons and M. O'Connell, *Married-Couple and Unmarried-Partner Households, 2000* (Washington, DC: U.S. Census Bureau, 2003), http://www.census.gov/prod/2003pubs/censr-5.pdf (accessed June 1, 2004).

18. *Boston Globe*, January 23, 2004.

19. Remarks by Mass. Gov. Romney to the Republican National Convention, FDCH E-Media, September 1, 2004, http://www.washingtonpost.com/wp-dyn/articles/A54468-2004Sep1.html (accessed May 11, 2006).

20. E. Perrin and Committee on Psychosocial Aspects of Child and Family Health, "Technical Report: Coparent or Second-Parent Adoption by Same-Sex Parents," *Pediatrics* 109, no. 2 (2002): 341–44.

21. C. Patterson, *Lesbian and Gay Parenting* (Washington, DC: American Psychological Association, 1995), http://www.apa.org/pi/parent.html (accessed November 1, 2002).

22. E. Ferrero, J. Freker, and T. Foster, *Too High a Price: The Case against Restricting Gay Parenting* (New York: American Civil Liberties Union Lesbian and Gay Rights Project, 2002).

23. American Psychoanalytic Association, "Position Statement on Gay and Lesbian Parenting" (New York: American Psychoanalytic Association, 2002), http://www.apsa.org/ctf/cgli/parenting.htm (accessed May 11, 2006).

24. J. Stoever, "Delegates Vote for Adoption Policy," *FP Report*, October 17, 2002, http://www.aafp.org/fpr/assembly2002/1017/7.html (accessed December 10, 2002).

25. L. Silverstein and C. Auerbach, "Deconstructing the Essential Father," *American Psychologist* 54, no. 6 (1997): 397–98.

26. J. Lansford, R. Ceballo, A. Abbey, and A. Stewart, "Does Family Structure Matter? A Comparison of Adoptive, Two-Parent Biological, Single-Mother, Stepfather, and Stepmother Households," *Journal of Marriage and Family* 63, no. 3 (2001): 840–51.

27. J. Stacey and T. Biblarz, "(How) Does the Sexual Orientation of the Parent Matter?" *American Sociological Review* 66, no. 2 (2001): 159–84.

28. K. Kelleher, "Turns Out the Happy Couple Is . . . Gay?" *Los Angeles Times*, February 5, 2001.

29. C. Patterson and R. Redding, "Lesbian and Gay Families with Children: Implications of Social Science Research for Policy," *Journal of Social Issues* 52, no. 3 (1996): 29–50.

30. C. Patterson, "Family Relationships of Lesbians and Gay Men," *Journal of Marriage and Family* 62 (2000): 1062.

31. D. H. Demo and M. J. Cox, "Families and Young Children: A Review of Research in the 1990s," *Journal of Marriage and the Family* 62, no. 4 (2000): 876–96.

32. R. Green, "Sexual Identity of 37 Children Raised by Homosexual or Transsexual Parents," *American Journal of Psychiatry* 135 (1978): 692.

33. T. White and R. Ettner, "Children of a Parent Undergoing a Gender Transition: Disclosure, Risk, and Protective Factors" (paper presented at the XVIth Symposium of the Harry Benjamin International Gender Dysphoria Association, London, August 17–21, 1999), http://www.symposion.com/ijt/greenpresidental/green17.htm (accessed May 11, 2006).

34. Ibid.

35. J. Battle, C. Cohen, D. Warren, G. Fergerson, and S. Audam, *Say It Loud, I'm Black and I'm Proud: Black Pride Survey 2000* (New York: Policy Institute of the National Gay and Lesbian Task Force, 2002), 14.

36. V. Mays, L. Chatters, S. Cochran, and J. Mackness, "African American Families in Diversity: Gay Men and Lesbians as Participants in Family Networks," *Journal of Comparative Family Studies* 29, no. 1 (1998): 73–87.

37. Bradford, Barrett, and Honnold, *The 2000 Census.* While only 23 percent of the white lesbians had given birth to one or more children, 30 percent of Asian/Pacific Islander lesbians, 43 percent of Hispanic lesbians, and 60 percent of black lesbians had biological children.

38. Dang and Frazer, *Black Same-Sex Households in the United States.*

39. Simmons and O'Connell, *Married-Couple and Unmarried-Partner Households, 2000.*

40. M. V. L. Badgett, *Money, Myths, and Change: The Economic Lives of Lesbians and Gay Men* (Chicago: University of Chicago Press, 2001).

41. M. V. L. Badgett, *Income Inflation: The Myth of Affluence among Gay Men, Lesbians, and Bisexuals* (New York: Policy Institute of the National Gay and Lesbian Task Force and Institute for Gay and Lesbian Strategic Studies, 1998).

42. Human Rights Campaign, news releases, http://www.hrc.org/template.cfm?section=Press_Room&CONTENTID=18783&TEMPLATE=ContentManagement/ContentDisplay.cfm (accessed May 11, 2006). The Human Rights Campaign and the Urban Institute analyzed data from half a dozen states (including California, Texas, Illinois, New York, and Massachusetts), made available by the Census Bureau in spring 2003.

43. Dang and Frazer, *Black Same-Sex Households in the United States.*

44. T. Dougherty, *Economic Benefits of Marriage under Federal and Massachusetts Law* (New York: Policy Institute of the National Gay and Lesbian Task Force, 2004).

45. S. Cahill and K. Jones, *Leaving Our Children Behind: Welfare Reform and the Gay, Lesbian, Bisexual, and Transgender Community* (New York: Policy Institute of the National Gay and Lesbian Task Force, 2001).

46. Ibid.

47. *D.C. Code Ann.* § 16-914(a)(1) ("With respect to matters of custody and visitation . . . sexual orientation of a party, in and of itself, shall not be a conclusive consideration").

48. *J.A.D. v. F.J.D.*, 978 S.W.2d 336 (Mo. 1998) (holding that "[a] homosexual parent is not ipso facto unfit for custody"); *Tucker v. Tucker*, 910 P.2d 1209 (Utah 1996) (holding that a mother's sexual orientation would not by itself disqualify her from being awarded custody); *Bottoms v. Bottoms*, 457 S.E.2d 102 (Va. 1995) (holding that a parent's sexual orientation does not by itself render that person unfit to have custody).

49. "Tennessee Reconsiders Ban on Gay Dad's Partner Meeting His Son," *Gay Today* 8, no. 22, http://www.gaytoday.com/world/021204wo.asp (accessed March 2, 2004).

50. *Ex parte H.H. (D.H. v. H.H.)*, Ala., No. 1002045, February 15, 2002. Eighteen months later, Moore was removed from office after refusing to abide by a federal court order, assented to by the U.S. Supreme Court, to remove a statue of the Ten Commandments from the court building.

51. As of June 2003, when the U.S. Supreme

Court struck down all sodomy laws, four states had gay-only sodomy laws (Texas, Oklahoma, Kansas, and Missouri), and nine states had laws banning oral and anal sex regardless of the sex of those engaging in the sexual activities (Idaho, Utah, Louisiana, Mississippi, Alabama, Florida, South Carolina, North Carolina, and Virginia). Two states (Michigan and Massachusetts) had on the books sodomy laws whose applicability had been restricted by court rulings, but the laws themselves had not been struck down.

52. P. Logue, *The Rights of Lesbian and Gay Parents and Their Children* (New York: Lambda Legal Defense and Education Fund, 2001), http://www.lambdalegal.org/binary-data/LAMBDA_PDF/pdf/115.pdf (accessed February 1, 2005).

53. For example, *Rubano v. DiCenzo*, 759 A.2d 959 (R.I. 2000); *V.C. v. M.J.B.*, 163 N.J. 200, 748 A.2d 539, cert. denied, 121 S. Ct. 302 (2000); *S.F. v. M.D.*, 751 A.2d 9 (Md. 2000); *E.N.O. v. L.M.M.*, 429 Mass. 824, 711 N.E.2d 886, cert. denied, 120 S. Ct. 500 (1999); *Holtzman v. Knott*, 195 Wis.2d 649, 533 N.W.2d 419, cert. denied, 116 S. Ct. 475 (1995); *T.B. v. L.R.M.*, 786 A.2d 913 (Pa. 2001).

54. *In re the Matter of Visitation with C.B.L.*, 723 N.E.2d 316 (Ill. App. Ct. 1999); *In re Thompson*, 11 S.W.3d 913 (Tenn. Ct. App. 1999), appeal denied (Jan. 24, 2000); *Kazmierazak v. Query*, 736 So. 2d 106 (Fla. Ct. App. 1999); *Guardianship of Z.C.W. and K.G.W.*, 71 Cal. App. 4th 524, 84 Cal. Rptr. 2d 48; *Lynda A.H. v. Diane T.O.*, 673 N.Y.S.2d 989 (N.Y. Sup. Ct. 1998).

55. Gay and Lesbian Advocates and Defenders, *Protecting Families: Standards for Child Custody in Same-Sex Relationships* (Boston: Gay and Lesbian Advocates and Defenders, 1999).

56. Florida, Mississippi, Utah, Arkansas, North Dakota, and Oklahoma limit adoption or foster parenting. Florida law bans homosexuals from adopting: the statute reads, "No person eligible to adopt under this statute may adopt if that person is a homosexual" (*Fla. Stat.* tit. VI, chap. 63, § 63.042, 2(d)3). Mississippi law bans same-sex couples from adopting: the statute reads, "Adoption by couples of the same gender is prohibited" (*Miss. Code* § 93-17-3(2) [1972]). Utah law (*Utah Code Ann.* § 78-30-9(3) [2004]) states "(b) A child may not be adopted by a person who is cohabitating in a relationship that is not a legally valid and binding marriage under the laws of this state." Arkansas regulations ban gays and lesbians from foster parenting but not from adopting. An anti-gay adoption bill was rejected by the Arkansas legislature in 2000. North Dakota adopted a law allowing adoption agencies receiving state contracts and licensure to refuse to place children in homes of prospective parents against whom the agencies have religious objections; the law (S 2188) was signed by North Dakota's governor on April 23, 2003 (D. Wetzel, "Senate Approves Measure to Protect Religious Adoption Agencies," Associated Press, January 29, 2003). Oklahoma's law stating that second-parent adoptions from other states involving same-sex couples are not recognized in that state was passed in May 2004 (Associated Press, "Henry Signs Measure on Gay Adoptions," May 4, 2004).

57. National Center for Lesbian Rights, "Adoption by Lesbian, Gay, and Bisexual Parents: An Overview of Current Law" (San Francisco: National Center for Lesbian Rights, 2004), http://www.nclrights.org/publications/adptn0204.htm (accessed May 11, 2006); Gay and Lesbian Advocates and Defenders, "Adoption Issues" (Boston: Gay and Lesbian Advocates and Defenders, n.d.), http://www.glad.org/Publications/CivilRightProject/Adopt.pdf (accessed June 1, 2003); Western PA Freedom to Marry Coalition, "Vermont Couples File Pro-Marriage Suit: Freedom to Marry Coalitions Continue National Fight," *Marriage Announcements* 2, no. 4 (August–September 1997), http://www.cs.cmu.edu/afs/cs/user/scotts/ftp/wpaf2mc/newsletter2-4.pdf (accessed November 2, 2002).

58. National Center for Lesbian Rights, "Legal Recognition of LGBT Families" (San Francisco: National Center for Lesbian Rights, 2002), http://www.nclrights.org/publications/lgbtfamilies.htm#12 (accessed November 1, 2002); *In re Dana*, 660 N.E.2d 397 (N.Y. 1995); *In re Adoption of Two Children by H.N.R.*, 666 A.2d 535 (N.J. Super. Ct. App. Div. 1995); *In re Petition of K.M. and D.M.*, 653 N.E.2d 888 (Ill. App. Ct. 1995); *In re M.M.D. & B.H.M.*, 662 A.2d 837 (D.C. 1995), all cited in Gay and Lesbian Advocates and Defenders, "Adoption Issues."

59. An Act concerning the Best Interest of Children in Adoption Matters (2000), *Conn. Legis. Serv.*

P.A. § 00-228 (S.H.B. 5830) (West), amending *Conn. Gen. Stat.* § 45a-724 (1993), cited in Gay and Lesbian Advocates and Defenders, "Adoption Issues."

60. S. Cahill, M. Ellen, and S. Tobias, *Family Policy: Issues Affecting Gay, Lesbian, Bisexual, and Transgender Families* (New York: Policy Institute of the National Gay and Lesbian Task Force, 2002). Updated by National Gay and Lesbian Task Force legislative lawyer Kara Suffredini, August 2006.

61. D. Rayside, "The Politics of Lesbian and Gay Parenting in Canada and the United States" (paper presented at the annual meeting of the Canadian Political Science Association, Toronto, Ontario, May 2002), 2.

62. J. Murphy, "Antilesbian Discrimination in Assisted Reproduction," in *Queer Families, Queer Politics*, ed. M. Bernstein and R. Reiman (New York: Columbia University Press, 2001), 182–200.

63. D. Blankenhorn, *Fatherless America: Confronting Our Most Urgent Social Problem* (New York: HarperCollins, 1995), 171–72.

64. Ibid., 184.

65. Ibid., 232–33.

66. Logue, *The Rights of Lesbian and Gay Parents and Their Children.*

67. Ibid.

68. *Ariz. Rev. Stat. Ann.* § 25-218 (West 1991); *Ark. Code Ann.* § 9-10-201 (West 1991); *D.C. Code Ann.* § 16-401-02 (Michie 1997); *Fla. Stat. Ann.* §§ 742.15, 742.16 (West 1997); *Ind. Code Ann.* §§ 21-20-1-1 to 20-3 (Burns 1997); *Ky. Rev. Stat. Ann.* § 199.590 (Michie 1999); *La. Rev. Stat. Ann.* § 2713 (West 1991); *Mich. Comp. Laws Ann.* §§ 722.851–53 (West 1997); *Neb. Rev. Stat.* § 25-21, 200 (1995); *Nev. Rev. Stat. Ann.* § 126.045 (Michie 1998); *N.H. Rev. Stat. Ann.* §§ 168-B:1 to B:32 (1994, Supp. 1998); *N.Y. Dom. Rel. Law* §§ 122, 123 (McKinney 1998, Supp. 1999); *N.D. Cent. Code* §§ 14-18-01 to 07 (Michie 1997); *Utah Code Ann.* § 76-7-204 (Michie 1995); *Va. Code Ann.* §§ 20-156 to 165 (1995); *Wash. Rev. Code Ann.* §§ 26.26.210–60 (West 1997).

69. Chicago-Kent College of Law, "Table IV: State Laws on Surrogacy," (Chicago: Chicago-Kent College of Law, n.d.) http://www.kentlaw.edu/islt/TABLEIV.htm (accessed November 2, 2002).

70. J. M. LaRue, *Homosexuals Hijack Civil Rights Bus* (Washington, DC: Concerned Women for America, March 22, 2004), http://www.cwfa.org/articles/5395/LEGAL/family/index.htm (accessed May 11, 2006).

71. Dang and Frazer, *Black Same-Sex Households in the United States.*

72. Associated Press, "Michigan Governor Pulls Same-Sex Benefits," *Bakersfield Californian*, December 1, 2004.

73. A version of this section first appeared as S. Cahill, "Welfare Moms and the Two Grooms: The Concurrent Promotion and Restriction of Marriage in U.S. Public Policy," *Sexualities* 8, no. 2 (2005): 169–87.

74. Cahill and Jones, *Leaving Our Children Behind;* W. Hirczy de Mino, "From Bastardy to Equality: The Rights of Non-marital Children and Their Fathers in Comparative Perspective," *Journal of Comparative Family Studies* 31, no. 2 (2000): 231–62.

75. G. Lewis and J. Edelson, "DOMA and ENDA: Congress Votes on Gay Rights," in *The Politics of Gay Rights*, ed. C. Rimmerman, K. Wald, and C. Wilcox (Chicago: University of Chicago Press, 2000), 193–216.

76. T. Zeller, "Two Fronts: Promoting Marriage, Fighting Poverty," *New York Times*, January 18, 2004, WK3.

77. *The Marriage Movement: A Statement of Principles* (New York: Institute for American Values, n.d.), http://www.marriagemovement.org/html/report.html (accessed January 16, 2004); *The Marriage Movement: Manifesto* (New York: Institute for American Values, n.d.), http://www.marriagemovement.org (accessed January 16, 2004); National Fatherhood Initiative, *History* (Gaithersburg, MD: National Fatherhood Initiative, n.d.), http://www.fatherhood.org/history.htm (accessed January 16, 2004); National Fatherhood Initiative, "Dispatches from the States: Mississippi," *Policy and Practice*, nos. 12–13 (Gaithersburg, MD: National Fatherhood Initiative, 1999), http://www.fatherhood.org/statelocal.asp (accessed November 1, 2001).

78. W. Horn, "Wedding Bell Blues: Marriage and Welfare Reform," *Brookings Review* 19, no. 3 (summer 2001): 39; W. Horn, D. Blankenhorn, and M. Pearlstein, eds., *The Fatherhood Movement: A Call to Action* (New York: Lexington, 1999); W. Horn and A. Bush, *Fathers, Marriage, and Welfare Reform* (Washington, DC: Hudson Institute, 1997), http://

welfarereformer.org/articles/father.htm (accessed November 1, 2001).

79. Bradford, Barrett, and Honnold, *The 2000 Census*.

80. G. Herdt and A. Boxer, *Children of Horizons*, 2nd ed. (Boston: Beacon, 1996).

81. A. H. Faulkner and K. Cranston, "Correlates of Same-Sex Behavior in a Random Sample of Massachusetts High School Students," *American Journal of Public Health* 88, no. 2 (1998): 262–66; J. Kosciw and M. Cullen, *The GLSEN 2001 National School Climate Survey: The School-Related Experiences of Our Nation's Lesbian, Gay, Bisexual, and Transgender Youth* (New York: Gay, Lesbian, and Straight Education Network, 2001).

82. J. Perrotti and K. Westheimer, *When the Drama Club Is Not Enough: Lessons from the Safe Schools Program for Gay and Lesbian Students* (Boston: Beacon, 2001).

83. J. Fontaine, "Evidencing a Need: School Counselors' Experiences with Gay and Lesbian Students," *Professional School Counseling* 1, no. 3 (1998): 8–14; Perrotti and Westheimer, *When the Drama Club Is Not Enough*, 108.

84. C. Ryan and D. Futterman, *Lesbian and Gay Youth: Care and Counseling* (New York: Columbia University Press, 1998).

85. M. Rosarlo, J. Hunter, and M. Rotheram-Borus, unpublished data on lesbian adolescents (HIV Center for Clinical and Behavioral Studies and New York State Psychiatric Institute, New York, 1992); E. Hetrick and A. Martin, "Developmental Issues and Their Resolution for Gay and Lesbian Adolescents," *Journal of Homosexuality* 14, nos. 1–2 (1987): 25–43.

86. B. Singer and D. Deschamps, *Gay and Lesbian Stats: A Pocket Guide of Facts and Figures* (New York: New Press, 1994); P. Gibson, "Gay Male and Lesbian Youth Suicide," in *Report of the Secretary's Task Force on Youth Suicide*, by U.S. Department of Health and Human Services (Washington, DC: U.S. Department of Health and Human Services, 1989).

87. Ryan and Futterman, *Lesbian and Gay Youth*.

88. J. Varney, "Undressing the Normal: Community Efforts for Queer Asian and Asian American Youth," in *Troubling Intersections of Race and Sexuality: Queer Students of Color and Anti-oppressive Education*, ed. K. Kumashiro (New York: Rowman and Littlefield, 2001), 87–104.

89. *Cal. Educ. Code* § 220 (West 2003); *Cal. Penal Code* § 422.6(a) (West 2003), § 422.76 (West 2003); *Conn. Gen. Stat.* § 10-15c (2003); *D.C. Code Ann.* § 2-1402.41 (2003); *Mass. Gen. Laws*, chap. 71, § 89(l) (2003), chap. 76, § 5 (2003); *Minn. Stat.* § 363A.02 (2003), § 363.03(5) (2003); *N.J. Stat. Ann.* § 10:5-5 (West 2003), § 10:5-12(f)(1) (West 2003), § 18A:37-15 (West 2003); *Vt. Stat. Ann.* tit. 9, §§ 4501–2 (2003), tit. 16, § 11(26) (2003), tit. 16, § 565 (2003); *Wash. Rev. Code* § 9A.36.080(1)(c) (2003), § 28A.300.285 (2003), § 49.60.030 (2003); *Wis. Stat.* § 118.13 (2003), § 118.40 (2003).

90. *Alaska Admin. Code* tit. 20 § 10.020(b)(6) (2003); *Fla. Admin. Code* r. 6B-1.006(3) (2003); *Mass. Regs. Code* tit. 603 § 7 (2003); 22 *Pa. Code* § 235.8 (2003).

91. Hawaii Dep't of Educ. Nondiscrimination Policy Mem., August 17, 1996; *Haw. Bd. of Educ. Admin. Rules* § 8-41-1-15; *Md. Regs. Code* tit. 13A, § 01.04.03 (2003); *Or. Admin. Rules* § 571-003-0025 (2003); *Pa. Bd. of Educ. Rules & Regs.* § 4.4(c) (1992); R.I. Dep't of Educ., State of R.I. and Providence Plantations, A Policy Statement of the State Board of Regents Prohibiting Discrimination Based on Sexual Orientation; *Wis. Admin. Code* § 9.01 (2003). This may not be a complete list of regulations. Check with your state education department.

92. P. Griffin and M. Ouellette, "Going Beyond Gay/Straight Alliances to Make Schools Safe for Lesbian, Gay, Bisexual, and Transgender Students," *Angles* (Institute for Gay and Lesbian Strategic Studies, Amherst, MA) 6, no. 1 (2002).

93. *No Child Left Behind Act of 2001, U.S. Code* 115 (2002), § 1425.

94. For more on these and other issues, see J. Cianciotto and S. Cahill, *Education Policy Issues Affecting Lesbian, Gay, Bisexual, and Transgender Youth* (New York: Policy Institute of the National Gay and Lesbian Task Force, 2003).

95. A. Shippy, M. Cantor, and M. Brennan, "Patterns of Support for Lesbians and Gays as They Age" (paper presented at the Symposium on Social Support Networks held at the 54th Annual Scientific Meeting of the Gerontological Society of America, Chicago, November 2001).

96. D. Wolfe, *Men Like Us: The GMHC Complete Guide to Gay Men's Sexual, Physical, and Emotional Well-Being* (New York: Ballantine, 2000), cited in "Lesbian, Gay, Bisexual, and Transgender Health:

Findings and Concerns," ed. L. Dean, I. Meyer, K. Robinson, R. Sell, R. Sember, V. Silenzio, D. Wolfe, D. Bohen, J. Bradford, E. Rothblum, J. White, and P. Dunn," *Journal of the Gay and Lesbian Medical Association* 4, no. 3 (January 2000): 102–51, http://www.glma.org/pub/jglma/vol14/3/j43text.pdf (accessed November 1, 2001).

97. G. Liu, "Social Security and the Treatment of Marriage: Spousal Benefits, Earnings Sharing, and the Challenge of Reform," *Wisconsin Law Review* 1 (1999): 1–64.

98. American Association of Retired Persons, *Your 401(k) Plan: Building toward Your Retirement Security* (Washington, DC: American Association of Retired Persons, n.d.).

99. Henry J. Kaiser Family Foundation, *Inside-OUT: A Report on the Experiences of Lesbians, Gays, and Bisexuals in America and the Public's Views on Issues and Policies Related to Sexual Orientation* (Menlo Park, CA: Henry J. Kaiser Family Foundation, 2001).

100. L. Dean et al., "Lesbian, Gay, Bisexual, and Transgender Health."

101. S. Greenberger, "Lawmakers Urge Medicaid Benefits for Same-Sex Couples," *Boston Globe*, November 25, 2005.

102. Lambda Legal Defense and Education Fund, "University of Maryland Medical System to Be Sued Wednesday by Gay Man Prevented from Visiting His Dying Partner at Shock Trauma Center in Baltimore," news release, February 26, 2002, http://www.lambdalegal.org/cgi-bin/iowa/documents/record?record=1011 (accessed April 10, 2002).

103. T. Emory, Associated Press, "Lesbian Couple Led Fight for Landmark Ruling," *Boston Globe*, November 18, 2003.

104. *Family and Medical Leave Act*, 29 CFR § 825.800.

105. G. Jones, "Davis to Sign Bill Allowing Paid Family Leave," *Los Angeles Times*, September 23, 2002.

106. National Gay and Lesbian Task Force, "Domestic Violence Laws in the United States" (New York: National Gay and Lesbian Task Force, n.d.), http://www.thetaskforce.org/downloads/domesticviolencelawsmap.pdf (accessed January 3, 2004).

107. C. Renzetti and C. Miley, eds., *Violence in Gay and Lesbian Domestic Partnerships* (Binghamton, NY: Harrington Park, 1996), 2. Renzetti and Miley cite V. Coleman, *Confronting Lesbian Battering* (St. Paul: Minnesota Coalition for Battered Women, 1990) (46 percent of lesbians experienced abuse); P. Brand and A. Kidd, "Frequency of Physical Aggression in Heterosexual and Female Homosexual Dyads," *Psychological Reports* 59 (1986): 1307–13 (25 percent of lesbians reported abuse in past); G. Lie, R. Schilit, J. Bush, M. Montagne, and L. Reyes, "Lesbians in Currently Aggressive Relationships: How Frequently Do They Report Aggressive Past Relationships?" *Violence and Victims* 6 (1991): 121–35 (26 percent of lesbians reported abuse in current relationship); E. Kelly and L. Warshafsky, "Partner Abuse in Gay Male and Lesbian Couples" (paper presented at the Third National Conference for Family Violence Researchers, Durham, NH, 1987) (46 percent of lesbians and gays used physical aggression with partner); Gay and Lesbian Community Action Council, "A Survey of the Twin Cities Gay and Lesbian Community: Northstar Project" (unpublished manuscript, Gay and Lesbian Community Action Council, Minneapolis, MN, 1987) (22 percent of nine hundred lesbians had been in a violent relationship).

108. Gay Men's Domestic Violence Project, "All You Want to Know . . . " (Boston: Gay Men's Domestic Violence Project, n.d.).

109. National Coalition of Anti-Violence Programs, *Lesbian, Gay, Bisexual, Transgender Domestic Violence in 2000* (New York: National Coalition of Anti-Violence Programs, 2001), http://www.avp.org/publications/reports/2000ncavpdvrpt.pdf (accessed November 2, 2002).

110. Gay Men's Domestic Violence Project, "Similarities and Differences: Same-Gender and Opposite-Gender Domestic Violence" (Boston: Gay Men's Domestic Violence Project, n.d.), http://www.gmdvp.org/pages/differences.html (accessed November 2, 2002).

111. National Coalition of Anti-Violence Programs, *Annual Report on Lesbian, Gay, Bisexual, Transgender Domestic Violence* (New York: National Coalition of Anti-Violence Programs, 1998), http://www.vaw.umn.edu/FinalDocuments/glbtdv.htm#concl (accessed January 7, 2000).

112. Gay Men's Domestic Violence Project, "Similarities and Differences."

113. Personal communication with Curt Rogers,

executive director of the Gay Men's Domestic Violence Project, August 20, 2002.

114. National Coalition of Anti-Violence Programs, *Lesbian, Gay, Bisexual, Transgender Domestic Violence in 2000.*

115. Renzetti and Miley, *Violence in Gay and Lesbian Domestic Partnerships.*

116. R. Davidson, "Gay-on-Gay Violence: The Gay Community's Dirty Secret—Domestic Violence —Is Finally Coming Out of the Closet," *Salon.com*, February 27, 1997, http://www.salon.com/feb97/news/news2970227.html (accessed November 2, 2002).

117. National Coalition of Anti-Violence Programs, *Lesbian, Gay, Bisexual, Transgender Domestic Violence in 2000.*

118. *Sommi v. Ayer*, 51 Mass. App. Ct. 207 (2001), (Judge may not issue "mutual restraining orders" without written findings). See Gay and Lesbian Advocates and Defenders, "Appeals Court Decides Cases of Domestic Violence Involving Gay Men," news release, March 28, 2001, http://www.glad.org/press37-3-28-01.html (accessed November 2, 2002).

119. Gunner Scott of the Network knew of eighteen such programs (personal communication with Gunner Scott, organizer/outreach coordinator of the Network/La Red, August 20, 2002). As of 2002, the National Coalition of Anti-Violence Programs listed fifteen LGBT organizations addressing domestic violence issues.

120. Personal communications with Curt Rogers and Gunner Scott.

121. Personal communication with Curt Rogers.

122. Personal communications with Curt Rogers and Gunner Scott.

123. Personal communication with Gunner Scott.

124. Gay Men's Domestic Violence Project, "GMDVP Partners with the Boston Police Department," news release, n.d., http://www.gmdvp.org/pages/news1.html (accessed November 2, 2002).

125. Empire State Pride Agenda, *Anti-Gay/Lesbian Discrimination in New York State* (New York: Empire State Pride Agenda, 2001), http://www.prideagenda.org/pride/survey.pdf (accessed January 20, 2005).

126. S. Minter and C. Daley, *Trans Realities: A Legal Needs Assessment of San Francisco's Transgender Communities* (San Francisco: National Center for Lesbian Rights; Transgender Law Center, 2003).

127. J. Keatley, T. Nemoto, D. Operario, and T. Soma, "The Impact of Transphobia on HIV Risk Behaviors among Male-to-Female Transgenders in San Francisco" (San Francisco: University of California, AIDS Research Institute, n.d.), http://ari.ucsf.edu/pdf/Posters/barcelona/keatley.pdf (accessed January 20, 2005).

128. R. Colvin, *The Extent of Sexual Orientation Discrimination in Topeka, KS* (New York: Policy Institute of the National Gay and Lesbian Task Force, 2004), http://www.thetaskforce.org/downloads/TopekaDiscrimination.pdf (accessed January 20, 2005).

129. J. Xavier, *The Washington Transgender Needs Assessment Survey*, Washington, DC: J. Xavier, 2000.

130. B. Ragins, "The Effect of Legislation on Workplace Discrimination on Gay Employees" (paper presented at the 106th Convention of the American Psychological Association, San Francisco, August 14–18, 1998).

131. National Gay and Lesbian Task Force, "National Gay and Lesbian Task Force Hails Passage of Washington State Bill Prohibiting Discrimination Based on Sexual Orientation and Gender Identity; 48% of Nation's Population will Now be Protected by Sexual Orientation Laws," news release, January 27, 2006, http://www.thetaskforce.org/media/release.cfm?print=1&releaseID=914 (accessed May 11, 2006).

132. By "a local jurisdiction," we mean a town, city, or county.

133. W. Washington, "White House, Counsel Split on Gay Rights; Official Had Questioned Antidiscrimination Law," *Boston Globe*, April 1, 2004.

134. J. Towey, *Protecting the Civil Rights and Religious Liberty of Faith-Based Organizations: Why Religious Hiring Rights Must Be Preserved* (Washington, DC: White House Office of Faith-Based and Community Initiatives, n.d. [sent to Congress in June 2003]), http://www.whitehouse.gov/government/fbci/booklet.pdf (accessed January 20, 2005).

135. *Dodge v. Salvation Army*, 1989 WL 53857 (S.D. Miss. January 9, 1989).

136. Towey, *Protecting the Civil Rights and Religious Liberty of Faith-Based Organizations.*

137. R. Smith, "Judge Dismisses Bias Claim against KY Agency," *Washington Blade*, July 27, 2001.

138. Lambda Legal Defense and Education Fund, "New Lawsuit Charges Methodist Children's Home Uses Tax Dollars to Discriminate in Employment and to Indoctrinate Foster Youth in Religion," news release, August 1, 2002, http://www.lambdalegal.org/cgi-bin/iowa/documents/record?record=1108 (accessed January 20, 2005).

139. Ibid.

140. A. Liptak, "A Right to Bias Is Put to the Test," *New York Times*, October 11, 2002, http://www.nytimes.com/2002/10/11/national/11CHUR.html?tntemail0 (accessed November 2, 2002).

141. Ibid.

142. Lambda Legal Defense and Education Fund, "New Lawsuit Charges Methodist Children's Home."

143. S. Goldberg, "Civil Rights, Special Rights, and Our Rights," in *Eyes Right! Challenging the Right-Wing Backlash*, ed. C. Berlet (Boston: South End, 1995), 111.

144. General Accounting Office, *Sexual Orientation–Based Employment Discrimination: States' Experience with Statutory Prohibitions*, GAO-02-878R (Washington, DC: General Accounting Office, 2002).

145. Ibid., 2.

146. Intern. Rev. Code §§ 105–6.

147. Intern. Rev. Code § 152 defines a dependent as an individual who receives half his or her support from the taxpayer and is a member of the taxpayer's residence, which is the dependent's principle place of residence. However, even if a same-sex partner fulfills these two requirements of §152, subsection (b)(5) of the same section requires the taxpayer's relationship to the dependent to be one recognized by local law, thus raising valid concerns about whether a same-sex relationship would qualify.

CHAPTER 3

1. C. Campbell and R. Davidson, "Gay and Lesbian Issues in the Congressional Arena," in *The Politics of Gay Rights*, ed. C. Rimmerman, K. Wald, and C. Wilcox (Chicago: University of Chicago Press, 2000), 360–62.

2. Associated Press, "Conn. Civil Union Bill Signed into Law," *Insurance Journal*, April 22, 2005, http://www.insurancejournal.com/news/east/2005/04/22/54179.htm (accessed June 20, 2005).

3. Rayside, "Politics of Lesbian and Gay Parenting"; Human Rights Campaign, *Domestic Partner Benefits* (Washington, DC: Human Rights Campaign, 2002), http://www.hrc.org/worknet/dp/index.asp (accessed December 4, 2003); Policy Institute of the National Gay and Lesbian Task Force, internal analysis, January 2005.

4. A. Levene, "World's First Legal Gay Weddings Held in Amsterdam," Reuters, April 1, 2001; "Belgium Approves Same-Sex Marriages," Associated Press, January 30, 2003.

5. Civil partnerships are distinct from marriage because they are exclusively for same-sex couples, created only through a civil procedure and through the signing of a document, rather than through the exchange of spoken words. See http://www.womenandequalityunit.gov.uk/lgbt/faq.htm.

6. L. Rohter, "Brazil Grants Some Legal Recognition to Same-Sex Couples," *New York Times*, June 10, 2000, A3; C. Hogg, "Taiwan Move to Allow Gay Unions," BBC News, October 28, 2003, http://news.bbc.co.uk/2/hi/asia-pacific/3219721.stm (accessed December 4, 2003); "Australian State Grants Partner Rights," *Gaynetsa*, http://www.gaynetsa.co.za/news2002/australian_state_grants_partner_.htm (accessed December 4, 2003).

7. General Accounting Office, "Tables of Laws in the United States Code Involving Marital Status, by Category" (Washington, DC: General Accounting Office, 1997), http://www.gao.gov/archive/1997/og97016.pdf (accessed November 2, 2002).

8. Associated Press, "Schwarzenegger Vetoes Gay Marriage Bill," MSNBC, September 29, 2005, http://www.msnbc.com/id/9535128/ (accessed May 12, 2006).

9. C. Levendosky, "Hawaii Court Rules in Favor of Gay Marriage, Legislators Disagree," *Casper (Wyo.) Star-Tribune*, February 18, 1997, http://www.stolaf.edu/people/leming/soc260fam/news/Feb_18.html (accessed May 12, 2006).

10. The Defense of Marriage Act (Public Law 104-199, *U.S. Statutes at Large* 110 [1996]: 2419) provides the following:

SECTION 1. SHORT TITLE.

This Act may be cited as the 'Defense of Marriage Act'.

SEC. 2. POWERS RESERVED TO THE STATES.

(a) IN GENERAL- Chapter 115 of title 28, United States Code, is amended by adding after section 1738B the following:
'Sec. 1738C. Certain acts, records and proceedings and the effect thereof
'No State, territory, or possession of the United States, or Indian tribe, shall be required to give effect to any public act, record, or judicial proceeding of any other State, territory, possession, or tribe respecting a relationship between persons of the same sex that is treated as a marriage under the laws of such other State, territory, possession, or tribe, or a right or claim arising from such relationship.'.
(b) CLERICAL AMENDMENT- The table of sections at the beginning of chapter 115 of title 28, United States Code, is amended by inserting after the item relating to section 1738B the following new item:
'1738C. Certain acts, records and proceedings and the effect thereof.'.

SEC. 3. DEFINITION OF MARRIAGE.

(a) IN GENERAL- Chapter 1 of title 1, United States Code, is amended by adding at the end the following:
'Sec. 7. Definition of 'marriage' and 'spouse'
'In determining the meaning of any Act of Congress, or of any ruling, regulation, or interpretation of the various administrative bureaus and agencies of the United States, the word 'marriage' means only a legal union between one man and one woman as husband and wife and the word 'spouse' refers only to a person of the opposite sex who is a husband or a wife.'.
(b) CLERICAL AMENDMENT- The table of sections at the beginning of chapter 1 of title 1, United States Code, is amended by inserting after the item relating to section 6 the following new item:
'7. Definition of 'marriage' and 'spouse'.

11. A backlash was felt in Hawaii as well, stoked by extensive right-wing organizing. In November 1998, after a divisive state campaign, voters amended the Hawaii Constitution and gave the state legislature the power to limit marriage to heterosexual couples only. This effectively preempted the Hawaii Supreme Court decision and ended the same-sex couples' marriage lawsuit. Earlier in the same year, an Alaska trial court ruled that marriage was a fundamental right that could not be denied same-sex couples. In the November 1998 elections, voters in Alaska also enshrined marriage discrimination in their state constitution by excluding same-sex couples.

12. Representative Charles Canady (R-FL), *DOMA Debate*, 104th Cong., *Congressional Record* (July 11, 1996): H 7443.

13. Reagan Administration White House Working Group on the Family, *The Family: Preserving America's Future* (Washington, DC: U.S. Department of Education, Office of the Under Secretary, 1986), 21, cited in M. Abramovitz, *Under Attack, Fighting Back: Women and Welfare in the United States* (New York: Monthly Review Press, 2000), 20.

14. R. Rector, "Combatting Family Disintegration, Crime, and Dependence: Welfare Reform and Beyond," *Heritage Foundation Backgrounder* (Washington, DC), April 8, 1994, 7, cited in Abramovitz, *Under Attack, Fighting Back*, 19.

15. Quoted in K. Sack, "In Mississippi, Will Poor Grow Poorer with Welfare Plan?" *New York Times*, October 23, 1995, A1, cited in Abramovitz, *Under Attack, Fighting Back*, 30.

16. A. Smith, "The Politicization of Marriage in Contemporary American Public Policy: The Defense of Marriage Act and the Personal Responsibility Act" (unpublished paper, Department of Government, Cornell University, Ithaca, NY, n.d.), 19.

17. Lambda Legal Defense and Education Fund, "Constitutional and Legal Defects in H.R. 3396 and S. 1740, the Proposed Federal Legislation on Marriage and the Constitution" (New York: Lambda Legal Defense and Education Fund, 1996), http://www.lambdalegal.org/cgi-bin/iowa/documents/record?record=80 (accessed November 2, 2002).

18. *Goodridge v. Department of Public Health*, 440 Mass. 309, *6 (2003).

19. Associated Press, "Massachusetts Court Clarifies Gay Marriage Ruling," February 4, 2004.

20. D. Stout, "San Francisco Officials Perform Gay Marriages," *New York Times*, February 4, 2004.

21. D. Murphy, "California Supreme Court Voids Gay Marriages in San Francisco," *New York Times*, August 12, 2004.

22. Ibid.

23. *M.T. v. J.T.*, 355 A.2d 204 (N.J. Super. Ct.

App. Div. 1976); *Vecchione v. Vecchione*, Civ. No. 96DO03769 (Cal. App. Dep't. Sup. Ct. 1997).

24. "Spouses Sex Change Clouds Residency Status," San Jose *Mercury News*, November 30, 2004, 14A.

25. S. Minter, *Transgendered Persons and Marriage: The Importance of Legal Planning* (San Francisco: National Center for Lesbian Rights, 2001), http://www.transgenderlaw.org/resources/transmarriage.htm (accessed November 1, 2002).

26. D. Rayside, "Recognizing Same-Sex Relationships: Profiling Change in Canada and the United States" (paper presented at the annual meeting of the American Political Science Association, Boston, August 29–September 1, 2002), 21–23; Human Rights Campaign, *Domestic Partner Benefits*.

27. See chapter 5 of this book for more discussion about Bush's position on civil unions.

28. *Baker v. State*, 170 Vt. 194, 744 A.2d 864 (2000).

29. *Vt. Stat. Ann.* tit. 15, § 23 (2000).

30. Vermont law allows people under eighteen to marry with parental consent or court certificate. This allowance does not extend to same-sex couples.

31. *Wall Street Journal*/NBC News poll conducted by Peter Hart and Robert Teeter, September 9–13, 1999, cited in Lambda Legal Defense and Education Fund, "Preliminary Notes on the Hawaii Supreme Court's 12/9/99 Decision" (New York: Lambda Legal Defense and Education Fund, 1999), http://www.lambdalegal.org/cgi-bin/iowa/documents/record?record=544 (accessed December 4, 2003).

32. I. Peterson, "Metro Briefing New Jersey: Poll Finds Support for Gay Marriage," *New York Times*, July 29, 2003, 4B (New Jersey voters favor same-sex marriage 55 to 41 percent in a July 2003 Zogby poll); "Poll: New Hampshire Residents Favoring Law for Same-Sex Marriages," Associated Press, May 23, 2003 (54 percent of New Hampshire voters favor same-sex marriage in May 2003 University of New Hampshire poll).

33. "2001–2 Freshmen Survey: Their Opinions, Activities, and Goals," *Chronicle of Higher Education*, February 1, 2002, http://chronicle.com/free/v48/i21/opinions.htm (accessed December 4, 2003).

34. According to Vermont law (*Vt. Stat. Ann.* tit. 15, § 1 [2001]), this means that "[a] man shall not marry his mother, grandmother, daughter, granddaughter, sister, brother's daughter, sister's daughter, father's sister or mother's sister."

35. General Accounting Office, *Tables of Laws in the United States Code Involving Marital Status*.

36. M. Bonauto, "Statement of Mary L. Bonauto, Attorney for Plaintiff Couples in Marriage Case (*Goodridge et al. v. Dept. of Public Health*), in Response to Recent Statements of Gov. Romney and Attorney General Reilly" (Boston: Gay and Lesbian Advocates and Defenders, 2003), http://www.glad.org/News_Room/press64-11-21-03.shtml (accessed December 3, 2003).

37. National Gay and Lesbian Task Force, internal analysis, December 2004.

38. K. Sherrill, "Same-Sex Marriage, Civil Unions, and the 2004 Presidential Election" (New York: Policy Institute of the National Gay and Lesbian Task Force, 2004), http://thetaskforce.org/downloads/MarriageCUSherrill2004.pdf (accessed January 10, 2005).

39. Lambda Legal, "A Historic Victory: Civil Unions for Same-Sex Couples; What's Next!" (New York: American Civil Liberties Union, 2000), http://www.lambdalegal.org/cgi-bin/iowa/news/fact.html?record=659 (accessed April 5, 2006).

40. *N.Y. Admin. Code* § 3-240 et seq. (New York City domestic partnership law).

41. S. Kohn, *The Domestic Partnership Organizing Manual for Employee Benefits* (New York: Policy Institute of the National Gay and Lesbian Task Force, 1999), 5.

42. C. Smith, "Couples Pick Up Domestic Partner Forms," *Press Democrat*, January 6, 2000, http://www.pressdemocrat.com/search/index.html#archives (accessed November 2, 2002).

43. California Alliance for Pride and Equality, "Senate Passes Inheritance Rights Bill: AB 2216 Supported 22–13 in Senate," news release, August 20, 2002, http://www.calcape.org/news/054.senate-passes-inheritance-rights.htm (accessed September 12, 2002).

44. *Cal. Fam. Code* § 297.5(a).

45. Human Rights Campaign, *Domestic Partner Benefits*.

46. Kohn, *Domestic Partnership Organizing Manual*.

47. M. Carlsen, "Domestic Partnership Benefits: Employer Considerations," *Employee Benefit*

Practices, 4th quarter, (Washington, DC: Bureau of Labor Statistics, 1994); U.S. Department of Labor, "Employer Costs for Employee Compensation, March 2000," *News: U.S. Department of Labor* (Washington, DC: U.S. Department of Labor, June 29, 2000).

48. *San Francisco, Ca., Administrative Code* § 12B.2(b) (1997).

49. P. Goodman, "Catholic Church at Odds with San Francisco Law," *Washington Post*, January 30, 1997, A-3.

50. *S.D. Myers, Inc v. City and County of San Francisco*, 253 F.3d 461 (9th Cir. 2001); *Air Transport Ass'n of America v. City and County of San Francisco*, 266 F.3d 1064 (9th Cir. 2001). These cases were brought by, respectively, a construction company contracting on city land and an airline trade organization on behalf of the airlines servicing San Francisco International Airport. The challengers argued that the ordinance violated, among other things, federal constitutional limits on commercial regulation and federal laws regulating the airline industry. However, the court upheld the ordinance in both cases.

51. *Berkeley, Cal., Mun. Code* § 13.29 (2001); *L.A., Cal. Admin. Code* § 10.8.2.1; *San Mateo County Code* § 2.93; *Seattle, Wash., Mun. Code* § 20.45; *Tumwater, Wash., Mun. Code* § 3.46.

52. S. Essoyan, "Hawaii Approves Benefits Package for Gay Couples," *Los Angeles Times*, April 30, 1997, 3.

53. 1997 *Haw. Sess. Laws* H.B. 117 § 2, at 1247.

54. Personal communication with Dr. Unaka from the Hawaii Health Department on August 13, 2001. The state does not post current data to the health department Web site.

55. Partners Task Force for Gay and Lesbian Couples, "Reciprocal Beneficiaries: The Hawaiian Approach" (Seattle: Partners Task Force for Gay and Lesbian Couples, 2000), http://www.buddybuddy.com/d-p-hawa.html (accessed November 10, 2002).

56. Ibid.

57. *Baker v. State*, 170 Vt. 194, 744 A.2d 864 (2000). See also C. Goldberg, "Marriage Law Roils Vermont," *New York Times*, October 25, 2000, A16; "Vermont Residents Split over Civil Unions Law," *New York Times*, September 3, 2000, 18.

58. In *Gilden v. Crooke* (414 S.E.2d 645 [Ga. Sup. Ct. 1992]), the Georgia Supreme Court overturned the ruling of the trial court that the property agreement between a lesbian couple was invalid because they were engaged in a sexual relationship in violation of the Georgia sodomy law. In a tersely worded decision that gave no hint whatsoever to the fact that the parties were a lesbian couple, the Georgia Supreme Court simply ruled that since the contract did not require either party to engage in illegal sexual activity, it was valid. In *Posik v. Layton* (695 So. 2d 759 [Fla. Ct. App. 1997]), the Florida Court of Appeals upheld a support agreement between two women where one was encouraged to give up her job, sell her home, and relocate by the promise that the other would support her and provide support payments should they cease living together. Acknowledging the state laws banning same-sex marriage and adoption of children by lesbians and gay men, the Florida court stated that although the state does not condone "the lifestyles of homosexuals or unmarried live-ins," it does recognize their constitutional private property and contract rights.

59. *Marvin v. Marvin*, 18 Cal.3d 660, 134 Cal. Rptr. 815, 557 P.2d 106 (1976).

60. While Michele Marvin was apparently able to rely on her status as a nonmarital homemaker for her famous, film-star partner, Lee Marvin, the California courts were initially reluctant to enforce a similar verbal agreement between two men. See *Jones v. Daly*, 122 Cal. App. 3d 500 (1981). Subsequent cases reveal the court's great relief in enforcing partner agreements that have more clearly defined business or financial provisions. See *Whorton v. Dillingham*, 202 Cal. App. 3d (1988).

61. In *Seward v. Mentrup* (87 Ohio App. 3d 601 [1993]), the court held that the trial court had no authority to assist a lesbian couple in dividing their property after a nine-year relationship, that power being only available for married couples.

62. *In re Thompson*, 11 S.W.3d 913 (Tenn. Ct. App. 1999), appeal denied (Jan. 24, 2000); *In the Matter of Alison D. v. Virginia M.*, 77 N.Y.2d 651 (Ct. App. 1991).

63. *J.A.L. v. E.P.H.*, 682 A.2d 1314 (Pa. Super. 1996).

64. Lesbian and Gay Immigration Rights Task Force (New York), "Congressman Nadler Reintroduces Legislation for Gay and Lesbian Couples,"

news release, February 14, 2001, http://www.lgirtf.org/nadler.html (accessed November 10, 2002).

CHAPTER 4

1. Some gay and lesbian couples sought the right to marry during the 1970s. Courts ruled against same-sex marriages, for instance, in Minnesota in 1971 and Kentucky in 1973. However, the dominant ethos of the 1970s and 1980s was unquestionably hostile to same-sex marriage.

2. P. L. Ettelbrick, "Since When Is Marriage a Path to Liberation?" *Out/Look* 6 (fall 1989): 14.

3. S. Jeffreys, *Unpacking Queer Politics* (Malden, MA: Polity, 2003), 11.

4. C. Pateman, *The Sexual Contract* (Stanford, CA: Stanford University Press, 1988), 164.

5. N. D. Polikoff, "We Will Get What We Ask For: Why Legalizing Gay and Lesbian Marriage Will Not 'Dismantle the Legal Structure of Gender in Every Marriage,'" *Virginia Law Review* 79 (1993): 1535–50, http://www.lexis-nexis.com (accessed February 15, 2005).

6. M. Bronski, "Over the Rainbow," *Portland Phoenix*, August 1–7, 2003, http://www.portlandphoenix.com/features/other_stories/multi1/documents/03057410.asp (accessed February 15, 2005).

7. A. Dworkin, *Our Blood* (London: Women's Press, 1976), 11, 12, 13.

8. P. L. Ettelbrick, "Since When Is Marriage a Path to Liberation?" 14.

9. J. Ross, "Sex, Marriage, and History: Analyzing the Continued Resistance to Same-Sex Marriage," *Southern Methodist University Law Review* 55 (2002): 1657–81, http://www.lexis-nexis.com (accessed February 15, 2005).

10. N. D. Hunter, "Marriage, Law, and Gender: A Feminist Inquiry," *Law and Sexuality* 1 (1991): 12.

11. Ibid., 16.

12. Ibid., 17.

13. M. Bronski, quoted in Jeffreys, *Unpacking Queer Politics*, 155.

14. M. Warner, "Beyond Gay Marriage," in *Left Legalism/Left Critique*, ed. W. Brown and J. Halley (Durham and London: Duke University Press, 2002), 264.

15. A. Jagose, quoted in Jeffreys, *Unpacking Queer Politics*, 10.

16. Warner, "Beyond Gay Marriage," 264.

17. Ibid., 265.

18. Ibid., 260.

19. J. Butler, "Is Kinship Always Heterosexual," in *Left Legalism/Left Critique*, ed. W. Brown and J. Halley (Durham and London: Duke University Press, 2002), 241–42.

20. Warner, "Beyond Gay Marriage," 267.

21. K. Yoshino, "Covering," *Yale Law Journal* 111 (2002): 769–939. Cheshire Calhoun's arguments on assimilation are also pertinent here. She notes: "To claim that same-sex marriage would necessarily assimilate gays and lesbians to mainstream culture ignores the fact that many heterosexuals (who, of course, do have the right to marry) have been anything but assimilationists. Evolution in both marriage law and marital and parenting practices has been a result of heterosexuals' *resistance* to the legal and social conception of traditional marriage" (C. Calhoun, *Feminism, the Family, and the Politics of the Closet: Lesbian and Gay Displacement* [Oxford: Oxford University Press, 2000], 113).

22. C. J. Cohen, "Punks, Bulldaggers, and Welfare Queens: The Radical Potential of Queer Politics," in *Sexual Identities, Queer Politics*, ed. M. Blasius (Princeton, NJ: Princeton University Press, 2001), 211. Many African-American members of the LGBT community do not consider themselves to be queer. The 2000 Black Pride Survey of nearly three thousand black LGBT people at Black Gay Pride events around the United States found that less than 1 percent of respondents identified as "queer"; most identified as "gay" or "lesbian," and more identified as "same-gender loving" or "in the life" than "queer." See Battle et al., *Say It Loud.*

23. Cohen, "Punks, Bulldaggers, and Welfare Queens," 204.

24. Ibid., 210.

25. Ibid.

26. P. L. Ettelbrick, "Wedlock Alert: A Comment on Lesbian and Gay Family Recognition," *Journal of Law and Policy* 5 (1996): 107–66.

27. P. L. Ettelbrick, "Domestic Partnership, Civil Unions, or Marriage: One Size Does Not Fit All," *Albany Law Review* 64 (2001): 905–14.

28. N. D. Polikoff, "Ending Marriage as We Know It," *Hofstra Law Review* 32 (2003): 210–32.

29. C. Kitzinger and S. Wilkinson, "The Rebranding of Marriage: Why We Got Married

instead of Registering a Civil Partnership," *Feminism and Psychology* 14 (2004): 127–50.

30. N. D. Hunter, "Marriage, Law, and Gender," 26.

31. J. Shapiro, "A Lesbian-Centered Critique of Second-Parent Adoptions," *Berkeley Women's Law Journal* 14 (1999): 17–39.

32. T. Boggis "Affording Our Families: Class Issues in Family Formation," in *Queer Families, Queer Politics*, ed. M. Bernstein and R. Reimann (New York: Columbia University Press, 2001), 176.

33. E. Wolfson, "Crossing the Threshold: Equal Marriage Rights for Lesbians and Gay Men and the Intra-community Critique," *New York University Review of Law and Social Change* 21 (1994): 586.

34. A. Sullivan, "Here Comes the Groom: A Conservative Case for Gay Marriage," *New Republic*, August 28, 1989, http://www.andrewsullivan.com/homosexuality.php (accessed February 1, 2005).

35. W. N. Eskridge, Jr., "A History of Same-Sex Marriage," *Virginia Law Review* 79 (1993): 1419–1513.

36. Ibid.

37. Ibid.

38. D. L. Hutchinson, "Out yet Unseen: A Racial Critique of Gay and Lesbian Legal Theory and Political Discourse," *Connecticut Law Review* 29 (1997): 561–645.

39. A. Sullivan, *Virtually Normal: An Argument about Homosexuality* (New York: Knopf, 1995), 185. The experience of Massachusetts has shown that the first of Hutchinson's claims is untrue; lesbian couples marrying outnumbered gay male couples marrying by nearly two to one (65 to 35 percent) in the first year of same-sex marriage, May 2004–May 2005. See "Gay Marriages in Massachusetts: One Year Later; May 2005," *Lesbian Life*, http://lesbianlife.about.com/od/wedding/a/MassOneYear.htm (accessed June 1, 2005).

40. Hutchinson, "Out yet Unseen." Suffredini and Finley argue that federal tax laws related to marriage are more likely to penalize low-income people and people of color: see K. Suffredini and M. Finley, "Speak Now: Progressive Considerations on the Advent of Civil Marriage for Same-Sex Couples," *Boston College Law Review* 45 (2004): 595–618.

41. L. Duggan, "Holy Matrimony," *Nation*, March 15, 2004, http://www.thenation.com/doc/20040315/duggan (accessed February 15, 2005).

42. Ibid.

43. Quoted in ibid.

44. T. B. Stoddard, "Why Gay People Should Seek the Right to Marry," *Out/Look* 6 (fall 1989): 12.

45. Quoted in J. Hanania, "The Debate Over Gay Marriages: No Unity," *Los Angeles Times*, June 13, 1996, quoted in Hutchinson, "Out yet Unseen."

46. Wolfson, "Crossing the Threshold," 574.

47. *Daniel Hernandez, et al., v. Victor L. Robles*, 7 Misc. 3d 459 (2005) http://www.lambdalegal.org/binary-data/LAMBDA_PDF/pdf/378.pdf.

48. U. Vaid, *Virtual Equality: The Mainstreaming of Gay and Lesbian Liberation* (New York: Anchor, 1995), 181.

49. Ibid., 180.

50. D. L. Hutchinson, "'Gay Rights' for 'Gay Whites'? Race, Sexual Identity, and Equal Protection Discourse," *Cornell Law Review* 85 (2000): 1358–91.

CHAPTER 5

1. D. Herman, "The Gay Agenda Is the Devil's Agenda: The Christian Right's Vision and the Role of the State," in *The Politics of Gay Rights*, ed. C. Rimmerman, K. Wald, and C. Wilcox (Chicago: University of Chicago Press, 2000), 140. Premillennials are those who believe that the biblical book of Revelations prophesies the end of the world, at which time Christ will come for a second time and rule for one thousand years. They interpret radical social changes, crises, wars, and natural disasters as evidence of the "end times."

2. J. Green, "Antigay: Varieties of Opposition to Gay Rights," in *The Politics of Gay Rights*, ed. C. Rimmerman, K. Wald, and C. Wilcox (Chicago: University of Chicago Press, 2000), 124.

3. This is ironic, as many evangelicals consider Catholics pagan idolators and believe that they and others who are not "born-again" Christians will eventually be destroyed following the rapture allegedly foretold in the book of Revelations. Many view the pope and the Vatican as the Antichrist.

4. Green, "Antigay," 124.

5. J. Hardisty, *Mobilizing Resentment: Conservative Resurgence from the John Birch Society to the Promise Keepers* (Boston: Beacon, 1999), 103.

6. C. Berlet and M. Lyons, *Right-Wing Populism in America: Too Close for Comfort* (New York: Guilford, 2000), 235.

7. Hardisty, *Mobilizing Resentment*, 120–22.

8. Ibid., 121.

9. Coalition for Marriage, *Coalition Position Statements: Special Rights and Protections for Homosexuals*, http://www.marriagepreservation.org/position.htm (accessed January 26, 2004).

10. L. Sheldon, *Discrimination and Tolerance*, Traditional Values Coalition Special Report 21, no. 1 (Anaheim, CA: Traditional Values Coalition, 2003).

11. Bay State Republican Council, *Individual Liberty*, http://www.baystaterepublicancounci.homestead.com/IndividuaLiberty~ns4.html (accessed March 1, 2004).

12. A. Yang, *The 2000 National Elections Study and Gay and Lesbian Rights: Support for Equality Grows* (Washington, DC: National Gay and Lesbian Task Force, 2001).

13. F. Newport, "Six out of 10 Americans Say Homosexual Relations Should Be Recognized as Legal, but Americans Are Evenly Divided on Issue of Legal Civil Unions between Homosexuals Giving Them Legal Rights of Married Couples," Gallup News Service, May 15, 2003.

14. T. Donovan and S. Bowler, "Direct Democracy and Minority Rights: Opinions on Anti-Gay and Lesbian Ballot Initiatives," in *Anti-Gay Rights: Assessing Voter Initiatives*, ed. S. Witt and S. McCorkle (Westport, CT: Praeger, 1997), 114–17; Vaid, *Virtual Equality*, 67, 113.

15. Hardisty, *Mobilizing Resentment*, 106.

16. Coalition for Marriage, *Position Statements*.

17. Massachusetts Family Institute, "Massachusetts Family Institute Criticizes Acting Governor Swift over the Extension of Special Rights for Homosexuals," news release, September 10, 2001, http://www.mafamily.org/Press%20Room%20Folder/Press%20Releases/PressRelease20.htm (accessed March 4, 2004); "Massachusetts Family Institute Criticizes Acting Governor's Decision to Extend Domestic Partner Benefits," news release, August 16, 2001, http://www.mafamily.org/Press%20Room%20Folder/Press%20Releases/PressRelease15.htm (accessed March 4, 2004).

18. Massachusetts Family Institute, *Issue in Focus: Same-Sex Marriage* (Newton: Massachusetts Family Institute, 2003), http://www.mafamily.org/samesexmarriage.htm (accessed December 16, 2003).

19. Baystate Republican Council, *The Family*, http://www.baystaterepublicancounci.homestead.com/Family~ns4.html (accessed March 8, 2004).

20. Catholic Action League, "Catholic Action League Condemns SJC Decision on Same-Sex Marriage," news release, November 18, 2003, http://www.frmcgivneyassembly.org/CatholicActionLeague.html (accessed March 8, 2004).

21. C. Barillas, "Mass. High Court Repeals Boston DP Ordinance," July 9, 1999, http://www.datalounge.com/datalounge/news/record.html?record=4439 (accessed March 8, 2004).

22. WorldNet Daily, "City Sued over 'Domestic Partnerships,'" August 13, 2003, http://www.inthedays.com/articles.php?articleId=619 (accessed March 8, 2004).

23. Faulkner and Cranston, "Correlates of Same-Sex Behavior."

24. T. Dailey, "Homosexuality and Children: The Impact for Future Generations," *Homosexuality and Children* (Family Research Council, Washington, DC) 15, no. 5 (February 2004), http://www.frc.org/get.cfm?I=FP02K&v=PRINT (accessed March 8, 2004).

25. For a review of the social science research on anti-gay harassment and violence and its impact on youth, see Cianciotto and Cahill, *Education Policy Issues*.

26. P. Sprigg, "Questions and Answers: What's Wrong with Letting Same-Sex Couples 'Marry'?" *In Focus* (Family Research Council), no. 256 (2003), http://www.frc.org/get.cfm?I=IF03H01&f=PG03I03 (accessed December 3, 2003).

27. L. Sheldon, *Homosexuals Recruit Public School Children: Activists Use Issues of "Safety," "Tolerance," and "Homophobia" as Tactics to Promote Homosexuality in Our Nation's Schools*, Traditional Values Coalition Special Report 18, no. 11 (Anaheim, CA: Traditional Values Coalition, n.d.).

28. W. C. Holmes and G. B. Slap, "Sexual Abuse of Boys: Definitions, Prevalence, Correlates, Sequelae, and Management," *Journal of the American Medical Association* 280, no. 21 (1998): 1855–62.

29. C. Jenny and T. A. Roesler, "Are Children at Risk for Sexual Abuse by Homosexuals?" *Pediatrics* 94, no. 1 (1994): 41–44; A. N. Groth and H. J. Birnbaum, "Adult Sexual Orientation and Attraction

to Underage Persons," *Archives of Sexual Behavior* 7, no. 3 (1978): 175–81.

30. G. Stanton, "Is Marriage in Jeopardy?" *Focus on the Family: Focus on Social Issues: Marriage and Family FAQs*, August 27, 2003, http://family.org/cforum/fosi/marriage/FAQs/a0026916.cfm (accessed October 3, 2003).

31. M. Ash, M. Badgett, N. Folbre, L. Saunders, and R. Albelda, *Same-Sex Couples and Their Children in Massachusetts: A View from Census 2000* (Amherst, MA: Institute for Gay and Lesbian Strategic Studies, 2004).

32. Links to articles and commentary by Maggie Gallagher are available at http://www.mafamily.org/commentary.htm.

33. M. Gallagher, "The Stakes: Why We Need Marriage," *National Review Online*, July 14, 2003, http://www.nationalreview.com/comment/comment-gallagher071403.asp (accessed March 8, 2004).

34. M. Gallagher, "What Marriage Is For: Children Need Mothers and Fathers," *Weekly Standard* 8, no. 45 (August 4–11, 2003), http://www.weeklystandard.com/Content/Public/Articles/000/000/002/939pxiqa.asp?pg=2, (accessed March 8, 2004).

35. J. Stacey and T. Biblarz, "(How) Does the Sexual Orientation of the Parent Matter?" *American Sociological Review* 66, no. 2 (2001): 159–84.

36. Y. Abraham, "O'Malley Calls Gay Marriage a Threat; Archbishop Opposes Definition Change,"*Boston Globe*, October 3, 2003.

37. The Vatican Congregation for the Doctrine of the Faith, *Considerations regarding Proposals to Give Legal Recognition to Unions between Homosexual Persons* (Vatican: Congregation for the Doctrine of Faith, 2003), http://www.vatican.va/roman_curia/congregations/cfaith/documents (accessed February 10, 2004).

38. L. Goodstein, "Two Studies Cite Child Sexual Abuse by 4% of Priests," *New York Times*, February 27, 2004, A1, A22; P. Belluck,"Boston Sexual Abuse Report Breaks Down Accusations," *New York Times*, February 27, 2004, A16.

39. Belluck, "Boston Sexual Abuse Report Breaks Down Accusations."

40. Quoted in J. Johnson, "Homosexuals Seek Survivor Benefits Intended for Families," Cybercast News Service, October 22, 2001, http://www.dadi.org/homogred.htm (accessed February 9, 2004).

41. J. Dobson, *Dr. Dobson's Newsletter* (Focus on the Family, Colorado Springs, CO), January 2002, http://www.family.org/docstudy/newsletters/a0019238.html (accessed February 9, 2004).

42. Quoted in People for the American Way Foundation, *Hostile Climate: Report on Anti-Gay Activity*, 8th ed. (Washington: People for the American Way Foundation, 2002), 31.

43. Quoted in ibid., 33.

44. Quoted in ibid., 31.

45. Quoted in ibid., 33; B. Berkowitz, "Religious Right on the Ropes," *AlterNet*, October 21, 2001, http://www.alternet.org/print.html?StoryID=11840 (accessed February 9, 2004).

46. Quoted in People for the American Way Foundation, *Hostile Climate*, 33.

47. Quoted in ibid.

48. People for the American Way Foundation, *Hostile Climate*, 31–32.

49. Quoted in R. Bluey, "Homosexuals Push for Same-Sex Marriage after Sodomy Ruling," Christian News Service, June 27, 2003.

50. J. Kimball, "Homosexuals Pose New Threat to U.S. Border Security," *Concerned Women for America*, September 29, 2003, http://www.cwfa.org/printerfriendly.asp?id=4629&department=cwa&categoryid=family (accessed September 29, 2003).

51. "Who Can Say 'I Do'?" *CNN Crossfire*, November 18, 2003, http://www.cnn.com/TRANSCRIPTS/0311/18/cf.00.html (accessed March 8, 2004).

52. Family Research Council, *FRC President Tony Perkins Reacts to State of the Union Address*, January 20, 2004, http://www.frc.org/get.cfm?i=PR04A07&v=PRINT (accessed March 8, 2004).

53. The Massachusetts Family Institute, *Timely Commentary*, http://www.mafamily.org/commentary.htm (accessed March 8, 2004).

54. D. Prager, "San Francisco and Islamists: Fighting the Same Enemy," *TownHall.com*, March 2, 2004, http://www.mafamily.org/commentary.htm (accessed March 5, 2004).

55. R. Flynn, letter reproduced in *Knights News*, January 29, 2004, http://www.massachusettsstatekofc.org/Knights_News.htm (accessed March 5, 2004).

56. Abraham, "O'Malley Calls Gay Marriage a Threat."

57. Web site searches were conducted on October 2, 2003.

58. K. Peterson, "USA's Women Have 'New Set of Priorities,' Poll Suggests," *USA Today*, June 23, 2003.

59. M. Vise, "Ex-Georgia Legislator Leads Foes of Gay Marriage," *Atlanta Journal-Constitution*, February 15, 2004.

60. Y. Abraham, "Transplant Targets Gay Marriage," *Boston Globe*, November 18, 2003.

61. B. Maher, *Why Marriage Should Be Privileged in Public Policy* (Washington, DC: Family Research Council, n.d.), http://www.frc.org/get.cfm?i=IS03D1&v=PRINT (accessed March 4, 2004).

62. B. Wilcox, *Sacred Vows, Public Purposes* (Washington, DC: Family Research Council, n.d.), http://www.frc.org/get.cfm?i=WT02G2&v=PRINT (accessed March 4, 2004).

63. Ibid.

64. J. LaRue, *Talking Points: Why Homosexual "Marriage" Is Wrong* (Washington, DC: Concerned Women for America, 2003).

65. Massachusetts Family Institute, *Massachusetts Marriage and Family Report, 2002* (Newton: Massachusetts Family Institute, 2002), http://www.mafamily.org/Marriage%20Report2002.pdf (accessed March 15, 2004).

66. Cited in S. Cahill, "Anti-Gay Groups Active in Massachusetts: A Closer Look." (New York: National Gay and Lesbian Task Force Policy Institute, 2004), http://www.thetaskforce.org/downloads/AntiGayMA.pdf (accessed May 12, 2006).

67. Abraham, "O'Malley Calls Gay Marriage a Threat."

68. People for the American Way, *Right Wing Organizations: Traditional Values Coalition*, http://www.pfaw.org/pfaw/general/default.aspx?oid=8992&print=yes (accessed March 1, 2004); Concerned Women for America, *Georgia School Board Ponders Creationism*, September 12, 2005, http://www.cwfa.org/articledisplay.asp?id=2059&department=CWA&categoryid=education (accessed March 5, 2004); Concerned Women for America, *Join CWA at the State Capitol!* February 23, 2004, http://www.cwfa.org/articledisplay.asp?id=5290&department=FIELD&categoryid=misc (accessed March 5, 2004).

69. People for the American Way, *Right Wing Organizations: Family Research Council*, http://www.pfaw.org/pfaw/general/default.aspx?oid=4211&print=yes (accessed March 1, 2004).

70. People for the American Way, *Right Wing Organizations: Concerned Women for America*, http://www.pfaw.org/pfaw/general/default.aspx?oid=3151&print=yes (accessed March 1, 2004).

71. "Stop ERA," http://www.eagleforum.org/era/index.html (accessed May 12, 2006).

72. P. Schlafly, "U.S. Social Security for Mexicans?" *Eagle Forum*, January 15, 2003, http://www.eagleforum.org/column/2003/jan03/03-01-15.shtml (accessed February 26, 2004).

73. R. Wockner, "Quote/Unquote," *Bay Windows* (Boston), November 27, 1997.

74. K. Conner, fund-raising letter for American Renewal, April 28, 2003. American Renewal is the legislative action arm of the Family Research Council.

75. Financial information on these organizations was obtained from http://www.guidestar.com, which posts Internal Revenue Service (IRS) Tax Forms 990 (or 990EZ) for nonprofit organizations that may accept tax-deductible contributions. In turn, this information comes from the IRS Business Master File of 501(c) nonprofits. 501(c)(3) organizations with twenty-five thousand dollars or more in annual revenue are required to file Form 990 with the IRS. We were not able to obtain financial data on six of fifteen member organizations of the Coalition for Marriage. There are a number of possible reasons: (a) some of the sponsoring organizations are not 501(c)(3) nonprofit organizations eligible to accept tax-deductible contributions (religious organizations, for-profits [e.g., Bott Broadcasting], and political advocacy 501(c)(4) organizations are not required to file Form 990); (b) the organization may be registered under a different name with the IRS; (c) the organization may be the program of a larger organization; (d) the organization may have lost its 501(c)(3) status; or (e) the organization may have been recently formed.

76. Family Research Council, *FRC Action and Pro-Family Coalition Launch $2 Million Ad Campaign*, February 27, 2004, http://www.american-renewal.org (accessed March 8, 2004).

77. Unless otherwise noted, all information in this section is drawn from "Coalition Members," *Boston Globe*, January 8, 2004, http://www.boston.com/news/specials/gay_marriage/coalition_marriage (accessed January 30, 2004).

78. L. Barstow, remarks to Morality in Media Event, Bear Hill Gold Club, Stoneham, MA,

October 26, 2000, http://www.moralmedia.net/tips5.html (accessed February 3, 2004).

79. A version of this section first appeared in Cahill, *Same-Sex Marriage in the United States*, 2–7.

80. In addition to the laws still in effect in thirteen states, sodomy laws were also still on the books in Michigan and Massachusetts as of June 2003, but their status was in dispute as court rulings had limited their reach.

81. D. Savage, "Ruling Seen as Precursor to Same-Sex Marriages; Supporters and Foes of Gay Civil Fights Say the Court's Overturning of Sodomy Laws Could Lead to Gay Unions," *Los Angeles Times*, June 28, 2003.

82. A. Gearan, "Scalia Blasts Court on Sodomy Ruling," Associated Press, June 26, 2003.

83. R. Santorum, "Americans Must Preserve the Institution of Marriage," *USA Today*, July 9, 2003.

84. Quoted in N. Lewis, "Conservatives Furious over Court's Direction," *New York Times*, June 27, 2003.

85. Savage, "Ruling Seen as Precursor to Same-Sex Marriages."

86. Ruth Harlow, cited in Santorum, "Americans Must Preserve the Institution of Marriage."

87. Quoted in Santorum, Ibid., 94.

88. R. McElvaine, "GOP 'Values'? Read Their Lip Service," *Los Angeles Times*, October 12, 1992; C. Berlet and M. Quigley, "Theocracy and White Supremacy: Behind the Culture War to Restore Traditional Values," in *Eyes Right! Challenging the Right-Wing Backlash*, ed. C. Berlet (Boston: South End, 1995), 15.

89. C. Bull and J. Gallagher, *Perfect Enemies: The Religious Right, the Gay Movement, and the Politics of the 1990s* (New York: Crown, 1996), 94.

90. Ibid., 129.

91. H. Rhoads, "Cruel Crusade: The Holy War against Lesbians and Gays," *Progressive* 53, no. 7 (March 1993): 18; Bull and Gallagher, *Perfect Enemies*, 95; R. Bailey, *Out and Voting II: The Gay, Lesbian, and Bisexual Vote in Congressional Elections, 1990–1998* (New York: Policy Institute of the National Gay and Lesbian Task Force, 2000).

92. A version of this section first appeared in Cahill, *Same-Sex Marriage in the United States*, 80–81.

93. Princeton Survey Research Associates/Pew Poll, May 31–June 9, 1996. Cited in "Attitudes About Homosexuality and Gay Marriage" (Washington, DC: America Enterprise Institute) http://www.aei.org/docLib/20050121_HOMOSEXUALITY.pdf (accessed May 12 2006).

94. Policy Institute of the National Gay and Lesbian Task Force, *Capital Gains and Losses: A State by State Review of Gay-Related Legislation in 1996* (Washington, DC: National Gay and Lesbian Task Force, 1996), http://www.thetaskforce.org/downloads/cgal96.pdf (accessed February 5, 2004).

95. Policy Institute of the National Gay and Lesbian Task Force, *Capital Gains and Losses: A State by State Review of Gay, Lesbian, Bisexual, Transgender, and HIV/AIDS-Related Legislation in 1998* (Washington, DC: National Gay and Lesbian Task Force, 1998), 13, http://www.thetaskforce.org/downloads/cgal98.pdf (accessed February 5, 2004). The Missouri Supreme Court overturned its 1996 anti-gay marriage law in May 1998, but the legislature passed another anti-marriage law two years later.

96. A version of this section first appeared in Cahill, *Same-Sex Marriage in the United States*, 82–83.

97. Log Cabin Repulicans, news release, "Anti-Gay Pledge Divides Struggling Far Right from Leadng GOP Candidates," August 25, 1999 (Washington, DC: Log Cabin Republicans), http://www.logcabinwa.com/archive/199908250741.shtml (accessed May 12, 2006).

98. H. Ramer, "Bauer: Gay Marriage Is Worse than Terrorism," Associated Press, December 27, 1999.

99. L. Keen, "An About Face for Bush? Opinion on Appointing Gays Remains Murky," *Washington Blade*, October 15, 1999.

100. "A Sodomy Law's Last Stand," *Advocate*, July 18, 2000. Then-governor Bush was originally quoted by David Elliot in *Austin-American Statesman*, January 22, 1994.

101. S. Cahill and E. Ludwig, *Courting the Vote: The 2000 Presidential Candidates on Gay, Lesbian, Bisexual, and Transgender Issues* (New York: Policy Institute of the National Gay and Lesbian Task Force, 1999).

102. National Gay and Lesbian Task Force, "Election Center 2000: VP Candidate Profile Richard 'Dick' Cheney" (New York: National Gay and Lesbian Task Force, 2000), http://www.ngltf.org/elections/cheney.htm (accessed January 8, 2004).

103. A version of this section first appeared in

Cahill, *Same-Sex Marriage in the United States*, 97–99.

104. S. Cahill et al., *The 2004 Democratic Presidential Candidates on Gay, Lesbian, Bisexual, and Transgender Issues* (New York: Policy Institute of the National Gay and Lesbian Task Force, 2003); National Gay and Lesbian Task Force, "The Presidential Candidates' Positions on LGBT Issues" (New York: Policy Institute of the National Gay and Lesbian Task Force, 2004), http://www.ngltf.org/election center/SummaryComparison.pdf (accessed January 30, 2004).

105. A. Dang, "The Democratic Presidential Candidates on Marriage Equality for Same-Sex Couples" (New York: Policy Institute of the National Gay and Lesbian Task Force, 2004), http://www.ngltf.org/electioncenter/DemsMarriage.pdf (accessed January 30, 2004).

106. A version of this section and the next section first appeared in S. Cahill, *Same-Sex Marriage in the United States*, 88–90.

107. Quoted in N. Anderson, "Candidates Leery of Gay Marriage Debate," *Los Angeles Times*, July 3, 2003.

108. "President Bush Discusses Top Priorities for the U.S.," news release, July 30, 2003, http://www.whitehouse.gov/news/releases/2003/07/20030730-1.html (accessed July 31, 2003).

109. S. Cahill et al., *"Marriage Protection Week" Sponsors: Are They Really Interested in "Building Strong and Healthy Marriages?"* (New York: Policy Institute of the National Gay and Lesbian Task Force, 2003), http://www.thetaskforce.org/community/marriage center.cfm (accessed February 14, 2005).

110. G. W. Bush, "President Defends the Sanctity of Marriage: Statement by the President," news release, November 18, 2003, http://www.whitehouse.gov/news/releases/2003/11/20031118-4.html (accessed December 17, 2003).

111. S. Jones, Cybercast News Service, "Bush's Comments on Marriage Draw Praise, Criticism," *CNSNews.com*, January 21, 2004.

112. M. Dobbin, "Enraged Foes of Gay Marriage Gear Up for Fight; Massachusetts Ruling Energizes Drive for a Constitutional Ban on Same-Sex Wedlock," *Sacramento Bee*, February 6, 2004.

113. W. Washington, "Bush 'Troubled' by Gay Marriage, but Is Quiet on Amendment Plans," *Boston Globe*, February 19, 2004.

114. A. Mitchell, "Bush Talks to Gays and Calls It Beneficial," *New York Times*, April 14, 2000, A26.

115. *Domestic Partners Benefits and Obligations Act*, HR 638, 107th Cong., 1st sess., 2003.

116. Press briefing by Scott McClellan, July 31, 2003, http://www.whitehouse.gov/news/releases/2003/07/20030731-9.html (accessed August 1, 2003).

117. *2004 Republican Party Platform: A Safer World and a More Hopeful America*, http://www.gop.com/media/2004platform.pdf (accessed November 10, 2004).

118. *Strong at Home, Respected in the World: The 2004 Democratic National Platform for America*, http://www.democrats.org/pdfs/2004platform.pdf (accessed November 10, 2004).

119. This figure is derived from an analysis of U.S. Census data on same-sex partner households and unmarried opposite-sex partner households by researcher Gary Gates for the National Gay and Lesbian Task Force: "Number of Same-Sex Couples and Opposite-Sex Unmarried Couples Affected by Anti-Gay Marriage Ballot Initiatives" (New York: Policy Institute of the National Gay and Lesbian Task Force, n.d.), http://www.thetaskforce.org/downloads/couplesaffected.pdf (accessed November 29, 2004).

CHAPTER 6

1. Polikoff, "Ending Marriage as We Know It."

2. Ibid.

3. N. D. Polikoff, "Why Lesbians and Gay Men Should Read Martha Fineman," *American University Journal of Gender, Social Policy, and the Law* 8 (2000): 167–76, http://www.lexis-nexis.com (accessed February 15, 2005).

4. J. Stacey, "Toward Equal Regard for Marriages and Other Imperfect Intimate Affiliations," *Hofstra Law Review* 32 (2003): 331–48, http://www.lexis-nexis.com (accessed February 15, 2005).

5. Ibid.

6. Calhoun, *Feminism, the Family, and the Politics of the Closet*, 127.

7. Ibid., 76.

8. Ibid., 160.

9. National Gay and Lesbian Task Force, *Gay Pride Survey: 2004 Presidential Election* (Washington, DC: National Gay and Lesbian Task Force, 2003), http://www.thetaskforce.org/downloads/gaypride survey.pdf (accessed February 15, 2005).

10. A. Dang and M. Hu, *Asian Pacific American Lesbian, Gay, Bisexual, and Transgender People: A Community Portrait; A Report from New York's Queer Asian Pacific Legacy Conference, 2004* (New York: Policy Institute of the National Gay and Lesbian Task Force, 2005), http://www.thetaskforce.org/downloads/APAstudy.pdf (accessed June 21, 2005).

11. Battle et al., *Say It Loud.*

12. M. Goebel, "Gays against Marriage," *New York Blade*, May 7, 2004.

13. Quoted in ibid.

14. Quoted in I. Monroe, "Defining the Movement for Same-Sex Marriage," *Advocate*, February 15, 2005, http://www.advocate.com (accessed February 25, 2005).

15. Monroe, "Defining the Movement."

16. Ibid.

17. I. Aguirre, "All in La Familia," *Girlfriends* (May 2004), 20.

18. V. A. Brownworth, "Our History Is Now," *Curve*, April 2005, 62.

19. Federalist 10, *The Federalist Papers* (New York: Penguin, 1987).

20. Quoted in D. Hernandez, "Gaily Ever After: Is Gay Marriage the New Civil Rights Struggle or Has It Co-opted a Legacy?" *Colorlines*, fall 2004.

SELECTED BIBLIOGRAPHY

Abramovitz, M. *Under Attack, Fighting Back: Women and Welfare in the United States.* New York: Monthly Review Press, 2000.

Aguirre, I. "All in La Familia." *Girlfriends,* May 2004, 20.

Ash, M., M. V. L. Badgett, N. Folbre, L. Saunders, and R. Albelda. *Same-Sex Couples and Their Children in Massachusetts: A View from Census 2000.* Amherst, MA: Institute for Gay and Lesbian Strategic Studies, 2004.

Badgett, M. V. L. *Income Inflation: The Myth of Affluence among Gay Men, Lesbians, and Bisexuals.* New York: Policy Institute of the National Gay and Lesbian Task Force, Institute for Gay and Lesbian Strategic Studies, 1998.

Battle, J., C. Cohen, D. Warren, G. Fergerson, and S. Audam. *Say It Loud, I'm Black and I'm Proud: Black Pride Survey 2000.* New York: Policy Institute of the National Gay and Lesbian Task Force, 2002.

Bell, A., and M. Weinberg. *Homosexualities: A Study of Diversity among Men and Women.* New York: Simon and Schuster, 1978.

Berlet, C., and M. Lyons. *Right-Wing Populism in America: Too Close for Comfort.* New York: Guilford, 2000.

Berlet, C., and M. Quigley. "Theocracy and White Supremacy: Behind the Culture War to Restore Traditional Values." In *Eyes Right! Challenging the Right-Wing Backlash,* ed. C. Berlet, 15–43. Boston: South End, 1995.

Blankenhorn, D. *Fatherless America: Confronting Our Most Urgent Social Problem.* New York: HarperCollins, 1995.

Boggis, T. "Affording Our Families: Class Issues in Family Formation." In *Queer Families, Queer Politics,* ed. M. Bernstein and R. Reimann, 175–200. New York: Columbia University Press, 2001.

Bradford, J., K. Barrett, and J. Honnold. *The 2000 Census and Same-Sex Households: A User's Guide.* New York: Policy Institute of the National Gay and Lesbian Task Force; Richmond: Survey and Evaluation Research Laboratory of Virginia Commonwealth University; Boston: Fenway Institute, 2002.

Bronski, M. "Over the Rainbow." *Portland Phoenix,* August 1–7, 2003. http://www.portlandphoenix.com/features/other_stories/multi1/documents/03057410.asp (accessed February 15, 2005).

Brownworth, V. A. "Our History Is Now." *Curve,* April 2005, 62.

Bull, C., and J. Gallagher. *Perfect Enemies: The Religious Right, the Gay Movement, and the Politics of the 1990s.* New York: Crown, 1996.

Butler, J. "Is Kinship Always Heterosexual?" In *Left Legalism/Left Critique,* ed. W. Brown and J. Halley, 229–58. Durham and London: Duke University Press, 2002.

Cahill, S., J. Cianciotto, and R. Colvin. *"Marriage Protection Week" Sponsors: Are They Really Interested in "Building Strong and Healthy Marriages?"* New York: Policy Institute of the National Gay and Lesbian Task Force, 2003.

Cahill, S., M. Ellen, and S. Tobias. *Family Policy: Issues Affecting Gay, Lesbian, Bisexual, and Transgender Families.* New York: Policy Institute of the National Gay and Lesbian Task Force, 2002.

Cahill, S., and K. Jones. *Leaving Our Children Behind: Welfare Reform and the Gay, Lesbian, Bisexual, and Transgender Community.* New York: Policy Institute of the National Gay and Lesbian Task Force, 2001.

Cahill, S., and E. Ludwig. *Courting the Vote: The 2000 Presidential Candidates on Gay, Lesbian, Bisexual, and Transgender Issues.* New York: Policy Institute of the National Gay and Lesbian Task Force, 1999.

Cahill, S., K. South, and J. Spade. *Outing Age:*

Public Policy Issues Affecting Gay, Lesbian, Bisexual, and Transgender Elders. New York: Policy Institute of the National Gay and Lesbian Task Force, 2000.

Calhoun, C. *Feminism, the Family, and the Politics of the Closet: Lesbian and Gay Displacement*. Oxford: Oxford University Press, 2000.

Campbell, C., and R. Davidson. "Gay and Lesbian Issues in the Congressional Arena." In *The Politics of Gay Rights*, ed. C. Rimmerman, K. Wald, and C. Wilcox, 347–76. Chicago: University of Chicago Press, 2000.

Cianciotto, J., and S. Cahill. *Education Policy Issues Affecting Lesbian, Gay, Bisexual, and Transgender Youth*. New York: Policy Institute of the National Gay and Lesbian Task Force, 2003.

Cohen, C. J. "Punks, Bulldaggers, and Welfare Queens: The Radical Potential of Queer Politics." In *Sexual Identities, Queer Politics*, ed. M. Blasius, 200–227. Princeton: Princeton University Press, 2001.

Colvin, R. *The Extent of Sexual Orientation Discrimination in Topeka, KS*. New York: Policy Institute of the National Gay and Lesbian Task Force, 2004.

Congregation for the Doctrine of the Faith. *Considerations regarding Proposals to Give Legal Recognition to Unions between Homosexual Persons*. Vatican: Congregation for the Doctrine of the Faith, 2003. http://www.vatican.va/roman_curia/congregations/cfaith/documents (accessed February 10, 2004).

Dailey, T. "Homosexuality and Children: The Impact for Future Generations." *Homosexuality and Children* (Family Research Council, Washington, DC) 15, no. 5 (February 2004), http://www.frc.org/get.cfm?I=FP02K&v=PRINT (accessed March 8, 2004).

Dang, A. *The Democratic Presidential Candidates on Marriage Equality for Same-Sex Couples*. New York: Policy Institute of the National Gay and Lesbian Task Force, 2004. http://www.ngltf.org/electioncenter/DemsMarriage.pdf (accessed January 30, 2004).

Dang, A., and S. Frazer. *Black Same-Sex Households in the United States: A Report from the 2000 Census*. New York: Policy Institute of the National Gay and Lesbian Task Force, 2004.

Dean, L., I. Meyer, K. Robinson, R. Sell, R. Sember, V. Silenzio, D. Wolfe, D. Bohen, J. Bradford, E. Rothblum, J. White, and P. Dunn. "Lesbian, Gay, Bisexual, and Transgender Health: Findings and Concerns." *Journal of the Gay and Lesbian Medical Association* 4, no. 3 (January 2000): 102–51. http://www.glma.org/pub/jglma/vol4/3/j43text.pdf (accessed November 1, 2001).

Demo, D. H., and M. J. Cox. "Families and Young Children: A Review of Research in the 1990s." *Journal of Marriage and the Family* 62, no. 4 (2000): 876–96.

Donovan, T., and S. Bowler. "Direct Democracy and Minority Rights: Opinions on Anti-Gay and Lesbian Ballot Initiatives." In *Anti-Gay Rights: Assessing Voter Initiatives*, ed. S. Witt and S. McCorkle, 107–25. Westport, CT: Praeger, 1997.

Dougherty, T. *Economic Benefits of Marriage under Federal and Massachusetts Law*. New York: Policy Institute of the National Gay and Lesbian Task Force, 2004.

Duggan, L. "Holy Matrimony." *Nation*, March 15, 2004.

Dworkin, A. *Our Blood*. London: Women's Press, 1976.

Eskridge, W. N., Jr. "A History of Same-Sex Marriage." *Virginia Law Review* 79 (1993): 1419–1513.

Ettelbrick, P. L. "Domestic Partnership, Civil Unions or Marriage: One Size Does Not Fit All." *Albany Law Review* 64 (2001): 905–14.

Ettelbrick, P. L. "Since When Is Marriage a Path to Liberation?" *Out/Look* 6 (fall 1989): 9, 14–17.

Ettelbrick, P. L. "Wedlock Alert: A Comment on Lesbian and Gay Family Recognition." *Journal of Law and Policy* 5 (1996): 107–66.

Faulkner, A. H., and K. Cranston. "Correlates of Same-Sex Behavior in a Random Sample of Massachusetts High School Students." *American Journal of Public Health* 88, no. 2 (1998): 262–66.

Fontaine, J. "Evidencing a Need: School Counselors' Experiences with Gay and Lesbian Students." *Professional School Counseling* 1, no. 3 (1998): 8–14.

Gallagher, M. "The Stakes: Why We Need Marriage." *National Review Online*, July 14, 2003, http://www.nationalreview.com/comment/comment-gallagher071403.asp (accessed March 8, 2004).

Gallagher, M. "What Marriage Is For: Children Need Mothers and Fathers." *Weekly Standard* 8, no. 45 (August 4–11, 2003).

Gay and Lesbian Advocates and Defenders. *Protecting Families: Standards for Child Custody in Same-Sex Relationships.* Boston: Gay and Lesbian Advocates and Defenders, 1999.

General Accounting Office. *Sexual Orientation–Based Employment Discrimination: States' Experience with Statutory Prohibitions.* GAO-02-878R. Washington, DC: General Accounting Office, 2002.

General Accounting Office. "Tables of Laws in the United States Code Involving Marital Status, by Category." Washington, DC: General Accounting Office, 1997. http://www.gao.gov/archive/1997/og97016.pdf (accessed February 2, 2003).

Goebel, M. "Gays against Marriage." *New York Blade*, May 7, 2004.

Goldberg, S. "Civil Rights, Special Rights, and Our Rights." In *Eyes Right! Challenging the Right-Wing Backlash*, ed. C. Berlet, 109–12. Boston: South End, 1995.

Gottman Institute. *12-Year Study of Gay and Lesbian Couples.* Seattle: Gottman Institute, 2004.

Graff, E. *What Is Marriage For? The Strange Social History of Our Most Intimate Institution.* Boston: Beacon, 2004.

Green, J. "Antigay: Varieties of Opposition to Gay Rights." In *The Politics of Gay Rights*, ed. C. Rimmerman, K. Wald, and C. Wilcox, 121–38. Chicago: University of Chicago Press, 2000.

Green, R. "Sexual Identity of 37 Children Raised by Homosexual or Transsexual Parents." *American Journal of Psychiatry* 135 (1978): 692–97.

Groth, A. N., and H. J. Birnbaum. "Adult Sexual Orientation and Attraction to Underage Persons." *Archives of Sexual Behavior* 7, no. 3 (1978): 175–81.

Hardisty, J. *Mobilizing Resentment: Conservative Resurgence from the John Birch Society to the Promise Keepers.* Boston: Beacon, 1999.

Herdt, G., and A. Boxer. *Children of Horizons.* 2nd ed. Boston: Beacon, 1996.

Herman, D. "The Gay Agenda Is the Devil's Agenda: The Christian Right's Vision and the Role of the State." In *The Politics of Gay Rights*, ed. C. Rimmerman, K. Wald, and C. Wilcox, 139–60. Chicago: University of Chicago Press, 2000.

Hernandez, D. "Gaily Ever After: Is Gay Marriage the New Civil Rights Struggle or Has It Coopted a Legacy?" *Colorlines*, fall 2004.

Hetrick, E., and A. Martin. "Developmental Issues and Their Resolution for Gay and Lesbian Adolescents." *Journal of Homosexuality* 14, nos. 1/2 (1987): 25–43.

Holmes, W. C., and G. B. Slap. "Sexual Abuse of Boys: Definitions, Prevalence, Correlates, Sequelae, and Management." *Journal of the American Medical Association* 280, no. 21 (1998): 1855–62.

Horn, W. "Wedding Bell Blues: Marriage and Welfare Reform." *Brookings Review* 19, no. 3 (summer 2001): 39–42.

Horn, W., D. Blankenhorn, and M. Pearlstein, eds. *The Fatherhood Movement: A Call to Action.* New York: Lexington, 1999.

Horn, W., and A. Bush. *Fathers, Marriage, and Welfare Reform.* Washington, DC: Hudson Institute, 1997. http://welfarereformer.org/articles/father.htm (accessed November 1, 2001).

Human Rights Campaign. *Domestic Partner Benefits.* Washington, DC: Human Rights Campaign, 2002.

Hunter, N. D. "Marriage, Law, and Gender: A Feminist Inquiry." *Law and Sexuality* 1 (1991): 9–30.

Hutchinson, D. L. "'Gay Rights' for 'Gay Whites'?: Race, Sexual Identity and Equal Protection Discourse." *Cornell Law Review* 85 (2000): 1358–91.

Hutchinson, D. L. "Out yet Unseen: A Racial Critique of Gay and Lesbian Legal Theory and Political Discourse." *Connecticut Law Review* 29 (1997): 561–645.

Jeffreys, S. *Unpacking Queer Politics.* Malden, MA: Polity, 2003.

Jenny, C., and T. A. Roesler. "Are Children at Risk for Sexual Abuse by Homosexuals?" *Pediatrics* 94, no. 1 (1994): 41–44.

Keatley, J., T. Nemoto, D. Operario, and T. Soma. "The Impact of Transphobia on HIV Risk Behaviors among Male-to-Female Transgenders in San Francisco." San Francisco: University of California, AIDS Research Institute, n.d. http://ari.ucsf.edu/pdf/Posters/barcelona/keatley.pdf (accessed January 20, 2005).

Kitzinger, C., and S. Wilkinson. "The Re-branding of Marriage: Why We Got Married instead of Registering a Civil Partnership." *Feminism and Psychology* 14 (2004): 127–50.

Kohn, S. *The Domestic Partnership Organizing Manual for Employee Benefits.* New York: Policy

Institute of the National Gay and Lesbian Task Force, 1999.

Kosciw, J., and M. Cullen. *The GLSEN 2001 National School Climate Survey: The School-Related Experiences of Our Nation's Lesbian, Gay, Bisexual, and Transgender Youth.* New York: Gay, Lesbian, and Straight Education Network, 2001.

Lansford, J., R. Ceballo, A. Abbey, and A. Stewart. "Does Family Structure Matter? A Comparison of Adoptive, Two-Parent Biological, Single-Mother, Stepfather, and Stepmother Households." *Journal of Marriage and Family* 63, no. 3 (2001): 840–51.

Lewis, G., and J. Edelson. "DOMA and ENDA: Congress Votes on Gay Rights." In *The Politics of Gay Rights*, ed. C. Rimmerman, K. Wald, and C. Wilcox, 193–216. Chicago: University of Chicago Press, 2000.

Liu, G. "Social Security and the Treatment of Marriage: Spousal Benefits, Earnings Sharing, and the Challenge of Reform." *Wisconsin Law Review* 1 (1999): 1–64.

Logue, P. *The Rights of Lesbian and Gay Parents and Their Children.* New York: Lambda Legal Defense and Education Fund, 2001. http://www.lambdalegal.org/binary-data/LAMBDA_PDF/pdf/115.pdf (accessed February 1, 2005).

Madison, J. "Federalist 10." In *The Federalist Papers*, ed. C. Rossiter, 71–79. New York: Signet Classic, 1999.

Massachusetts Family Institute. *Massachusetts Marriage and Family Report, 2002.* Newton: Massachusetts Family Institute, 2002. http://www.mafamily.org/Marriage%20Report2002.pdf (accessed March 12, 2004).

Mays, V., L. Chatters, S. Cochran, and J. Mackness. "African American Families in Diversity: Gay Men and Lesbians as Participants in Family Networks." *Journal of Comparative Family Studies* 29, no. 1 (1998): 73–87.

Minter, S. *Transgendered Persons and Marriage: The Importance of Legal Planning.* San Francisco: National Center for Lesbian Rights, 2001. http://www.transgenderlaw.org/resources/transmarriage.htm (accessed November 1, 2002).

Minter, S., and C. Daley. *Trans Realities: A Legal Needs Assessment of San Francisco's Transgender Communities.* San Francisco: National Center for Lesbian Rights; Transgender Law Center, 2003.

Monroe, I. "Defining the Movement for Same-Sex Marriage." *Advocate*, February 15, 2005.

Murphy, J. "Antilesbian Discrimination in Assisted Reproduction." In *Queer Families, Queer Politics*, ed. M. Bernstein and R. Reiman, 182–200. New York: Columbia University Press, 2001.

National Center for Lesbian Rights. "Legal Recognition of LGBT Families." San Francisco: National Center for Lesbian Rights, 2002. http://www.nclrights.org/publications/lgbtfamilies.htm#12 (accessed November 1, 2002).

National Coalition of Anti-Violence Programs. *Lesbian, Gay, Bisexual, Transgender Domestic Violence in 2000.* New York: National Coalition of Anti-Violence Programs, 2001.

National Gay and Lesbian Task Force. *Gay Pride Survey: 2004 Presidential Election.* Washington, DC: National Gay and Lesbian Task Force, 2003. http://www.thetaskforce.org/downloads/gaypridesurvey.pdf (accessed February 15, 2005).

Pateman, C. *The Sexual Contract.* Stanford, CA: Stanford University Press, 1988.

Patterson, C. "Family Relationships of Lesbians and Gay Men." *Journal of Marriage and Family* 62 (2000): 1052–69.

Patterson, C. *Lesbian and Gay Parenting.* Washington, DC: American Psychological Association, 1995. http://www.apa.org/pi/parent.html (accessed November 1, 2002).

Patterson, C. "Lesbian Mothers, Gay Fathers, and Their Children." In *Lesbian, Gay, and Bisexual Identities over the Lifespan*, ed. A. D'Augelli and C. Patterson, 262–90. New York: Oxford University Press, 1995.

Patterson, C., and R. Redding. "Lesbian and Gay Families with Children: Implications of Social Science Research for Policy." *Journal of Social Issues* 52, no. 3 (1996): 29–50.

People for the American Way Foundation. *Hostile Climate: Report on Anti-Gay Activity.* 8th ed. Washington, DC: People for the American Way Foundation, 2002.

Peplau, L., and L. Spalding. "The Close Relationships of Lesbians, Gay Men, and Bisexuals." In *Psychological Perspectives on Lesbian, Gay, and Bisexual Experiences*, ed. L. Garnets and D. Kimmel, 449–74. 2nd ed. New York: Columbia University Press, 2003.

Perrin, E., and Committee on Psychosocial Aspects

of Child and Family Health. "Technical Report: Coparent or Second-Parent Adoption by Same-Sex Parents." *Pediatrics* 109, no. 2 (2002): 341–44.

Perrotti, J., and K. Westheimer. *When the Drama Club Is Not Enough: Lessons from the Safe Schools Program for Gay and Lesbian Students.* Boston: Beacon, 2001.

Polikoff, N. D. "Ending Marriage as We Know It." *Hofstra Law Review* 32 (2003): 210–32.

Polikoff, N. D. "We Will Get What We Ask For: Why Legalizing Gay and Lesbian Marriage Will Not 'Dismantle the Legal Structure of Gender in Every Marriage.'" *Virginia Law Review* 79 (1993): 1535–50.

Polikoff, N. D. "Why Lesbians and Gay Men Should Read Martha Fineman." *American University Journal of Gender, Social Policy, and the Law* 8 (2000): 167–76.

Prager, D. "San Francisco and Islamists: Fighting the Same Enemy." *Townhall.com,* March 2, 2004, http://www.townhall.com/opinion/columns/dennisprager/2004/03/02/10932.html (accessed June 14, 2006).

Ragins, B. "The Effect of Legislation on Workplace Discrimination on Gay Employees." Paper presented at the 106th Convention of the American Psychological Association, San Francisco, August 14–18, 1998.

Rayside, D. "The Politics of Lesbian and Gay Parenting in Canada and the United States." Paper presented at the annual meeting of the Canadian Political Science Association, Toronto, Ontario, May 2002.

Rayside, D. "Recognizing Same-Sex Relationships: Profiling Change in Canada and the United States." Paper presented at the annual meeting of American Political Science Association, Boston, August 29–September 1, 2002.

Renzetti, C., and C. Miley, eds. *Violence in Gay and Lesbian Domestic Partnerships.* Binghamton, NY: Harrington Park, 1996.

Rimmerman, C., K. Wald, and C. Wilcox, eds. *The Politics of Gay Rights.* Chicago: University of Chicago Press, 2000.

Ross, J. "Sex, Marriage, and History: Analyzing the Continued Resistance to Same-Sex Marriage." *Southern Methodist University Law Review* 55 (2002): 1657–81.

Ryan, C., and D. Futterman. *Lesbian and Gay Youth: Care and Counseling.* New York: Columbia University Press, 1998.

Shapiro, J. "A Lesbian-Centered Critique of Second-Parent Adoptions." *Berkeley Women's Law Journal* 14 (1999): 17–39.

Sheldon, L. *Homosexuals Recruit Public School Children: Activists Use Issues of "Safety," "Tolerance," and "Homophobia" as Tactics to Promote Homosexuality in Our Nation's Schools.* Traditional Values Coalition Special Report 18, no. 11. Anaheim, CA: Traditional Values Coalition, n.d.

Sherrill, K. "Same-Sex Marriage, Civil Unions, and the 2004 Presidential Election." New York: Policy Institute of the National Gay and Lesbian Task Force, 2004. http://thetaskforce.org/downloads/MarriageCUSherrill2004.pdf (accessed January 10, 2005).

Shippy, A., M. Cantor, and M. Brennan. "Patterns of Support for Lesbians and Gays as They Age." Paper presented at the Symposium on Social Support Networks held at the 54th Annual Scientific Meeting of the Gerontological Society of America, Chicago, November 2001.

Silverstein, L., and C. Auerbach. "Deconstructing the Essential Father." *American Psychologist* 54, no. 6 (1997): 397–98.

Simmons, T., and M. O'Connell. *Married-Couple and Unmarried-Partner Households, 2000.* Washington, DC: U.S. Census Bureau, 2003. http://www.census.gov/prod/2003pubs/censr-5.pdf (accessed February 20, 2004).

Sprigg, P. "Questions and Answers: What's Wrong with Letting Same-Sex Couples 'Marry'?" *In Focus* (Family Research Council), no. 256 (2003).

Stacey, J. "Family Values Forever: In the Marriage Movement, Conservatives and Centrists find a Home Together." *Nation,* July 9, 2001.

Stacey, J. "Toward Equal Regard for Marriages and Other Imperfect Intimate Affiliations." *Hofstra Law Review* 32 (2003): 331–48.

Stacey, J., and T. Biblarz. "(How) Does the Sexual Orientation of the Parent Matter?" *American Sociological Review* 66, no. 2 (2001): 159–84.

Stoddard, T. B. "Why Gay People Should Seek the Right to Marry." *Out/Look* 6 (fall 1989): 9–13.

Suffredini, K., and M. Finley. "Speak Now: Progressive Considerations on the Advent of Civil Marriage for Same-Sex Couples." *Boston College Law Review* 45 (2004): 595–618.

Sullivan, A. "Here Comes the Groom: A Conservative Case for Gay Marriage." *New Republic*, August 28, 1989. http://www.andrewsullivan.com/homosexuality.php (accessed February 1, 2005).

Sullivan, A. *Virtually Normal: An Argument about Homosexuality*. New York: Knopf, 1995.

Towey, J. *Protecting the Civil Rights and Religious Liberty of Faith-Based Organizations: Why Religious Hiring Rights Must Be Preserved.* Washington, DC: White House Office of Faith-Based and Community Initiatives, n.d. http://www.whitehouse.gov/government/fbci/booklet.pdf (accessed January 20, 2005).

U.S. Census Bureau. *Profile of General Demographic Characteristics, 2000.* Washington, DC: U.S. Census Bureau, 2001. http://www.census.gov/Press-Release/www/2001/tables/dp_us_2000.PDF (accessed June 5, 2004).

Vaid, U. *Virtual Equality: The Mainstreaming of Gay and Lesbian Liberation.* New York: Anchor, 1995.

Varney, J. "Undressing the Normal: Community Efforts for Queer Asian and Asian American Youth." In *Troubling Intersections of Race and Sexuality: Queer Students of Color and Anti-oppressive Education*, ed. K. Kumashiro, 87–104. New York: Rowman and Littlefield, 2001.

Warner, M. "Beyond Gay Marriage." In *Left Legalism/Left Critique*, ed. W. Brown and J. Halley, 259–89. Durham and London: Duke University Press, 2002.

White, T., and R. Ettner. "Children of a Parent Undergoing a Gender Transition: Disclosure, Risk, and Protective Factors." Paper presented at the XVIth Symposium of the Harry Benjamin International Gender Dysphoria Association, London, August 17–21, 1999. http://www.symposion.com/ijt/greenpresidental/green17.htm (accessed May 11, 2006).

Wolfson, E. "Crossing the Threshold: Equal Marriage Rights for Lesbians and Gay Men and the Intra-community Critique." *New York University Review of Law and Social Change* 21 (1994): 568–615.

Xavier, J. *The Washington Transgender Needs Assessment Survey.* Washington, DC: J. Xavier, 2000.

Yang, A. *The 2000 National Elections Study and Gay and Lesbian Rights: Support for Equality Grows.* Washington, DC: National Gay and Lesbian Task Force, 2001.

Yoshino, K. "Covering." *Yale Law Journal* 111 (2002): 769–939.

INDEX